ROADS TO PROSPERITY AND RUIN

ROADS TO PROSPERITY AND RUIN

Infrastructure and the Making of Neoliberal Yucatán

FERNANDO ARMSTRONG-FUMERO

THE UNIVERSITY OF NORTH CAROLINA PRESS

Chapel Hill

Designed by Jamison Cockerham
Set in Scala, Scala Sans, DIN Condensed, and Futura Now
by codeMantra

Manufactured in the United States of America

Cover art: Cenote Carwash in Tulum, Riviera Maya,
Mexico © Adobe Stock/Nomadic DNA

Library of Congress Cataloging-in-Publication Data
Names: Armstrong-Fumero, Fernando author
Title: Roads to prosperity and ruin : infrastructure and the making
of neoliberal Yucatán / Fernando Armstrong-Fumero.
Description: Chapel Hill : The University of North Carolina Press,
[2025] | Includes bibliographical references and index.
Identifiers: LCCN 2025020644 | ISBN 9781469691206 cloth alk. paper |
ISBN 9781469691213 paperback alk. paper |
ISBN 9781469688015 epub | ISBN 9781469691220 pdf
Subjects: LCSH: Tren Maya—Political aspects | Mayas—Political activity—
Mexico—Pisté | Mayas—Mexico—Pisté—Economic conditions | Rural
development projects—Political aspects—Mexico—Yucatán (State) |
Infrastructure (Economics)—Mexico—Yucatán (State)—History—20th
century | Infrastructure (Economics)—Mexico—Yucatán (State)—
History—21st century | Tourism—Government policy—Mexico—Yucatán
(State) | Neoliberalism—Mexico—Yucatán (State) | BISAC: SOCIAL SCIENCE
/ Anthropology / General | SOCIAL SCIENCE / Indigenous Studies
Classification: LCC F1435.1.Y89 A76 2025 |
DDC 320.0897/427—dc23/eng/20250701
LC record available at https://lccn.loc.gov/2025020644

This book will be made open access within three years of publication
thanks to Path to Open, a program developed in partnership between
JSTOR, the American Council of Learned Societies (ACLS), the University
of Michigan Press, and the University of North Carolina Press to bring
about equitable access and impact for the entire scholarly community,
including authors, researchers, libraries, and university presses around
the world. Learn more at https://about.jstor.org/path-to-open/.

For product safety concerns under the European Union's General Product
Safety Regulation (EU GPSR), please contact gpsr@mare-nostrum.co.uk
or write to the University of North Carolina Press and Mare Nostrum
Group B.V., Mauritskade 21D, 1091 GC Amsterdam, The Netherlands.

Este libro es dedicado

a la memoria de

EDIWILMA CIMÉ PADILLA

CONTENTS

ILLUSTRATIONS

ACKNOWLEDGMENTS

The research behind this book developed from ideas that started percolating in the mid-2010s and that took firmer shape between 2019 and 2021. During those years, I have been fortunate to be able to rely on the help and support of numerous friends, relatives, and colleagues, particularly during the months of pandemic shutdown when the current text slowly emerged.

I'd like to thank the anonymous external reviewers who offered generous and insightful readings of previous drafts and helped to make this a much stronger and effective book. I am likewise grateful to the staff at UNC Press, particularly María García and Valerie Burton, for their support and encouragement throughout the process.

A number of nonanonymous colleagues provided invaluable information, feedback, and moral support during the research and writing of this book. I owe an immense debt to Julio Hoil Gutiérrez, who has been a close friend for over two decades, and who has been endlessly generous with his insights. I am also very indebted to Ben Fallaw, whom I have known for fewer years, but who has become a sort of midcareer mentor to me. As this project neared completion, Bianet Castellanos and Matilde Córdova Azcárrate provided very valuable input and support. Finally, I am grateful to the faculty at the Universidad del Caribe, Cancún, for their insight into regional tourism development. I'm afraid that I may be missing the names of some people with whom I met at UCaribe in 2018, but I would like to thank Myrna Beltrán

Pérez, Alejandra Cazal, Francisco Domínguez, Christine Elizabeth McCoy Cador, Pedro Moncada Jiménez, and Veronica Ochoa.

A special thank-you goes to Jon Caris, Kalaʻi Ellis, Nicolás Reyes and Heather Rosenfeld at the Smith College Spatial Analysis Lab, who created the maps that are included in this text. Some of my own travel for archival and ethnographic research was financed with a Smith College CFCD faculty development grant.

I owe another special debt to the staff at the various archives that I have consulted for this project, which include the Archivo General del Estado de Yucatán, the Archivo General de la Nación de México, the Mapoteca Orozco y Berra, the Archivo Histórico del Banco de México, and the library archives of the Universidad del Caribe.

As with all of my ethnographic work, I am very deeply indebted to the families in Pisté, Popolá, Xcalakoop, and other communities where I have conducted research. This includes people who have generously shared their time and knowledge as informants, as well as dozens of friends who have kindly offered me meals, transportation, or just plain moral support over nearly a quarter century. Your kindness and friendship are written, again and again, in my mind and heart.

Of course, as with all I do, I am indebted to my parents, Fernando Armstrong Rivera and Dafne Fumero Pugliesi, for their endless moral support and for the efforts that they made since my childhood to keep me on this course.

Acknowledgments

ROADS TO PROSPERITY AND RUIN

Introduction

ROADS TO PROSPERITY, AND ROADS THAT RUIN

In October 2022, a regional Mexican newspaper announced the impending "death" of a community where I have conducted ethnographic fieldwork since the late 1990s. Pisté is a town of around 6,000 predominantly Indigenous Maya residents in the state of Yucatán. In 2022, changes to an infrastructure project known as the Tren Maya threatened to direct tourist traffic away from businesses that were the economic heart of the community. Initiated during the presidency of Andrés Manuel López Obrador (2018–24), the megaproject will link major tourist sites in five Mexican states with modern rail service. When it was first announced in 2018, people in Pisté greeted the news with a mix of skepticism and optimism. Experience had taught them that such ambitious projects often floundered before they could be completed. But their town was situated between the state capital of Mérida and the resort city of Cancún, and was strategically located to benefit from any increase in commercial traffic.

Most of Pisté's residents are employed in various tourist service jobs, or as sellers of handicrafts at Chichén Itzá, an archaeological site located just two kilometers from downtown. In 2020, when the COVID-19 pandemic closed the archaeological zone to tourists, municipal leaders were able to leverage their control of local lands that were needed for the Tren Maya project to secure federal funding for the foundation of a small university. A second round of federal funding paid for the restoration of the town's colonial church, which became the centerpiece of a small historical and tourist district in the heart of the community. As local residents began to recover from the initial economic blows of the pandemic, they had reason to feel optimistic about their community's ability to derive a range of benefits from the rapidly emerging rail project.

Two years later, their luck changed. Fernando Barbachano, the millionaire owner of a luxury hotel on the periphery of the archaeological zone, sold a large parcel of land well outside of Pisté's downtown to the federal agencies in charge of the train project. Along with several other regional tourism magnates, Barbachano seemed poised to benefit from a new train station and museum complex that would divert traffic away from the town, its businesses, and local handicraft vendors. As the newspaper report stated, this simple rerouting of rail infrastructure would "kill" the most important economic sector of the community (Osorio 2022).

When I made my annual visit to Pisté in the summer of 2023, frustration over the development of the Tren Maya was palpable. But the wheels seemed to already be turning on the next round of local negotiations with the state and federal governments. The 2024 election was only a year away. President López Obrador's party, the Movimiento de Regeneración Nacional (Movement of National Regeneration), which had no presence in the town's political scene during the 2018 election cycle, now had thousands of local adherents. Public indignation about the fate of the Tren Maya notwithstanding, many of López Obrador's policies had proved very popular in town. Perhaps more important, the consolidation of the relatively new Movimiento de Regeneración Nacional as a major force in Mexican politics seemed inevitable. Generations of experience had taught the people of Pisté that pragmatic engagement with mainstream political parties was essential in turning projects that had the potential to "kill" the local economy into a source of prosperity.

When people in Pisté attempt to influence the routing of a project like the Tren Maya, or to mitigate its worst local impacts, they draw on a political common sense that developed over the course of generations. This book is a historical and ethnographic account of how several key political strategies emerged during a period of relatively rapid economic development in the mid-twentieth century, and of how they continue to be relevant in the "neoliberal" era that began in the 1980s. Transport infrastructure like the Tren Maya and the roads and highways that preceded it play the most prominent role in this story. But as other examples will demonstrate, many rural Yucatecans apply the same cultural logics when they seek to influence state-sponsored development projects that range from educational institutions to the regional landscape of museums and performance spaces that is often referred to as "cultural infrastructure."

My friends and informants in Pisté and neighboring communities recognize a common thread in different kinds of state-sponsored development. Just as new transportation projects like the Tren Maya threaten to divert profitable traffic from communities that grew around older routes, investment in specific economic sectors tends to exercise negative externalities on others. For example, heavy government investment in the tourist industry has generated millions of service sector jobs but also has tended to limit the employability of college graduates trained in other fields. New destinations for museumgoers and fans of the performing arts can create opportunities in underserved regions but also tend to siphon away visitors from established sites like Chichén Itzá. Framed within this vernacular common sense, political participation becomes a struggle against competing regions and elite interests that divert opportunities from local families. I will refer to these negative externalities of development projects with the umbrella term of "negative infrastructure."

Throughout this book, I will focus on how political tactics that emerged in the wake of infrastructural developments that began at the end of the 1930s continue to be relevant to local communities today, in spite of the formal political and economic changes that marked the neoliberal transition of the 1980s. This reflects the ambiguity of that transition in the lived experience of many rural Mexicans. One of the insights that has emerged in contemporary political anthropology is that neoliberalization has been experienced differently and is imagined in distinct ways at the different sites where it has made an impact (see Ganti 2014). Accordingly, I will employ a somewhat flexible use of the term that balances its various comparative, realpolitik, and commonsense dimensions.

By "comparative," I refer to the work of influential authors like David Harvey (2005, 2), who characterized neoliberalism as a hegemonic global order in which the primary role of the state is to protect "strong private property rights, free markets, and free trade" (see also Harvey 2007). Mexico's neoliberalism is, in many ways, an instance of this global process. The privatizations and free trade policies that have transformed Mexico's economy and society since the 1980s were shaped by transnational political pressure, conditions set by international financial institutions, and the ideology of a generation of native technocrats trained in elite US institutions. Not surprisingly, some of the most prominent Mexican critics of these policies point to these same globalizing interests as the source of many of their country's current ills.

While this transnational vision provides a broad understanding of the dynamics of capital and the state at the turn of the millennium, it can be less useful for explaining the realpolitik that shapes Mexico's distinct national experience with neoliberalism. For many scholars and journalists working in Mexico, the term "neoliberalism" refers to a period of national history as much as it does to the technical specifies of an economic model. Privatization, the removal of tariff barriers, and monetary reforms were all calculated responses to a crisis of legitimacy that challenged Mexico's distinctive political system in the 1980s. The approaches to economic development and political legitimation that Mexican leaders employed before and after their "neoliberal" transition were quite heterodox and complicate the idea of a single coherent transformation in the country's hegemonic order. In these contexts, "neoliberalism" tends to refer to a distinctly national set of political actors and media narratives that emerged during this period of crisis and reorganization.

If Mexico's distinct national experience brings added layers of contextual meaning to the term "neoliberalism," a similar expansion of the term is implied at what I refer to as the "common sense" level. As authors like Wendy Brown (2017) and Adam Kotsko (2018) have argued, neoliberalism must be understood as a symbolic order that legitimates the logic of capitalism by applying it to diverse experiences of everyday life. But this process of legitimation does not only work from the top down. Insofar as different communities have experienced Mexico's neoliberal era in different ways, they have created different symbolic orders to make national processes intelligible within local realities. That is, when rural Yucatecans interpret local experiences of life, labor and politics through the moral order of capitalism, they also place a distinctly local stamp on this hegemonic global system.

As I will show, many rural Mayan speakers frame their experience of regional politics and economic development in ways that defy the expectations of both Mexican policymakers and academic theorists of Indigenous resistance. In contrast to the explicitly anticapitalist discourses employed by activists like the Ejército Zapatista de Liberación Nacional (Zapatista National Liberation Army) of Chiapas (Collier and Quaratiello 1999; Nash 1997; Stephen 2002), many residents of Pisté articulate personal identities that embrace the entrepreneurial values of a tourist market in which their own ethnicity becomes a saleable commodity. In this regard, they employ a bottom-up articulation of the kind of "ethnic entrepreneurship" discussed by Monica Dehart (2010, 12), in which Indigenous individuals become "autonomous, enterprising ethnic subjects" capable of representing the commodified cultures that they embody in a globalized economy (see also Hota 2019). But just as the political strategies employed by Mexico's neoliberalizing policy elites bear traces of older regimes of state-driven development, the self-identified entrepreneurs of rural Yucatán continue to value institutions associated with the corporatist politics of the early twentieth century. For example, early twentieth-century agrarian institutions that once embodied rural dependency have been redeployed as a means of asserting local control over valuable real estate. Throughout the text, I will use the phrase "vernacular neoliberalism" to refer to this heterodox local discourse and the political strategies that it informs.

This vernacular, commonsense dimension of neoliberalism brings us back to the questions of infrastructure and development. As recent ethnographies have emphasized, access to public goods such as roads or communication technologies is not simply a question of material benefits. Access provides a series of symbolic anchors for the social identities with which communities in the Global South situate themselves inside a hierarchical and often exclusionary modernity (Fredericks 2018; Harvey and Knox 2015; Melly 2017). Part of this symbolic work lies in the creation of social and political networks whose function cannot be reduced to the materiality of roads or irrigation schemes (Larkin 2013, 329–32). Modern infrastructure also provides a tangible expression of the more intangible subjectivities—what I have referred to as "commonsense" ones—that legitimate a given social order. Writing about the role of public water resources in the evolution of liberal governance in India, Nikhil Anand (2017, 20) notes that the maintenance of modern pumps and pipes was "not only productive of liberal expertise, but also enabled a series of constitutive divisions necessary for the operation of liberal rationalities in everyday life." That is, water infrastructure instantiates the logics of power through which the human subjects of "modernization" are governed, even as it satisfies their physical needs.

As a number of studies have shown, *exclusion* from the benefits of infrastructural developments is a form of coercion wielded by government agencies, or simply a possible outcome in the struggle for limited public goods (see Bleynat 2021; Paerregaard, Stensrud, and Andersen 2016; and Wutich and Brewis 2018, 445–47). These forms of coercion and competition are at the heart of the histories of local infrastructure that I will discuss in this book. However, my approach to these conflicts diverges slightly from that of authors like Anand (2017, 25–30), who focus on forms of narrated and embodied political subjectivity that are diffuse within a larger system of technologies and actors, and are therefore "irreducible" to formal structures of administration and representative governance. This interpretation of technical landscapes, shaped by Foucauldian notions of biopower (see also Kennelly 2015; Mitchell 2002; and Stern 1999), has offered invaluable insight about the pervasive and sometimes invisible workings of power in everyday experiences of modern infrastructure. But it would be a somewhat awkward fit for the stories told by my friends and informants in Yucatán, who take pride in successfully leveraging municipal elections and formal bureaucratic institutions to influence the behavior of political elites who initiate projects like the Tren Maya. Rural Yucatecans *do* employ the same kinds of personalistic relationships to officials and forms of protest that are central to Anand's (2017, 31) discussion of subaltern political engagement in Mumbai. But effective engagement with formal political institutions, both real and aspirational, is at the heart of the discourses of vernacular neoliberalism that evolved at the turn of the millennium.

As I will show, the vernacular neoliberalism of rural Yucatán is closely tied to the multigenerational experience of economic and social change brought on by the creation of Cancún. For people living on the peninsula, the development of a regional tourist economy around the resort city is the chief embodiment of the benefits and potential harms of state-sponsored development and private capital investment (see Córdoba Azcárate 2020; and Castellanos 2020). The Cancún project was initiated in 1968 as a means of creating employment in Mexico's underdeveloped Southeast and creating new sources of foreign revenue. Funded by a loan from the Inter-American Development Bank, several newly created federal agencies built hotels and urban infrastructure that would eventually transition to private ownership. Given this timing, the project impacted the regional economy for nearly a decade before the 1980s financial crises that precipitated neoliberal reforms on a national level. Communities like Pisté, which were strategically located in the tourism infrastructure that developed around the resort, experienced unprecedented prosperity in the last third of the twentieth century. In contrast, communities on the peripheries of the major tourism artery experienced negative infrastructure, as more state investment and private capital drifted to the peninsula's most profitable industry. Throughout this generation-long struggle for access to infrastructural goods, vernacular critiques of older

6

styles of personalist and clientelistic politics developed alongside new strategies of local-level electioneering.

The timing of the Cancún project and its diverse impacts on the economies and political identities of rural Yucatecans also poses an interesting challenge to the "classic" narrative of Mexico's neoliberalization. For example, a series of authoritative economic histories of Mexico published in the early 2000s (see Ávila 2006; and Gracida 2004) draw a clear boundary between "neoliberalism" and a period of state-driven "Stabilizing Development" that ended amid mounting economic crises in the 1970s.[1] That is, these studies posit a neoliberal "transition" that took place well over a decade after many rural Yucatecan communities had experienced the impacts of the Cancún project. The idea of an interventionist state that entered a period of crisis and transformation in the last quarter of the twentieth century makes considerable sense for analyzing the "big picture" of national-level policy decisions and social movements. But, again, it is an awkward fit for lived experience of people in much of rural Yucatán during the same period. Yucatán's economy remained dependent on an increasingly obsolete henequen industry through much of the Stabilizing Development era, making it one of the most impoverished Mexican states. Paradoxically, rural Yucatecans who were fortunate enough to live near emerging tourist sites remember experiencing a new prosperity during the economically and politically turbulent 1970s, which only expanded during subsequent decades of neoliberal reform. This reality was not invisible to Mexican policy elites, for whom it underscored the exceptional nature of the Yucatán Peninsula within the larger national polity. As I will discuss in chapters 3 and 4, economists who played a key role in national development policy disagree regarding whether the Cancún project properly belongs to the Stabilizing Development era, or whether it anticipated the neoliberal policies with which they sought to pull the country from a decade of crisis.

Abstract debates about the neoliberal or developmentalist roots of the Cancún project float around the periphery of the political imagination of many rural Yucatecans. But more localized and concrete struggles over access to the region's touristic cash cows have become a central drama of local electoral politics. For example, residents of an isolated rural village might recall the pavement or expansion of a particular roadway as a far more transformative event than national-level free trade reforms that had a smaller impact on the local economy. For another community, the key moment might be the opening of a successful peripheral tourist attraction that created local employment opportunities and freed young people from the need to relocate to larger cities in search of work. In either case, these economic gains can be reversed by the rerouting of a road, or by preferential investments in a different region or industry. In the following section, I will provide a series of historical and ethnographic sketches of these wins and losses in competition over infrastructural development, before turning to the structures of national realpolitik that determine the rules of the game.

HITTING THE ROAD

As for most anthropologists working in rural Mexico, buses and bus routes have played a central role in my fieldwork. This was particularly true during eighteen months between 2004 and 2005, when I split my time between Mérida, where I was conducting archival research, and the town of Pisté, where I rented a room from friends. Those months were marked by multiple weekly trips on the hourly "second-class" service that was the main commuter transit for people traveling to rural communities between Mérida and Cancún. Until 2007 or 2008, the itineraries of the departing buses were announced over the loudspeaker by the cashiers who operated the ticket booths at the terminal. Today, the verbal announcements have been replaced by a computer-generated voice. The litany of place names remains the same. "ADO is pleased to welcome you to our imminent departure with service to Tahmek, Hoctún, Xocchel, Kantunil, Holcá, Libre Unión, Pisté, Kaua, Valladolid, Chemax, Leona Vicario, and intermediate points heading to the city of Cancún."

These chanted itineraries instantiate a geography of settlement and commerce that is taken for granted today but was imposed on the Yucatán Peninsula by a series of projects that began in the late 1930s. Specifically, it reflects the formation of the eastern terminus of Federal Highway 180, which today spans over 1,300 miles from Cancún to Matamoros, Tamaulipas, in the Mexican Northeast. The eastern extension of this road was originally intended to link the state capital of Mérida to the sparsely inhabited Caribbean coast (see map 0.1). Decades later, it was an artery between Mérida and the emergent resort city of Cancún.

The construction of major roads like Federal Highway 180 played a prominent role in the social mandate and electoral politics of the modern Mexican state. In the nineteenth century, the construction of rail infrastructure embodied aspirations for the development and economic modernization of the countryside, with concurrent "civilizing" effects on the rural population (Matthews 2013). As automobile travel became more feasible and

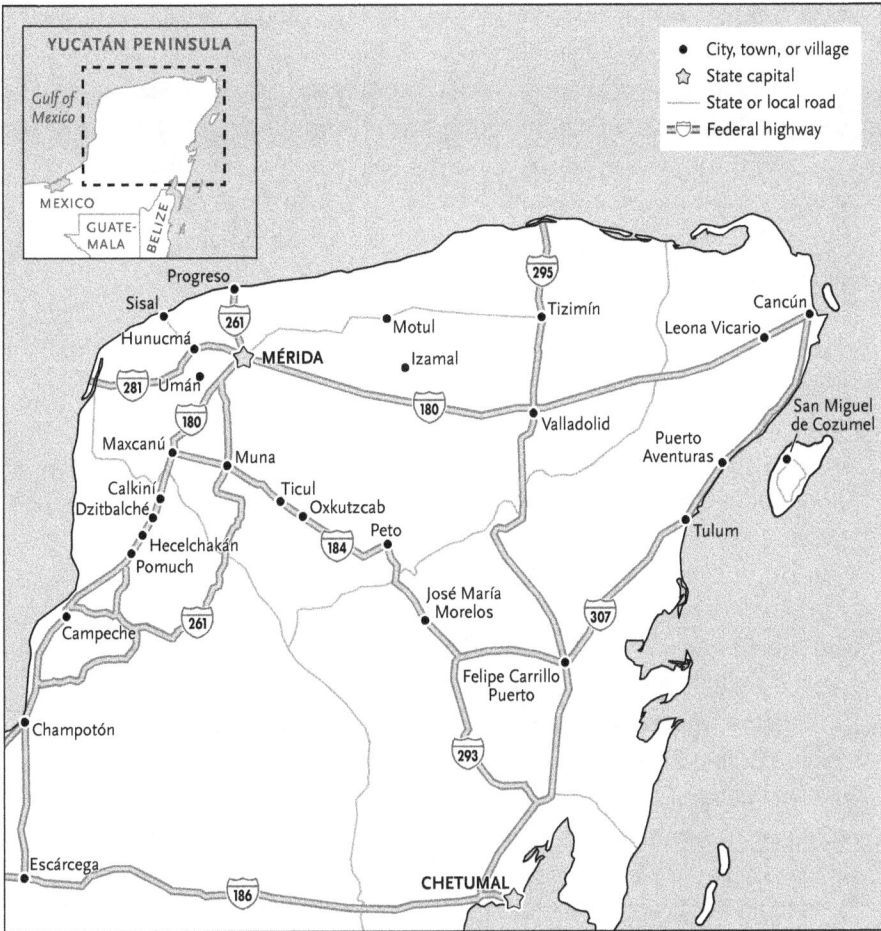

Map 0.1. Transpeninsular road network.
*Map created by Nicolás Reyes, Heather Rosenfeld, and Kalaʻi Ellis
at the Spatial Analysis Lab, Smith College, Northampton, MA.*

popular in the 1920s and 1930s, roadways embodied similar aspirations for the post-Revolutionary state (Núñez Tapía and Méndez Reyes 2018; Waters 1998). But as several studies of road development in different regions of Mexico have noted, this process tended to be both economically precarious and politically contentious. Tracing construction in the states of Veracruz and Nuevo León, Michael Bess (2017) has documented how the intervention of a constellation of rural community groups, urban civic organizations, and moneyed elites complicate any unified vision of centralized state planning of this vital infrastructure (see also Waters 1999). These factional contentions were compounded by frequent shortages of funds and materials, which led to the suspension or abandonment of entire projects (Mijares Lara 2019). Other studies have pointed to unintended secondary consequences of road construction, from conflicts with Indigenous communities in Chiapas (Otto 2018), to the growth of a generation gap between homebound parents and more mobile children in Tepoztlán (Waters 1998), to moral panics about the threats to life and limb posed by a rapidly expanding national "car culture" (Freeman 2011).

The current routing of Federal Highway 180 reflects its own history of suspensions, political contestation, and unintended consequences. The planning of this corridor, which patched together existing roads between Mérida and Valladolid and created new stretches from Valladolid to the Caribbean, was initiated through presidential decree in 1936. After a series of suspensions and slowdowns, the span was completed by the end of the 1950s. It was later amplified in the 1990s by the construction of a roughly parallel four-lane toll road that bypasses many of the communities along the original corridor. Still, with the exception of tourists and local travelers willing to pay the rather steep tolls, the vast majority of transit and commerce in the region takes place along the original path laid out in the late 1930s.

In many respects, the Highway 180 corridor embodies the transformation of the Yucatán Peninsula, its economy, and the stakes of different local and regional political actors in the second half of the twentieth century. With the emergence of tourism as a dominant regional industry, traffic from inland Yucatán to the coast displaced an older economic polarity that centered on the monocrop henequen industry of the north and west of the peninsula. But the dramatic development on the peripheries of Highway 180 does not represent the only possible evolution of the peninsula's economy. This corridor also displaced a series of possible posthenequen futures that were imagined in the decades after the Second World War, and that slowly withered and died on the edges of roads less traveled.

The first of these alternative routes consists of a series of roads known as the "Mérida-Chetumal" corridor—which today consists of various combinations of Federal Highways 184 and 307 (see map 0.1). These roads link the state capitals of Yucatán and Quintana Roo through the major commercial town of Peto. Between the 1940s and 1960s, these roads offered the possibility of linking a promising region of commercial maize and sugar production to Mérida and the ports of the Caribbean. For more than twenty years, a diverse group of local Maya agriculturalists and Mérida-based businessmen wrote to several presidential administrations to boost the potential of this route. In the end, construction lagged far behind that of Highway 180, and the thriving commercial agriculture that was imagined for the south of the state of Yucatán never fully emerged.

This struggle against the dominance of the future 180 corridor was even more difficult for stakeholders in the third, southernmost transpeninsular road that was commissioned in 1936, or what today consists of the eastern-most segment of Federal Highway 186. Linking the town of Escárcega in the south of the state of Campeche to Chetumal, this road passes through the swampy, densely forested region where the scrub trees of the Yucatán Peninsula proper give way to the tall canopies of the Southern Maya Lowlands. Historically, this has been the narrowest and least traveled and maintained of the three transpeninsular corridors.

Today, residents of towns along the Mérida-Chetumal corridor have experienced some prosperity connected to the rise of a few local public universities. The Tren Maya megaproject offers unprecedented infrastructural and economic developments to the communities of the Highway 186 corridor. However, the fact that these communities are only "catching up" today is itself a testament to a much longer period during which they had been disadvantaged in the struggle for public and private investment in infrastructure. The benefits derived by those fortunate enough to live near what would become Highway 180 came at their long-term loss.

These various wins and losses in the competition for development resources embodies the dichotomy that I will employ between "positive" and "negative" infrastructure. Many factors influence policy decisions regarding the development of road corridors. These include the size of the populations that can be served by the roads, the contribution that paid roadwork will make to different local economies, and the benefits to the larger national and regional economies that can be gained from connecting particular sites to the road infrastructure. In some cases, these decisions are also motivated by the venal ends of politicians who hope to divert funds from extended construction projects to businesses owned by their political allies. But in either case, the tendency is for roads that benefit one region or series of communities to take traffic and economic importance away from other claimants for limited infrastructure funds. This negative infrastructure is the loss of access, traffic, and opportunity that is experienced by a given community or region as a result of projects that benefit others.

If the generation-long evolution of the three transpeninsular corridors reflects the phenomenon of negative infrastructure on a regional scale, far more local and historically punctuated incidences of this phenomenon are even more common. The case of the towns of Kantunil and Holcá, located a little less than halfway between Pisté and the city of Mérida, offers a good example. Whenever my friends from Pisté give me a ride to or from Mérida, our itinerary looks a bit different than the route chanted by human and computerized voices at the bus terminal. Most local drivers who leave rural towns choose to avoid the toll highway (Federal Highway 180D) that runs parallel to the old 180 and links Cancún to Mérida. Or, at least, they do so until they reach the town of Holcá, where there is an exit leading to the final, toll-free stretch of the newer four-lane highway. This bypasses the towns of Kantunil, Xocchel, Hoctún, and Tahmek, which the bus passes through on the "old" 180. Entering the "new" four-lane highway at the fork outside of Holcá shaves close to an hour from the trip to Mérida.

Over the years, friends have pointed out to me the stark differences between the Kantunil and Holcá downtown areas that have resulted from the effects of the highway extensions. Of the two towns, Kantunil has a deeper history as a municipal seat and market area, as evidenced by its colonial-era church and numerous large downtown buildings of nineteenth-century provenance. Holcá, a *comisaría* or outlying community of the county seat of Kantunil, lacked major downtown architecture until fairly recently, and even its church betrays a twentieth-century construction.

Despite the formal political dominance of Kantunil, the construction of the toll-road exit clearly tipped the balance of economic fortune in Holcá's favor. Holcá is now the last stop for food for travelers heading to Mérida on the highway extension. For those heading east, it is in a sweet spot between a largely barren stretch of highway and the towns closer to Chichén Itzá, where "touristic" prices become more common. Day or night, the main street bustles with mostly female vendors who sell food from small stands built into their own homes. Different homes offer grilled chicken and beans during the day, and *panuchos* or empanadas fried up at night. Holcá even has a tourist attraction of its own. A local family that had drawn water from a cave on their land noticed the carloads of Mexican travelers that stopped in town to eat chicken, and decided to open their own subterranean swimming attraction. It has become a favorite of Yucatecan day-trippers who wish to avoid the more crowded and expensive cenote attractions on the periphery of Chichén Itzá.

Kantunil presents a striking, and rather bleak, contrast. At night, the main street through which second-class buses pass is largely deserted. The few women who sell fried food to passersby do so from the shelter of a municipal market built in the 1960s, where most of the posts seem to be permanently shuttered.

Whether it's the formal transit itinerary chanted from the ADO station in Mérida or the more informal decisions with which drivers shave a few minutes or hours from their travels, road landscapes reflect a history in which benefits to one community often entailed significant detriments to others. As I will discuss further in chapter 1, the politicians and planners who approved the different transpeninsular corridors assumed that "seminomadic" Maya agriculturalists would naturally pick up stakes and relocate nearer to the newly built roads. But this happened less often than they anticipated in the 1930s, and even less so decades later, when the granting of usufruct ejido titles bound once-mobile communities to fixed sites where they enjoyed access to agricultural land (see Armstrong-Fumero 2013, 23–49). By the time that Kantunil was cut off from the main traffic artery to Mérida, falling victim to negative infrastructure was a familiar experience to the residents of hundreds of communities throughout the state. The "death" of downtown Kantunil, like the heralded "death" of downtown Pisté, embodies the dangers behind the larger processes of state-sponsored development and national politics that will be the focus of the next section.

ELITE POLITICIANS AND THE "SEXENIO CURSE"

As I noted earlier, development and neoliberalization in Mexico must be partly understood within the context of elite realpolitik, and the consequences of national and regional elections. For my friends and informants in Pisté, projects that have inflicted negative infrastructure on their community are intimately tied to the elected official who promoted them. But, notwithstanding geographical, cultural, and linguistic differences that separate them from the urban halls of power, Pisteños have a number of tools that they are able to leverage to influence policy and electoral outcomes. The evolution of these formal and informal mechanisms in twentieth-century Mexico is a complex topic and the subject of a vast secondary literature. Some of these complexities will be teased out in the specific chapters of this book. But by way of introduction, I will highlight some key features of this political system that will emerge in most of the specific incidents that will be discussed in more detail later.

The story that I tell in this book begins with the single-party rule of the Partido Revolucionario Institucional (Institutional Revolutionary Party, or

PRI), which consolidated its national hegemony at the end of the 1920s.[2] Much of the PRI's initial success rested on securing votes among the country's peasantry and urban working class through clientelistic labor and agrarian organizations (McCormick 2016). Outright fraud supplemented this electioneering when necessary. The party also averted conflict among political elites through informal networks of patronage that circulated power among major factions (Ai Camp 1995, 2002). As the national economy evolved over the course of the twentieth century, these intraelite negotiations dovetailed with the creation of policies that were favorable to national business magnates who were themselves closely tied to the PRI (Alexander 2016; Carmona [1970] 1990).

This system was seemingly stable for a period of almost seventy years that is somewhat deceptively called the *pax priísta*. In reality, the stability of this period was maintained through the accommodation of certain forms of dissent and the violent repression of groups deemed to be too subversive (Aviña 2014). But by the 1970s, fractures were evident in the different coalitions that maintained PRI control. A combination of political missteps, economic crises, and increases in political repression led to the unravelling of single-party rule, which ended definitively when Vicente Fox Quesada of the opposition Partido Acción Nacional (National Action Party) won the presidency in 2000.

Despite the formal transition to competitive democracy, many aspects of the structures of national power that were established under the PRI continue to shape the political lives of people in communities throughout the country. Though battered by a generation of neoliberal reform, the ejido, a federal agrarian institution that bound peasant agriculturalists to the state in the 1930s, clings to life. Collectively managed ejido lands continue to generate a limited agricultural subsistence and provide a means of controlling local territory for many rural communities, like Pisté. Also, despite extensive electoral reforms, the actual processes through which parties bring voters to the polls in rural areas continue to bear traces of older forms of clientelism. Just as the PRI cultivated voter reserves and elite consensus through informal networks, the years leading up to recent elections continue to see extensive "backroom" negotiations through which different parties woo promising candidates and well-placed supporters ahead of the formal campaign.

Another aspect of political culture that has remained consistent over time, and that is particularly relevant to the planning and completion of major development projects, is the dominance of national presidents and state governors over the legislative and judicial branches of the government. Major development projects like the Tren Maya are intimately linked to the personalities of elected executives who are highly motivated to complete them by the end of their terms. Journalists and laypersons often speculate on how a given project reflects an individual's desire to cement their legacy, or whether it is meant to improve the electoral chances of a hand-picked successor. As a tradition of investigative reporting has demonstrated, these projects also offer an opportunity to skim cash from the public treasury.

This dominance of chief executives over political projects has important implications for understanding the rhythm of infrastructure and other forms of development in Mexico. It's no coincidence that the historian and prominent public intellectual Enrique Krauze (1987) titled his epic history of the modern Mexican presidency *Biografía del Poder* (*The Biography of Power*). For Krauze, the historical tendency for Mexican political systems to grant more or less autocratic powers to the presidency makes the biography of powerful individuals the primary means of exploring the national life of a given period. Understandably, this approach has often raised the ire of scholars trained in various critiques of "great men" approaches to historiography (see Lomnitz 2001, 214–18). But, insofar as the timing of infrastructural projects coincides with the tenure of specific politicians, Krauze's anthropomorphic temporality bears some considering. At the very least, this suggests that the six-year presidential period, or *sexenio*, must play a central role in understanding the rhythms of development and local politics.

As the Yucatecan governor Carlos Loret de Mola observed, a Mexican president is at their most powerful in the final year of a sexenio (1978, 1–5). During this period, they are courted by all of the main national and regional factions within their party, who seek to exercise influence during the next administration.[3] As the sexenio winds down, the successful completion of infrastructure projects that were proposed at the beginning of the sitting president's tenure is seen as essential to enhancing the prestige of the party and securing a positive electoral result for the successor (see Krauze 2013; Lomnitz 2001; Zaid [1987] 2012). These two political concerns motivate the exercise of the president's considerable power in influencing the election of legislators, state governors, and even mayors who can help to consolidate this legacy (Aliskym 1980; Hernández Rodríguez 2008). As in several cases that I will discuss in chapters 2 and 3, governors who "lost" too many municipalities to opposition-party candidates often risked being forced from office by the nation's chief executive. By extension, pressure on governors to "deliver" for their respective parties creates an opening in which rural communities can stage protests, threaten major political defections, or elect their own opposition candidates to wrest concessions from urban political elites. As I will show, these key moments of regional and national electoral cycles can turn the municipal leaders of small rural towns like Pisté into key actors in regional and even national political dramas.

This cycle of electoral politics has contributed to what policy analysts refer to as the "*sexenio* curse" (Heath 1999). The work of political succession often leads sitting presidents to spearhead a glut of social and infrastructure spending at the end of a sexenio, sometimes with little consideration of the long-term viability of different projects. Conversely, the desire to establish an independent institutional legacy might lead a chief executive to cancel or unnecessarily transform successful programs instituted by their predecessor (see Mijares Lara 2019). As will become clear in later chapters of this book, the "*sexenio* curse" is a constant factor in the strategies adopted by both technocratic elites and local stakeholders in different projects as they adjust their planning and expectations for incoming presidents and governors.

CANCÚN AS EXCEPTION AND ASPIRATION

Earlier, I referred to the somewhat idiosyncratic place of Cancún in the history of Mexican development, as a project that seems to straddle the age of free market neoliberalism and the age of Stabilizing Development. This exceptionalism extends to the relationship between the resort city and the consequences of Mexico's electoral politics. The development of Cancún survived the sexenio curse, and management of much of its tourism infrastructure made a relatively smooth transition to private hands by the 1980s.[4] The success and durability of the project was key to the prosperity of communities across the Yucatán Peninsula. Many rural people whose families benefited materially from this process claim that Cancún provides a model for what becomes possible when private enterprise survived and superseded the worst tendencies of Mexico's political system. This assumption, based on the lived experience of several generations of tourism development, is at the heart of the vernacular neoliberalism that plays a prominent role in the political identity of many of my friends and informants in Pisté.

In hindsight, the completion of Cancún was one of the few bright spots of the Stabilizing Development era in the Yucatán Peninsula. As I will discuss in more detail in chapters 2 and 3, a glut in government spending at the end of the 1970s is interpreted by many economists as a catalyst for the financial crises that devastated the national economy in the early 1980s. For many natives of the Yucatán Peninsula, this ill-advised public spending was exemplified by almost desperate attempts to secure rural votes by propping up a flagging henequen industry, even as a more promising touristic alternative was rapidly emerging. These sentiments were echoed in the popular regional press and informed local discourses about negative infrastructure and related externalities of poorly planned development. As many rural Yucatecans in their sixties and seventies have told me, the diversion of vast sums of public money to maintain the henequen industry unnecessarily slowed the development of the parts of the state that were best poised to take advantage of the tourism boom.

Fortunately for the population of Yucatán and its neighboring state of Quintana Roo, the ultimate expansion of the "Cancún effect" on the regional economy tempered some of the worst impacts of the financial crises that assailed Mexico from the end of the 1980s to the mid-1990s. Some economists, boosters for free trade, privatization, and other aspects of neoliberal reform framed the Cancún project as anticipating the reorientation of the Mexican economy that would take place in the late 1980s and 1990s. Prophetic or not, the developments that had been promoted in the late 1960s created an industry that often benefited from the increased international demand generated by the "cheap" peso of the crisis years.

With half a century of hindsight, the impacts of the tourist industry that developed around Cancún seem more equivocal. Throughout this book, I will make several references to recent work by Matilde Córdoba Azcárate (2020), who has characterized tourism as a "sticky" industry that has remained the primary route to prosperity in Yucatán even as it perpetuates different forms of social inequality and environmental harm across the region. As Bianet Castellanos (2020) has observed, these negative impacts include rampant commodification of land and other basic resources, contributing to the precarity of the large population of Maya people who live and work in Cancún and other overdeveloped areas on the tourism circuit. Córdoba Azcárate and Castellanos speak to larger trends both within the academic literature and a broader global reckoning with the effects of mass tourism. By the turn of the millennium, damage to popular sites like Venice and Pompeii, the rampant gentrification of destination cities, and adjustments to local subsistence patterns to accommodate the demands of tropical ecotourism had all attracted the attention of mainstream transnational media (see Becker 2016). These global concerns are paralleled in an ethnographic literature increasingly focused on economic and environmental impacts that are obscured by the "bubble" in which tourists move through space (Carrier and Macleod 2005; see also Babb 2011; Fabinyi 2010; González Velarde 2018; and Herzfeld 2010).

The mass tourism that moves between Cancún and Chichén Itzá has inflicted a range of harms on local Maya communities, particularly as it has been dominated by several large regional conglomerates. Even those who have prospered from the industry often struggle to reconcile new lifestyles and social identities with those of their elders and less fortunate kin (Castellanos 2010; Re Cruz 1996; Taylor 2018). But in the vernacular narratives of communities like Pisté, these negative effects tend to be offset by the memory of newfound economic opportunities that also broadened the political horizons of local residents. These positive associations reflect the experience of established communities that are fortunate enough to have tourist attractions abutting locally controlled lands and municipal jurisdictions. Rural Mayan speakers in communities like Pisté have legal mechanisms for determining the use of local land resources and are the dominant force in local municipal elections. Both of these factors grant them a degree of control over their collective economic destinies that is virtually unattainable for their counterparts living in more urbanized areas like Cancún and other major cities along the Caribbean coast.

These historical experiences are at the root of the political discourse that I have termed "vernacular neoliberalism." As I will discuss in detail below, many of my friends and informants express pride in their Maya heritage even as they are highly critical of the early twentieth-century agrarian institutions that were the primary nexus between Indigenous agriculturalists and the state. Instead, they articulate a notion of Indigenous autonomy based on local entrepreneurialism and benefits that trickle down from wealthy merchants to their poorer neighbors. As I will discuss in chapters 4, 5, and 6, this emphasis on entrepreneurialism tends to inform a broader moral economy that many rural people apply to discussions of municipal politics and voter behavior in general.

Adam Kotsko has approached this simultaneously political and moralistic dimension of neoliberal culture by adapting Carl Schmitt's concept of "political theology." That is, he argues that the logic of markets, efficiency, and private property escape the bounds of the economy to provide a consistent normative framework for numerous terrains of human experience (Kotsko 2018, 12–16). Kotsko pays close attention to how political actors cite popular stock characters that embody certain values without making explicit reference to formal political platforms. For example, neoliberalism's boosters in the United States popularized "demonic" figures like the Reagan-era "welfare queen," a mythical character that reframed older racist stereotypes into a libertarian nightmare of economic underproductivity and sexual overproductivity. Kotsko (2018, 78–90) argues that "demonic" foils such as these provide a coherent moral order that unites the economic, domestic, and social realms.

As I will show in the chapters that follow, vernacular narratives of politics and economic development in the communities where I conduct research are also densely populated with "demons." These include predictable characters, like inefficient workers in bloated government bureaucracy, or ambitious politicians for whom electoral gains trump sensible development strategy. But they also include stereotypical characters who imply a vernacular critique of what are considered traditional lifeways. Some of my friends' and informants' sternest criticisms are reserved for their own ancestors and older relatives, whose long dependence on the government subsidies that propped up an inefficient agrarian economy turned them into a reliable "voter reserve" of the PRI. These critiques of traditional agrarian occupations are invoked side-by-side with a celebration of Maya culture, which many younger people view as perfectly compatible with entrepreneurial participation in the tourism industry. This vision of Indigeneity is often difficult to reconcile with the "official" multiculturalism of government agencies or the expectations of the international public. But for many rural Yucatecans, it is an Indigeneity that coherently integrates cultural and linguistic heritage with economic aspirations and participation in mainstream politics.

ETHNOGRAPHY AND HISTORY OF THE TWENTIETH CENTURY: A CHAPTER SUMMARY

This book tells the story of how several generations of rural Yucatecans participated in political institutions that were dominated by elite interests in order to derive what benefits they could from an often-volatile economy. Drawing on material from a number of national and regional archives, my narrative begins with the creation of the three transpeninsular highway corridors that defined a regional geography of development. Over the course of several decades, this landscape saw the decline of parastatal industrial agriculture and the rise of tourism as the cornerstone of the regional economy. Those communities fortunate enough to be situated on major arteries of the tourism circuit prospered, albeit amid frequent struggles against rival regions and business elites that threatened to cut them off from the roads to prosperity. This is the larger historical context for the emergence of vernacular neoliberalism, which continues to define local aspirations and struggles for political self-determination.

Later chapters of his story will focus more on ethnographic materials from a number of communities in Yucatán and its neighboring state of Quintana Roo. As will become clear, the bulk of my ethnographic examples focus on towns and villages on the periphery of the major archaeological zone of Chichén Itzá. The most important of these is the town of Pisté, where I have conducted research for over twenty years. Pisté has also been the focus of writing by several previous ethnographers (Breglia 2006; Castañeda 1996). In examining the quotidian life and municipal politics of this community, I will draw on decades of my own ethnographic observations, informal surveys, and over forty long-form interviews that I recorded between the early 2000s and 2016. The latter represent the perspectives of persons ranging from artisans who are part-time agriculturalists, to well-off merchants, multilingual tour guides and food service staff, university-educated professionals, blue-collar workers, and elders who were major political players in the events of the 1960s and 1970s. Just as important, my perspective on the politics of Yucatán as a whole has been shaped by countless informal conversations in which local friends and informants shared their insight on reporting in regional and national newspapers.

This field site is, in many ways, at the geographical, economic, and infrastructural heart of the story that I tell in this book. A community of around 6,000 today, Pisté is home to almost half of the population of the municipality of Tinum, which also includes the town of Tinum, the villages of San Francisco, Tohopkú, and Xcalakoop, and other small settlements. Perhaps the most outstanding characteristic of Pisté and its closest neighbors is access to the tourism economy. Although there is a lack of fine-grained municipal- and town-level reporting of economic data from rural Mexico, it is possible to draw some broad contours from published census materials. Due to the volume of tourism at Chichén Itzá, the municipality of Tinum's service and commercial sector boasted an annual income of at least US$4 billion at the end of the 2000s.[5] As I will discuss in later chapters, government agencies, luxury hotels, and major tourism corporations absorb the lion's share of the net income. Still, in this municipality, a population of around 13,000 lives and works in a local economy that brings in well over twice the combined total of the five neighboring municipalities, which are home to close to 33,000 people. Long-standing business arrangements and kinship networks tend to give residents of Pisté privileged access to the most desirable jobs in the tourism economy. Access to coveted points of sale near and in the archaeological zone has also allowed many of the town's residents to become retailers of handicrafts that are produced in outlying communities.

Many residents of Pisté also employ commuters from these more rural towns and villages to perform manual jobs that range from yardwork and house-cleaning to moving goods to and from points of sale.

In chapter 1 of this book, I explore how this privileged access to a tourism hotspot reflects a process of territorial configuration that began decades before the foundation of Cancún. Pisté emerged among the clearest "win-ners" in a series of road infrastructural developments that began in 1936 when President Lázaro Cárdenas decreed the construction of three trans-peninsular highway corridors. The road projects evolved slowly over several decades, amid changing political priorities and the rise and fall of several state-subsidized industries. Specific decisions regarding the routing of the roads, and which spans to prioritize at which time, have embodied forms of positive and negative infrastructure for generations of people in the state's rural periphery. As I will show, this decades-long process was also crucial in determining the "when" and "where" for the eventual foundation of Cancún and its sprawling commercial geography.

As I noted earlier, Cancún has as much of a symbolic as a material im-portance for people living and working in its peripheries. By the end of the 1970s, the resort city represented a rare success story amid the collapse of other industries that had been built around state-directed development projects. Chapter 2 focuses on the fate of Yucatán's once-powerful hene-quen industry, along with several agrarian alternatives that were promoted between the 1950s and 1970s. Journalistic critiques of the "failures" of state-sponsored agrarian development became particularly acute during a glut of parastatalization in the mid-1970s, which coincided with the rise of tourism as a dominant industry across the peninsula. As I will argue in sub-sequent chapters, this contrast between the emergent potentials of tourism and the evident failures of state-subsidized agriculture projects shaped the vernacular neoliberalism that influences the political participation of many rural Yucatecans today.

Chapters 3 and 4 will slightly shift the emphasis from the contours of regional development to the political realignments that marked the transition from Stabilizing Development to neoliberalism. As I noted earlier, uses of the term "neoliberalism" in Mexico evoke political personalities and historical moments as much as they do the particulars of an economic model. In Yu-catán, this historical transition is embodied by a particularly powerful figure within the PRI, the state governor and kingmaker Víctor Cervera Pacheco. In chapter 3, I will examine the electoral strategies, public rhetoric, and signature development projects that allowed Cervera and his collaborators to blur the boundary between postcrisis economic realities and the legacies of populism and state-driven development. Tourism infrastructure was one cornerstone of this strategy. Though this style of politics was successful for over a decade, the gradual unravelling of Cervera's power base led to the rise of political opposition in rural communities like Pisté. This ultimately contributed to the election of the first governor from an opposition party in 2000. In chapter 4, I use a series of ethnographic vignettes to discuss how the vernacular discourse on neoliberalism that is common today reflects both the *cerverista* syncretism of market-based values and rural populism, and the local grievances that ultimately led many rural people to break with the PRI.

The remaining chapters of this book will focus on the intersections of this vernacular neoliberalism with more recent struggles over development and concurrent forms of positive and negative infrastructure. One factor behind the rise of vernacular neoliberalism is the expansion of public education opportunities for residents of rural communities. This expansion reflects a series of federal programs that were intended to ease Mexico's transition into the free market realities of a neoliberal world in the wake of the North American Free Trade Agreement (NAFTA). Chapter 5 will look more closely at local experiences of expanding educational horizons in Pisté and neighboring communities. Though education is highly valued in these communities, recent graduates are left to face a job market that is far less favorable for professionals than it is for blue-collar service sector workers. The depth of public and private investment in the tourist sector that has been the source of many Pisteños' prosperity continues to inflict negative infrastructure on alternative industries that could accommodate their better-educated children. This relative lack of occupational mobility sets the stage for an endemic conflict between local tourism entrepreneurs, the state government, and major tourism firms.

Chapter 6 will focus on a particularly dramatic series of municipal-level conflicts that emerged in the 2010s. In 2007, Governor Ivonne Ortega Pacheco returned the statehouse to the PRI, ushering a two-sexenio period of the party's dominance in Yucatán. Just as her uncle and political predecessor Víctor Cervera Pacheco had partnered with major tourism operators during his tenure, Ortega Pacheco strengthened the regional PRI's ties to major tourism firms, most notably the Xcaret Group. This collaboration was reflected in a series of reforms that gave the state government of Yucatán unprecedented control over regional archaeological sites. Another important component of this collaboration was a reconfiguration of the spatial dynamics of state-sponsored infrastructural development in ways that were compatible with the decentered, logistics-focused model of tourism employed by Xcaret and related firms.

These projects brought Ortega Pacheco and her immediate successor into direct conflict with opposition politicians in Pisté and other communities in the municipality of Tinum. A project proposed in the early 2010s involved the construction of a road that would have imposed a significant degree of negative infrastructure on the municipality. Though local residents were ultimately successful in preventing the project's completion, the resulting tensions contributed to a series of particularly violent election cycles during which state-level PRI politicians sought to marginalize a popular opposition figure in town. Community members responded with a range of strategies that were consistent with lessons learned during the 1970s and 1980s. This blend of participation in mainstream electoral politics, time-tested forms of direct action, and the mobilization of identities that blend Indigeneity and entrepreneurialism encapsulates the political ramifications of vernacular neoliberalism.

Chapter 7 will take a closer look at some of the ideological underpinnings of this local political resistance. In the 2010s, time-tested strategies of electioneering and direct action were augmented by the use of social media, particularly Facebook. However, in contrast to more widely studied cases of digital activism in Indigenous communities, these uses of social media rarely made any attempt to link local partisan conflicts to broader Indigenous or anti-neoliberal struggles. Furthermore, they draw on platforms, genres of content, and references to popular media that many intellectuals in Mexico and abroad associate with "mainstream" and apolitical consumption. But as I argue, these practices are consistent with the social identities and political common sense that emerged in many rural communities at the end of the twentieth century. Like the narratives of Maya heritage that I discussed in chapter 4, this political engagement through consumerist media melds locally meaningful experiences with participation in the global economy.

I conclude this book with a discussion of the Tren Maya megaproject that was initiated in 2019 by the administration of left-of-center President Andrés Manuel López Obrador. Under the aegis of a new political party, López Obrador took the presidency offering a radical post-neoliberal transformation of Mexican society. The massive influx of travelers who would arrive in the peninsula with the proposed train would not only increase tourism to existing sites but also "open" new regions in the South. But just as many of President López Obrador's programs stumbled in the face of local political opposition and the global crisis of COVID-19, the Tren Maya has faced resistance from some of the very communities it was intended to serve. Pisté was no exception, and many of the techniques of negotiation and direct action that local political factions used as a check against *priísta* administrations in the 2010s were applied against the new government. This still-evolving situation offers further evidence of a persistent tension between the interests of local communities and elite-driven innovations in infrastructural development. Just as important, it highlights the historical continuity and adaptability of the strategies with which rural Mayan speakers face these threats to their livelihood.

A NOTE ON THE NAME OF PLACES AND PEOPLE

Unlike some ethnographers, I have not used pseudonyms for the different towns and villages where I have conducted research. Given that this book combines ethnography with historiography, and that it is not typical to use place pseudonyms in historiography, this was necessary to meld different parts of the narrative and argument. Further, given that many of the incidents I will discuss involve the specific spatial relationship between towns and villages, any coherent narrative would have made the disguising of place names moot. Because of this, I have taken some additional steps to protect the anonymity of the interviewees who figure in some of the chapters. Besides using pseudonyms for all people interviewed here, I have intentionally avoided providing extensive or detailed biographical information about them. In some cases, I have changed the profession of individuals, or their specific age and family relationships.

Chapters 5 through 7 include some detailed discussion of a series of election cycles in the past ten years. Some of the information that shaped these chapters was derived from ethnographic interviews. However, I have intentionally omitted some specific sensitive information about those election cycles. Incidents of political violence that I discuss here have all been reported in the regional press. Thus, while my analysis of those incidents is informed by discussions in the community, I will not present any specific facts about those incidents that have not already been made public.

1

THE CREATION OF A MODERN GEOGRAPHY

In the introduction, I referred to the planning of the three transpeninsular road corridors in 1936 as a foundational act that defined the geographical parameters for twentieth-century development on the Yucatán Peninsula. Writing about the development of comparable interregional road networks in Peru, Penny Harvey and Hannah Knox (2015, 48) refer to the "rhythms of hope and disappointment" with which residents of isolated communities contemplate the promises, starts, and stops of projects that represent a physical and symbolic link to prosperity (see also Bess 2017). A similar pattern is evident in the documentary record of road construction in the Yucatán Peninsula, and in the narratives with which rural Yucatecans discuss the more recent experiences of positive and negative infrastructure. The three transpeninsular road corridors developed over a generation, during which the optimism of local stakeholders waxed and waned as resources were juggled between three distinct regions. As with other development projects, these moments of "hope and disappointment" coincided closely with the timing of presidential sexenios, each of which offered a new opportunity to seek redress for neglect by earlier leaders.

By the 1940s and 1950s, when much of the heavy work on the road corridors took place, rural communities also contended with changes in the ideology of Mexico's political elite. By the Second World War, the generals who had fought in the Mexican Revolution between 1910 and the 1920s were being replaced by a cohort of civilian leaders who had been born into the post-Revolutionary state. When the latter age cohort began their careers, institutions that had been prioritized in the 1920s were undergoing significant transformations (see Alexander 2016). The most economically significant of these for the state of Yucatán was a heavily subsidized henequen industry, which was concentrated in the northwest of the peninsula. I will discuss the fate and impacts of this industry at length in chapter 2. In this chapter, I will focus more on the southern and eastern portions of the Yucatán Peninsula, which were the primary targets for new road infrastructure in the 1930s. This was a historically "underdeveloped" region, where the first Revolutionary governments had made significant territorial and economic concessions to autonomous Maya communities that were involved in the transnational chicle trade. As urban boosters for commercial agriculture pushed for the creation of new productive zones, they criticized "inefficient" uses of forest resources by "nomadic" natives. As I will show, these elite critics often employed a discourse of terra nullius (see Watson 2014) to erase earlier histories of agriculture and settlement, and to constitute the far south and southeast of the peninsula as an "unclaimed" frontier of development. There are historical parallels between these plans for the development of the Yucatán Peninsula and contemporaneous projects for the infrastructural and economic development of Mexico's Northwest. But where the latter was seen as a site for negotiation between Mexicans and their cross-border neighbors in the United States (Kim 2015; Núñez Tapía and Méndez Reyes 2018), the infrastructural and economic development of the peninsula was initially envisioned as a strictly national affair.

Something that is clear from the historical accounts is that the early Revolutionary state had left a minimal infrastructural footprint on vast swaths of the Yucatán Peninsula. Note, for example, the itinerary that Undersecretary of Public Education Moisés Sáenz followed when he led an exploratory commission through Quintana Roo in 1929. Flying into Guatemala, they traveled to Belize on the Caribbean coast, and from there to Payo Obispo, the future site of the city of Chetumal. After touring the Río Hondo, the traditional border between Mexican territory and the British settlement, Sáenz and his companions traveled by mule to the old fortress town of Bacalar. From there, they traveled north into Santa Cruz del Bravo. This was the traditional territory of the Cruzo'ob, a cluster of allied Maya communities that had retained political autonomy since the so-called Caste War of the mid-nineteenth century. Returning to the coast, Sáenz and his companions visited the island of Cozumel before returning to the mainland to travel west to the colonial town of Tizimín in the state of Yucatán (in Beteta 1951, x).

The fact that it was impractical to reach Payo Obispo in the Bay of Chetumal without exiting Mexican territory is a clear testament to the fragmentary nature of the peninsula's road infrastructure. The various routes that Sáenz followed from Bacalar to Chan Santa Cruz and from the coast adjacent Cozumel to the town of Tizimín consisted of narrow bush paths and rough, seasonally impassible roads. In the 1920s, the isolation of southern and central Quintana Roo from the rest of the republic, like the general difficulty of land travel in the peninsula, were cited as two of the principal impediments to its economic development.

Though some key historical documents are missing from Mexico's national archive, references in letters from the late 1930s to 1950s establish 1936 as the approval date for three transpeninsular road projects. This links them to a larger investment in transport infrastructure during the sexenio of Lázaro Cárdenas (1934–40). More specifically, these roads were decreed in the same year that saw the completion of the span of the Pan American Highway that linked Mexico to the United States (Bess 2017, 71–72; Gruel Sández 2017). Situated at the southeastern extreme of Mexico, these roads seem to embody the desire for an infrastructure that spanned the full extent of the nation's territory.

The formal names of the roads have changed over the decades, but the three routes described in the late 1930s are essentially the same three transpeninsular corridors that exist in the present day. The most important of these is the eastern extension of the Federal Highway 180 corridor that links the Yucatecan capital of Mérida to what is today Cancún. Between the 1930s and 1960s, this was referred to as the Mérida–Puerto Juárez road.

A second planned road corridor would link Mérida to the settlement of Payo Obispo, now the city of Chetumal, located near the Belizean border. Today, this consists of a combination of Federal Highways 194 and 307. When it was first conceived in the late 1930s, this corridor expanded on existing road and rail networks linking Mérida to the southern Yucatecan town of Peto, and was referred to as the Peto-Chetumal road or Mérida-Chetumal road. Constructed in the decades following the definitive peace between the autonomous Cruzo'ob and Mexico's federal government, this was envisioned as a means of both bringing the benefits of development to these once-isolated autonomous communities and of opening promising economic opportunities for agrarian capitalists from Yucatán.

The third road corridor planned under Cárdenas is both the least traveled and the least documented historically. This is today a part of Federal Highway 186, which links the town of Escárcega in the far south of Campeche to Chetumal in Quintana Roo. When formal construction began in 1939, Escárcega didn't exist as such, and the western terminus of the road was the train depot of Matamoros. In theory, this roadway would have linked several rich chicle-producing regions to the Bay of Chetumal in the east and the Bay of Campeche in the west. It would open a vast area of sparsely populated tropical forest and swampland to development. And, running roughly parallel to the border with Guatemala, it would prove an important piece of security infrastructure against often-hostile regimes in Mexico's southern neighbor.

As I noted in the introduction, the Highway 180 corridor emerged as the crown jewel of the peninsula's road infrastructure. After the creation of Cancún, it became the direct link between the peninsula's two most urbanized regions and some of its most densely populated rural areas. In the following sections, I will discuss a series of processes, events, and basic facts of geography that led to the consolidation of the 180 corridor's dominance at the expense of the two other roadways that were planned in 1936. If the dynamic between Holcá and Kantunil that I described in the previous chapter presents a microcosmic view of negative infrastructure, the histories that I will discuss here show similar phenomena evolving on a scale that would define the lives of millions of rural and urban people across three Mexican states.

TRACING HIGHWAY 180:
CHICLE COUNTRY AND WORLD WAR II

In late November 1939, President Lázaro Cárdenas wrote to the general of the military garrison in Mérida, asking that he select two officers to lead a commission that would reconnoiter the path from the city of Valladolid to the Caribbean coast.[1] This commission would determine the route of what would ultimately become the easternmost extreme of Federal Highway 180. Almost thirty years before the planning of Cancún, the idea of a beach resort was far from Cárdenas's mind. The purpose of this military commission was to help supply a newly constructed naval base on Isla Mujeres, the easternmost point of Mexico's national territory.

The fact that the civilian construction project decreed in 1936 had been placed under military jurisdiction in 1939 reflects some of the difficulties that marked Cárdenas's final years in office. One of the hallmarks of his sexenio was an unprecedented public investment in the construction of transportation and economic infrastructure (see Aguilar Camín and Meyer 1993; and Bess 2017, 72–76). Still, work on the transpeninsular corridors appears to have been limited before the outbreak of the Second World War. The sluggish pace of this development coincided with an economic slump that followed the accelerated expropriation of land from large private estates during the Cárdenas sexenio, as well as the immediate aftermath of the oil nationalization of March 1938 (see Aguilar Camín and Meyer 1993, 133).

In the case of the Mérida–Puerto Juárez road, military expediency seems to have trumped the economic factors that slowed the development of the other two corridors. By the fall of 1939, after several years of plotting a relatively noncommittal diplomatic course between the Allied and Axis powers, the Cárdenas administration found itself forging closer military ties to the United States (Schuler 1999, 161). This alliance made developing Mexico's military infrastructure, especially along the coast, essential. Cárdenas and his immediate successor, Manuel Ávila Camacho, feared that gringo offers of direct aid in Mexico's homeland security would result in a politically unacceptable presence of foreign forces on their soil and national waters (Jones 2014, 43–50). Located on the easternmost point in Mexican territory, the base on Isla Mujeres played a symbolic as much as a practical role in representing Mexico's sovereignty over its national boundaries.

Supplying a base on the Caribbean coast from Mexican soil posed particular problems. Large-scale land transportation from the city of Mérida to the coast was difficult under the best conditions and all but impossible during the late summer rains. Maritime shipping routes that used the port of Belize—like those on which Moisés Sáenz had relied a decade earlier—threatened an excessive dependence on an already-contentious British colony. Any route through the south of the peninsula was ruled out by the intractability of the terrain and the proximity to Guatemala. In 1939, Mexico's southern neighbor was governed by the caudillo Jorge Ubico, who deeply distrusted the "Bolshevik" Cárdenas and had a historically cozy relationship with the Axis powers (see Grieb 1979, 219–34, 248–54).

Faced with these options, the northern route offered multiple benefits. It was crisscrossed by relatively well-traveled bush paths and even some basic modular rail lines associated with the chicle trade. It was deeply embedded in Mexico's national territory, far from the Guatemalan border and British holdings. It also boasted access to a more densely settled and productive agricultural region than the far south of the peninsula.

In contrast to later documentation of the transpeninsular corridors that was produced by the Secretaría de Obras Públicas (Secretariat of Public Works, or SOP), the orders and reports pertinent to the 1939 expedition highlight the military nature of the project. Besides finding the most viable terrain for constructing the road, Cárdenas also requested that the leaders of the expedition provide detailed observations of "the general conditions of the territory and natural resources that are apt for the needs of the military." By the end of November, equipped with 11,000 pesos of federal and state funds and accompanied by civilian engineers, Lieutenants Ricardo Ramos Flores and Félix García Mejía departed from Valladolid. Eleven days later, on 8 December, they arrived at the pre-Hispanic ruins of El Meco, near the village of Puerto Juárez and the nearest point of coast to Isla Mujeres.

The commission's route took them from Valladolid, a regional capital and market center, to the small town of Chemax. From there, they traveled to the village of Xcan, just across the state border from the Territory of Quintana Roo. Notwithstanding the presence of trained engineers in the expedition, there is little actual surveying in the report. Rather than tracing a straight route through the bush, the expedition explored a somewhat winding path through existing bush trails and short spans of Decauville rails (a modular system for steam- or mule-driven transport that was common on haciendas throughout the peninsula). Unlike later projects that would involve clearing large stretches of bush to sight and chart more or less linear paths through the peninsula, Lieutenant García Mejía's task seems to have been one of exploring and curating a corpus of paths created by more than a century of trade and transportation to determine which deserved to be canonized as federal road infrastructure.

The lieutenant's professional eye is immediately evident in the emphasis he placed on the fitness of existing infrastructure for military transport. He observed which paths were suited for the movement of artillery carts, which could be traversed by cavalry, and which could only be traversed by infantry in single file. He took note of which stretches passed through forest that was so densely canopied that they could not be observed from the air. His observations of the utility of different tree species reflect either a detailed knowledge of Mayan-language terms for different woods or his reliance on local informants. For example, García Mejía refers to plants such as *kitamché* (*Caesalpinia gaumeri*), which is good for firewood, and *jabím* (*Piscidia piscipula*), which is useful for railway ties.[2]

García Mejía's descriptions of the population of different communities he encountered likewise focus on their usefulness to the military, and are tinged with obvious urban biases. In Chemax, he observed that "primitive" forms of agricultural production meant that there was limited availability of maize, beans, yucca, and sesame, which was evidenced by the poor health of the Mayan-monolingual inhabitants. The need for modern and gainful employment was also evidenced by what he saw as the "relatively high" incidence of alcoholism. García Mejía observed that, though they lacked any military training, the men of this community could be employed as infantry if necessary. Their attitude toward the military, he noted, was one of "neither repulsion nor sympathy . . . but of respect." Given that the expedition was entering a region that had maintained a strong degree of autonomy in the decades following the Caste War of 1847, and that Chemax itself was the site of frequent political unrest through most of the twentieth century (see Brown 2007), this comment seems to offer reassurance that the residents of this crucial waypoint would not offer serious resistance to the planned road project.

Lieutenant García Mejía and his companions traveled through the village of Catzín and the abandoned settlement of Xpuxkú on the way to Xcan. There, he described the thickening of the bush, a narrowing of trails, and a similarly "unhealthy" population to the one he had observed in Chemax. However, when they arrived in Kantunilkín, about forty kilometers to the northwest of Xcan, García Mejía observed a "properly healthy place," and a population with true "sympathy" for the military. He also observed "great enthusiasm" for the construction of a road, and the fact that it would be easy to recruit laborers from the local population.

Notwithstanding this observation about the community, the commission's report concluded that the final road should be built over existing trails as far as Xcan but then blaze a new transect through the bush directly to the settlement of Leona Vicario (see map 1.1). Thus, what is today Highway 180 passes well to the south of Kantunilkín. I have not found any records of this decision being protested by residents of Kantunilkín, but it's easy to imagine that many in the village viewed being cut off from this new transpeninsular infrastructure as a betrayal of faith that their ancestors had placed in the Mexican government. The community was first founded in 1859 when a faction of Caste War rebels sued for peace and were granted amnesty and a temporary autonomy in their local affairs. In the decades that followed, the people of Kantunilkín would be harassed and raided by their former allies, the Cruzo'ob, and also would contribute men and supplies to the state and federal governments' expeditions against remaining rebel factions (see Sullivan 2004, 35–37).

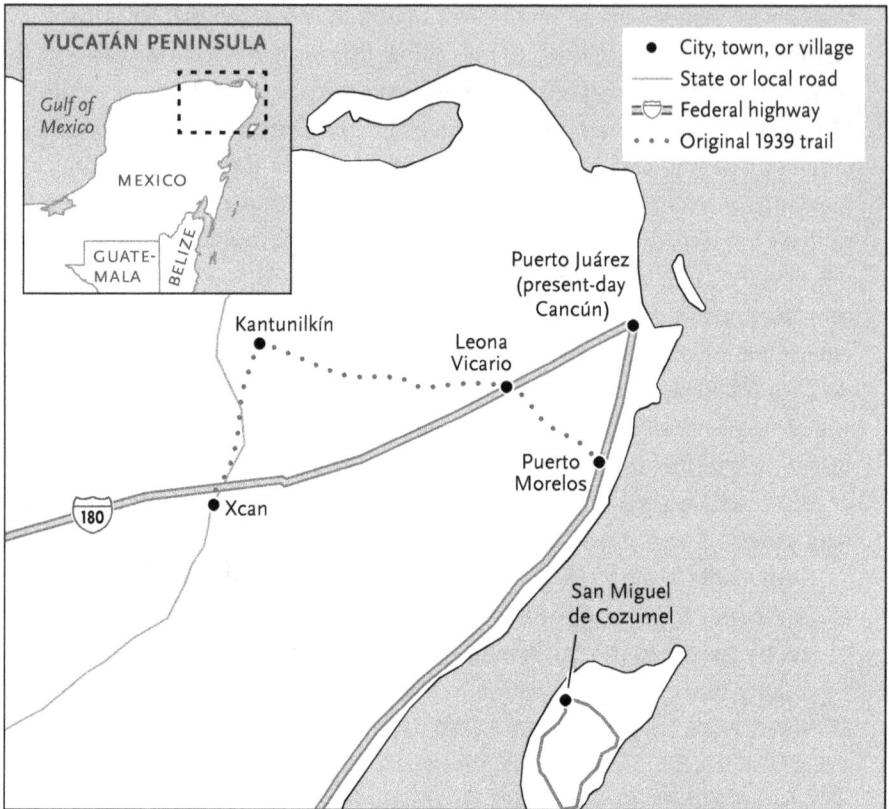

Map 1.1. The easternmost extension of Federal Highway 180.
Completed in the late 1950s, its trajectory reflects the route proposed
by the 1939 expedition. The dotted line represents the trail from Xcan to
Kantunilkín, the trail from Kantunilkín to Leona Vicario, and the Decauville
rail from Leona Vicario to Puerto Morelos. These were part of late
nineteenth-century infrastructure for transporting chicle to what was then the
busiest port on the Mexican Caribbean. They were still in use in the 1930s
but were excluded from the final plan of the Highway 180 corridor.
*Map created by Nicolás Reyes, Heather Rosenfeld, and Kala'i Ellis
at the Spatial Analysis Lab, Smith College, Northampton, MA.*

By the second half of the twentieth century, the decision to route the new
road directly from Xcan to Leona Vicario would inflict a significant degree
of negative infrastructure on Kantunilkín. The village was transformed from
an essential waypoint in most west-to-east travel to a distant satellite of what
would become the Highway 180 corridor. In fact, the consolidation of Highway 180 had impacts beyond Kantunilkín to an entire economic microregion

of the extreme northeast of the Yucatán Peninsula. In the second half of the nineteenth century, Kantunilkín was a key stop between the center of the peninsula and a number of sugar haciendas, like the ill-fated Xuxub, whose violent demise at the hands of a rebel Maya group was chronicled by Paul Sullivan (2004). Had García Mejía and his companions followed trails leading north, as Moisés Sáenz and his commission had a decade earlier, they would have encountered a lively small-scale fishing industry and settlements with a long history of exploiting naturally occurring salt pans all along the northern coast of the state of Yucatán.

This region possesses its own distinctive identity, and is popular among Yucatecans today as a more affordable beach area and for events associated with the annual fair of Tizimín. But until quite recently, it was peripheral to the east-west touristic corridor defined by Highway 180. Even today, it's rare to see significant groups of foreign tourists at the annual fair of Tizimín, despite this being one of the best attended in southeastern Mexico. Visitors to Caribbean resorts can purchase a package tour to snorkel with whale sharks off Holbox Island or see the flamingo habitat in Río Lagartos on the north coast. But both spots are relatively late additions to the tourist circuit after the "saturation" of Cancún, Playa del Carmen, and Tulum (see Córdoba Azcárate 2020, 1–4, 67).

If Lieutenant García Mejía had considered the long-term ramifications of the negative infrastructure that his recommendation would inflict on the far north of the peninsula, he didn't record it in his report. The scale of twenty-first-century tourist development would have been inconceivable in 1939, when he and his companions forged eastward from Kantunilkín through a heavily wooded region whose communities were isolated from each other. This seemingly "empty" territory had had a complex and violent history in the previous century. Home to dozens of Indigenous communities and small private haciendas at the beginning of the nineteenth century, it was largely depopulated in the wake of the Caste War. In the last third of the nineteenth century, as the Cruzo'ob and other rebel communities were increasingly contained in the southeast of the peninsula, the federal government under Porfirio Díaz declared this portion of the territory of Quintana Roo to be "baldío" (abandoned). The subsequent constitution of Quintana Roo as a federal territory allowed the national government to grant a series of concessions to private developers.[3] By 1939, when they were visited by Lieutenant García Mejía and his companions, the former concessions had been renationalized, and the region was being slowly resettled by transitory groups of independent chicle gatherers. These itinerant groups and the small footprint they left on the landscape are the only local population recorded in the 1939 report.

Though it's highly unlikely that later tourism developers were familiar with Lieutenant García Mejía's unpublished report, his characterization of this region as "empty" reiterated an official narrative that had been established since those lands were designated as "abandoned" at the end of the 1800s. Drawing on the same institutional common sense, the Banco de México technocrats who engineered the Cancún project in the 1960s treated it as an "open" frontier for economic development (Martí 1985). In this, they invoked classic tropes that legitimated Western expansion at the expense of Indigenous territoriality (Wilkins and Lomawaima 2001; Watson 2014). This "frontier" logic continued to resonate in decades of touristic development and promotion. In an analysis of maps published in popular guidebooks to the Mexican Caribbean, Bianet Castellanos notes a persistent tendency to erase signs of human habitation between coastal resorts and inland archaeological attractions. Along with text that plays on adventure narratives of "mystery" and "dense jungle," they present the peninsula through a classic settler colonialist trope, as a "terra nullius waiting to be discovered" by foreign tourists (Castellanos 2023, 182). Insofar as Lieutenant García Mejía's report was an instance of this official narrative of "emptiness," it contributed to an erasure of the complex human history of the area to the south of Kantunilkín.

The end of García Mejía's journey was in sight when the expedition arrived at the chicle camp known as Mil Novecientos (Nineteen hundred), which was linked by a Decauville light rail to the settlement of Leona Vicario, fifteen kilometers away. Where they had found communities of maize agriculturalists in Chemax, Xcan, and Kantunilkín, Leona Vicario was a settlement of 200 individuals dedicated almost exclusively to the harvesting of chicle and lumber. The settlement was on land that had been part of a private concession and was previously known as the Hacienda Santa María. Today, it is the easternmost town of significant size on Highway 180 before entering the municipal periphery of Cancún.

At Leona Vicario, Lieutenant García Mejía observed that a second set of Decauville tracks moved southeast to the port of Puerto Morelos, which was the primary point of export for chicle and timber (Macías Zapata 2002, 131). But seeking a stretch of coast that was closer to Isla Mujeres, he and his companions veered northward to the pre-Hispanic ruins of El Meco and the tiny fishing village of Puerto Juárez. Today, Puerto Juárez has been essentially absorbed into the urban footprint of Cancún. It is familiar to millions of Mexican and international tourists as the point of departure for twice-hourly ferries to Isla Mujeres and Cozumel. The nearby Playa de los Niños is considered by locals to be the last stretch of beach that is not in some way access-restricted by hotels, and therefore a destination of choice for blue-collar Cancún residents. But in Lieutenant García Mejía's day, the entire stretch of mainland coast was home to just a few hundred transient fishermen and settlers for whom "town" was one of the slightly larger villages on Isla Mujeres.

It's unclear from the 1939 documentation whether or not President Cárdenas envisioned the road corridor from Valladolid to Puerto Juárez as initiating the development of the north-central coast of Quintana Roo. It's likely that he had yet to look beyond the military exigencies of the Second World War. A little over a decade later, however, this area seems to have been on its way to eclipsing the newly minted territorial capital of Payo Obispo/Chetumal as Mexico's gateway to the Caribbean.

This early integration of Puerto Juárez into what would become the Highway 180 corridor also casts some doubt on claims that would be made by representatives of the Banco de México in the 1970s. As I noted earlier, the bankers' narrative leaned heavily on the characterization of Quintana Roo as a terra nullius and stressed the originality of the technical processes they had employed in identifying this "virgin" stretch of coast for the development of a new resort city (Martí 1985). A 1972 promotional article in the *New York Times* proclaimed that "the computer chose Cancún," noting that the selection of the barren but beautiful stretch of coast had been based on careful calculations of weather and travel times from major US airports (Dunphy 1972). In reality, existing road infrastructure largely determined the fact that a planned resort city on the northern Caribbean coast of the Yucatán Peninsula would be somewhere in the vicinity of Puerto Juárez. In all likelihood, whatever "computer" was employed in 1968 played a smaller role in choosing Cancún than Lieutenant García Mejía had thirty years earlier.

FROM PETO TO CHETUMAL: AUTONOMOUS CRUZO'OB AND EAGER CAPITALISTS

Besides the military expediencies of 1939, the inevitable "choice" of Cancún/Puerto Juárez also reflects the more arduous process of establishing road communications with southern parts of the Caribbean coast. What is today the city of Chetumal, capital of the state of Quintana Roo, was founded in 1898 as Payo Obispo, an outpost meant to regularize trade between Mexico and the neighboring colony of British Honduras. In the years following the military defeat of the Cruzo'ob at Chan Santa Cruz, the new entrepot would seek to establish control over the extraction of chicle, lumber, and other tropical resources that had, for half a century, left the peninsula through the British port of Belize. The settlement of Payo Obispo grew slowly and was so isolated from other Mexican population centers that it depended on cross-border trade with Belize for most of its manufactured goods (Romero Mayo and Benítez López 2014, 127). The population was a mere 2,790 souls in 1930, a figure that increased to 4,672 a decade later (Romero Mayo and Benítez López 2014, 135).

The road corridor linking Mérida to Chetumal presented a vital conduit to stock the emergent capital with Mexican food and construction materials, and to populate it with more Mexican settlers. But documentation preserved in the Archivo General de la Nación (General Archive of the Nation) suggests that the course of the Mérida-Chetumal corridor was more contested than that of the Mérida–Puerto Juárez corridor. Where the route of the latter was determined by a military commission and apparently confirmed by presidential decree, the exact trajectory of the former was debated by a number of officials, chambers of commerce, and Maya communities from the 1930s to the 1950s. In this regard, the building of the Mérida-Chetumal corridor involved more of the kinds of interventions by diverse local stakeholders that Michael Bess (2017) observed in road construction in Veracruz and Nuevo León. I have not found any documentary evidence that the people of Kantunilkín had much to say regarding the negative infrastructure that was inflicted on their town by the final routing of the road between Valladolid and Puerto Juárez. But many of their contemporaries to the south left a record of their dissenting opinions regarding the Mérida-Chetumal corridor.

Some of this dissent began before construction had launched in earnest. In June 1937, residents of the Maya villages of Cruz Chico, Carrillo Puerto, Filomeno Mata, and Ichmul requested that the proposed route from Peto to Chetumal be altered to pass through their communities. From the practical perspective, they noted that the current plan entailed construction through a swampy region, which would increase costs. Given these issues, they suggested that a more winding path through various villages posed fewer technical challenges. As an added benefit, this less direct path would connect their villages to "the rest of the country," allowing them to transport their lumber and chicle southeast to Chetumal or northwest to Peto. This petition seems to have been prepared in coordination with an ethnographic report sent to President Cárdenas by Professor Graciano Sánchez, the director of Indigenous affairs for the territory of Quintana Roo.[4]

President Cárdenas's secretary sent this report to the directorate of the SOP for comments. The response included the pragmatic observation that the increased cost of creating a longer "zigzag" route outweighed that of working through any swampy territory. But the bulk of the SOP's response consisted of a scathing indictment of the habits of the "tribal" population of central Quintana Roo, and of the governmental and private actors who enabled their current lifestyle. The response noted that

> given that the area is populated by Indigenous [*sic*] towns, it can-
> not be considered a region of fixed population, because, as is well
> known, the Maya tribes that form the population of this region are
> . . . nomadic tribes. It is normal for this population to migrate to sites
> of more abundant water, in the most intractable parts of the jungle
> where they can find security in isolation and tall forests that are ad-
> equate for their agricultural labor. [This is because] of their eternal
> custom of cutting and burning forest for their crops or tapping chicle
> tree trunks for the chicle trade. They only mark the place of their
> varied residences with a single house that more often than not is des-
> tined to be a shrine in which they keep the crosses that they worship.
> For this reason, Professor Sánchez's rationale for varying the path of
> the Peto–Payo Obispo road, which is to provide communication to
> the different towns of the Indigenous Zone, should not be taken into
> account.[5]

The response from the SOP further noted that geographical isolation and the relative ease of subsistence agriculture and seasonal chicle labor were contributing to the "racial degeneration" of the "tribal" villages. It stated that chicle cooperatives that had been organized in Indigenous communities were full of "mystification," controlled undemocratically by the "Generals, Captains, and Sergeants" and other leaders who had ruled their communities with an iron fist since the times of the Caste War. This exploitation of Indige-nous Mexicans at home was compounded by the machinations of the "Syrian and Lebanese" middlemen who purchased chicle and lumber on the coast. Making his own sociological arguments, the director of the SOP suggested that the construction a more direct route between Peto and Chetumal would induce these "nomadic" populations to settle in larger communities on the edges of the road, thus escaping the structures that bound them to corrupt tribal leaders at home and dishonest middlemen in Puerto Morelos.

The SOP's assessment of social conditions in central Quintana Roo in 1937 reflects a particular moment in Mexico's reckoning with the legacy of the Caste War, and requires some unpacking. On some level, the characterization of Indigenous communities as "nomadic" reflected the realities of swidden agriculture, in which households and whole communities relocated when the distance between homes and active horticultural fields became too great (Ford and Nigh 2016). But much of the "nomadism" to which the report refers was a response to the generations-long conflict between Cruzo'ob communities and the Mexican state. The town of Felipe Carrillo Puerto, in the heart of the "tribal" area traversed by the Mérida-Chetumal road, had developed on the site of Chan Santa Cruz, the original capital of the Cruzo'ob. Though the conquest and occupation of Chan Santa Cruz in 1901 is often cited as the official end to the half-century of conflict, several groups of Cruzo'ob sought out new spaces of autonomy to the south and west (see Reed 1977; and Dumond 1997).

Relations between Cruzo'ob descendants and the Mexican state shifted with the Mexican Revolution, as the new government made pragmatic decisions to guarantee peace along its southern border. The Revolutionary government transferred the capital of the territory of Quintana Roo to Payo Obispo/Chetumal, and the Indigenous leaders of the former Cruzo'ob capital were granted official recognition and limited political autonomy by the national government. The historical literature often cites the career of General Francisco May Pech as an example of this changing and often fraught relationship between Indigenous leaders in the former rebel territory and the post-Revolutionary Mexican state. In 1918, the national government of Venustiano Carranza recognized May as the de facto governor of the Maya population of the former rebel area. This status granted the Indigenous general a large degree of control over the chicle cooperative founded in the 1920s, and additional government concessions for the exploitation of lumber and other forestry resources (Ponce Jiménez 1990, 25–27; Redclift 2004).

The SOP's negative assessment of chicle cooperatives in 1937 seems to reference some unforeseen consequences of the Mexican state's embrace of Francisco May Pech. May Pech's style of governance, and perhaps resentment of the privileges he had been granted by distant rulers in Mexico City, spawned conflicts with rival leaders (see Sullivan 1991). He was driven out of Quintana Roo in 1932 and would not be able to return for decades (Redclift 2004, 68–74).

Thus, when representatives of the SOP debated the best route for the Mérida-Chetumal road in 1937, the "problem" of the semiautonomous Maya groups of central Quintana Roo was very different from what it had been a generation earlier. For Mexico City policymakers, the political and social rationale for the pact that the Cruzo'ob had negotiated in 1918 was wearing thin. With hindsight, the SOP argued that the hasty embrace of May Pech and other "tribal" leaders had introduced unnecessary "mystification" into local municipal politics and the state-sponsored system for exploiting chicle and other forest resources. Echoing the narrative of terra nullius that pervaded the official discourse on the territory of Quintana Roo, the SOP denied that these "nomadic" tribes had any true usufruct claim on the territory that they had occupied for generations. By creating a new microregional geography around the Mérida-Chetumal road, Mexico's federal government had an opportunity to overwrite these early "missteps."

Notwithstanding the SOP's scathing report, some Mexican politicians saw the road and future development schemes as a means of legitimating Indigenous claims to territory. Still, even more sympathetic policymakers seemed to assume that Maya communities would relocate to enjoy the benefits of emerging road infrastructure. General Rafael Melgar, named governor of the Federal Territory of Quintana Roo in 1935, embarked on a series of tours in which he laid out a multifaceted development plan that involved granting more formalized rights to land and forestry resources to local communities. This hinged on creating a viable transportation and commercial corridor to the coast: the Mérida-Chetumal road (Villa Rojas [1978] 1992, 132–33). In a book-length panegyric to Melgar's work in Quintana Roo, the Yucatecan poet and politician Luis Rosado Vega (1940, 331) noted, "In this road are placed the greatest expectations, and with good reason. It would be a vital nerve for the territory, especially if care is taken that the road truly benefits the communities through which it passes, rather than the interests of a few landholders who attempt to promote special reroutings of the road for their benefit."

Notwithstanding the populist tone struck by Cárdenas, by Melgar, and by commentators like Rosado Vega, landowners and urban capitalists provided some of the loudest voices for the completion of this corridor. Even as Governor Melgar and President Cárdenas promised local Indigenous communities exclusive title to the exploitation of chicle and other wild resources, urban capitalists of the 1930s and 1940s looked to the center and southeast of the Yucatán Peninsula as an area ripe for the development of large-scale agriculture. Seeking alternatives to the declining fortunes of henequen, they imagined reviving a sugar industry that had been destroyed by the Caste War, expanding the production of beef cattle, or establishing large-scale modern maize cultivation that would turn the Southeast into an exporter of grain (see Baklanoff 1980; Cámara Barbachano 1958; Fabila 1941). These developmentalist aspirations were the rationale behind the Bank of Commerce of

Yucatán, which was chartered in 1956 with a specific mandate of promoting the development of alternative agro-industries in new frontiers beyond the old henequen zone.[6] As I will discuss in the following chapter, many of the schemes for posthenequen commercial agriculture in the center and south of the peninsula floundered in the 1960s and 1970s. Even the more successful ones were less than competitive in the national and international market, and were only kept alive through government subsidies and parastatalization. Still, impassioned calls for the completion of Melgar's "vital nerve" through southern Quintana Roo would continue to arrive at the desks of Mexican presidents in succeeding sexenios. These calls became more urgent, and frustrated, as the full scale of the negative infrastructure being generated by the Highway 180 corridor became clear.

THE ESCÁRCEGA-CHETUMAL CORRIDOR:
A BUSY NO-MAN'S LAND

In his classic *The Folk Culture of Yucatan*, Robert Redfield (1941, 2) noted that the Yucatán Peninsula was, "in everything but literal truth," an island, its southern extent being shrouded by "a dense tropical forest penetrated by no road or railroad." Here, he was referring specifically to the vast zone of swampland and forest that is today the southern third of the states of Campeche and Quintana Roo. This is the region that was crosscut by the road corridor that links the town of Escárcega in Campeche to the city of Chetumal. In fact, the first tentative steps of "penetrating" roads into these forests were taking place around the time that Redfield wrote his book. But, confirming Redfield's assertion, I have found little evidence of significant advancement before the presidency of Manuel Ávila Camacho (1940–46).

Formal roads or not, the forests of the southern lowlands were not quite as unpopulated as Redfield's "island" analogy implied. Along with inland British Honduras and the Guatemalan Petén, the southern wilds of Campeche and Quintana Roo had been places of refuge for Indigenous and Hispanic families displaced by the Caste War. Historical accounts suggest that the porous border between the two nation-states and the British colony was subject to a small-scale but steady movement of people and goods in the first decades of the twentieth century. Besides the chicle trade, Norman Schwartz (1990, 107–9) has documented clandestine commerce in beef cattle between producers in the Petén and buyers on the Mexican side of the border, which irked Mexican customs officials and cattle producers. Likewise, Guatemalan authorities often accused chicle traders who operated in southern Campeche of prospecting too far south and robbing resources from their national territory (Schwartz 1990).

Direct military conflicts between Mexico and its neighbors to the south were relatively rare, but the threat of transnational violence had lain over this region for half a century by the 1930s. Fears of attack by Cruzo'ob based in Quintana Roo led to a brief transfer of the capital of the Guatemalan department of Petén from Flores to Sacluk in the 1880s. During the same period, Guatemalan residents of Petén contended with threats from Mexican troops in the south of the state of Campeche. Schwartz (1990, 95) suggests that this harassment was meant to apply pressure in border negotiations that ultimately led to Guatemala's concession of more than 10,000 square kilometers in 1883.[7]

These losses in the border negotiations of 1883 remained a point of contention for Guatemalan leaders. When Cárdenas assumed the Mexican presidency in 1934, the old grudge was undergoing a revival in the policies of Guatemalan dictator Jorge Ubico. Ubico held a deep distrust of Cárdenas, whom he considered to be a thinly disguised "Bolshevik" and enabler of insurgents in Guatemala (Grieb 1979, 207). One of Ubico's own signature projects was the expansion of the road network from Guatemala City to the isolated coffee-growing region of Alta Verapaz. From there, the road would have extended into the Petén, where it would establish effective control over the border territory (Grieb 1979, 135). These cross-border tensions continued into Manuel Ávila Camacho's sexenio (1940–46), amid negotiations that sought to determine the formal status of British Honduras.[8] It was during this period that work on the Escárcega-Chetumal road corridor began in earnest, suggesting that the Mexican politicians sought to flex their own infrastructural muscles over this contested region.

Unlike the Mérida-Chetumal road, there seems to have been relatively little contestation among local communities regarding the route of the Escárcega-Chetumal road, which simply runs parallel to the Guatemalan border. But like the other roads leading to the new capital of Quintana Roo, progress was painfully slow. The delays in road construction through southern Campeche and Quintana Roo were complicated by a family quarrel of sorts, which highlights how some instances of negative infrastructure are the result of quirks in the behavior of political elites.

At the time of the first major work on the southernmost road corridor, the SOP was headed by Maximino Ávila Camacho, the brother of then-president Manuel Ávila Camacho (Bess 2017, 92). Maximino was a former governor of the state of Puebla and still held vast informal powers as a regional cacique.

A flamboyant figure prone to raucous entertainments, shocking acts of violence, and liberal appropriations of government funds, he was known to be an embarrassment to his younger brother, the president (Alexander 2016, 73–74; Krauze 2013, 39–46). It was suggested by some contemporaneous observers that an appointment as head of the SOP allowed Manuel to appease his mercurial brother with a position that would grant him ample opportunities for graft, while keeping him from interfering in higher-level decision-making (Jones 2014, 25).

Only a few letters exist in the national archive regarding the development of the Escárcega-Chetumal project under Maximino's tenure at the SOP. In 1942, the current workforce consisted of 800 men, and was soon to be expanded to 1300. In a letter to his brother, Maximino observed that there was not a single nucleus of population in the 274 kilometers between Escárcega and Chetumal. Given the "special character" of the workforce that was available in the frontier zone, he suggested that federal police and soldiers needed to be deployed throughout the project, "particularly on payday."[9] It's unclear from this letter whether Maximino was implying that force was needed to defend the few agricultural hamlets in the region from drunk and rowdy workers or simply to keep itinerant chicleros and loggers from melting back into the forest after receiving their first week's pay. In either case, it suggests that the local population of southern Campeche and Quintana Roo was far less enthusiastic about road construction than the residents of Kantunilkín.

Other incidents recorded during the Ávila Camacho sexenio suggest that the relationship between the two brothers may have spilled into the larger process of decision-making regarding road construction in the peninsula. Maximino seemed determined to divert funds to the southernmost route, even if this meant slowing progress on the more economically important Mérida-Chetumal road. In August 1943, President Ávila Camacho ordered that work on the Mérida-Chetumal road be stopped so that priority could be given to finishing the basic, rough transept that would mark the course of the southern Escárcega-Chetumal route. This cessation seems to have come as an unpleasant surprise to General Gabriel Guevara, Rafael Melgar's successor as governor of the Federal Territory of Quintana Roo. After learning that the southern route would be finished at the expense of the artery linking his own territorial capital to Mérida, Guevara requested that he be allowed to use funds already allocated to complete the road to Peto. He suggested that work on the southernmost corridor could be completed with a "special fund."[10] He later elaborated on this suggestion by noting that heavy equipment owned by the firm Constructora Azteca would be idle after the completion of two airstrips in Chetumal and Ciudad del Carmen, more or less at opposite extremes of the planned road. This would thus allow the transept from Chetumal to Escárcega to be completed in a year or so if bonds were issued to complete the funding.[11]

This arrangement seems to have been unacceptable to the president's brother. The files at the Archivo General de la Nación preserve a typed summary of a now-missing letter that suggests that Maximino threatened to resign as the head of the SOP for lack of resources to complete the Escárcega-Chetumal road. Provided with only 1.5 million pesos, and expected to raise a half million on his own, Maximino would be unable to commit to the plan of delivering the finished project "four or five months" before the end of the Ávila Camacho sexenio.[12]

Given Maximino's reputation, it is fair to wonder if the requests for additional resources reflected more than the typical expenses of roadwork in the 1940s. In the southern forests of Campeche and Quintana Roo, there were far fewer eyes to observe whether funds and resources were reaching their intended destination. Insofar as President Ávila Camacho's prioritizing of different road corridors was influenced by his mercurial brother, this incident speaks to critiques of elite behavior that figure prominently in the political common sense of rural people throughout Mexico. In essence, a family quarrel could inflict negative infrastructure on the thousands of citizens whose livelihood depended on the completion of the Mérida-Chetumal corridor. A generation later, resentment of this kind of elite behavior would empower the emergence of new kinds of political opposition in the Mexican countryside.

THE UPS AND DOWNS OF REGIONAL INFRASTRUCTURE

The fraternal relationship between Maximino and Manuel Ávila Camacho may be unusual, but the fact that seemingly arbitrary decisions taken at the very top could shift resources from one of the transpeninsular corridors to another would be a recurring issue from the 1940s into the 1960s. Combined with budgetary shortfalls and outright theft of resources, work on all three roads slowed to a crawl in the late 1940s. In the end, the Mérida–Puerto Juárez segment of Federal Highway 180 emerged as the first and the most structurally sound of the three corridors. By extension, it would continue to inflict a strong degree of negative infrastructure on its southern counterparts.

The success of the Mérida–Puerto Juárez corridor reflects the fact that the SOP and its local contractors could count on many of the existing trails that had been documented by Lieutenant García Mejía in 1939. It was also built on considerably less challenging terrain than what existed to the south. In this regard, the process of completing what of what would become Federal Highway 180 seems to have been fairly smooth by the standards of similar projects in early twentieth-century Mexico. As Marcela Mijares Lara (2019) noted in discussing the federal road to Acapulco, repeated suspensions and renewals of construction were a persistent drama in the infrastructural development of Mexico's Pacific coast. This problem became particularly acute as wartime shortages in fuel and strategic materials limited road construction throughout Mexico during the early 1940s (see Bess 2017, 93–97). Indeed, work on the Mérida–Puerto Juárez road was suspended several times between 1944 and 1951. But a big push between 1952 and 1954 led to a widening of existing transects and the first works of petrolization or pavement.[13] In 1958, a number of local business committees in Puerto Juárez and other communities along this road wrote to President Adolfo López Mateos to request the pavement of the last kilometers of road between Valladolid and the coast.[14] This implies that this route was more or less transitable at least a decade before either of the corridors to Chetumal.

There is less official documentation of how the Escárcega-Chetumal road developed in the late 1940s and 1950s. In 1950, it consisted of forty-two kilometers of consolidated dirt road and seventy-three kilometers of dirt road that was minimally consolidated and largely impassible for much of the year.[15] The road would not be completely paved until the end of the 1960s (Moncada Jiménez 2011), and it remains today the least traveled and worst maintained of the transpeninsular corridors.

There is more archival documentation for the historical development of the Mérida-Chetumal road for the simple fact that more local stakeholders wrote to the Mexican president to register their opposition to repeated delays. As it had been during the earlier years of construction, these stakeholders ranged from the members of rural Maya communities to urban business and labor groups seeking new investment opportunities. Construction had ground to a halt during the sexenio of Miguel Alemán Valdés (1946–52). In 1953, the Mérida branch of the Cámara Nacional de la Industria de Transformación (National Chamber of the Transformation Industry) and the Asociación Regional de Caminos de Yucatán (Regional Association of Roads of Yucatán) reminded President Adolfo Ruiz Cortines about the importance of this road for fomenting new agricultural opportunities and creating more demand for construction in the Southeast.[16] Construction resumed, and by the 1950s, the former Cruzo'ob stronghold of Felipe Carrillo Puerto was connected to both Peto and Valladolid by good roads (Villa Rojas [1978]

1992, 537). However, the final stretches linking Carrillo Puerto to Chetumal were indefinitely suspended during the presidency of Adolfo López Mateos (1958–64). In 1966, the Asociación de Ejecutivos de Venta y Mercadotecnia de Mérida (Association of Sales and Marketing Executives of Mérida) and the Club Rotario de Mérida (Mérida Rotary Club) joined the leaders of rural communities to the southeast of Peto to plead that President Gustavo Díaz Ordaz continue work on the "vital nerve" of the peninsula.[17]

By the end of the 1960s, both transpeninsular routes to Chetumal were complete. But by then, the status of the Highway 180 corridor as the dominant avenue for touristic and economic development was already secure. As I noted earlier, the early completion of this route at the site of Puerto Juárez largely determined the ultimate location of the resort city of Cancún. In fact, something like Cancún might have emerged at the end of the sexenio of Adolfo Ruiz Cortines (1952–58), when the near-completion of the road sparked the interest of Mérida-based capitalists. But, as the last miles of road into Puerto Juárez were to be paved, representatives of the SOP seemed to have second thoughts about shouldering the full expense. With nothing more than very basic accommodations and a shabby fishing village at the end of the road corridor, they proposed to resume the project once adequate hospitality resources had been built.[18]

Coastal development was at an impasse. The lack of finished roads or commercial ports discouraged private investors from building new hotels on this "frontier" of development. In late 1959, representatives of the Concilio para el Fomento y Coordinación de Producción Nacional (Council for the Promotion and Coordination of National Production), along with the Cámara Nacional de Comercio de Mérida (National Chamber of Commerce of Mérida), wrote to incoming president Adolfo López Mateos to lament the "paralysis" of the road project. In this instance, they proposed that the federal government build a new international port in Puerto Juárez. The latter would allow ferry boats from Cuba, the Antilles, and even Florida to dock on the Caribbean coast, bringing tourists to archaeological sites in the interior of the peninsula. A 1960 plan for tourism development created by the López Mateos administration offered further projections for possible work in Cozumel, Puerto Juárez, and Isla Mujeres. But tourism development doesn't seem to have been a priority, and it wasn't until 1961 that López Mateos made serious inquiries to the navy regarding the feasibility of a ferry port in Puerto Juárez.[19]

It's not clear to what extent the Mexico City–based planners of Cancún were aware of these repeated "paralyses" when they solicited funds from the Inter-American Development Bank a decade later. It is worth noting that Antonio Ortiz Mena, the legendary economist and financier who would play a role in the origins of the Cancún project, served as secretary of finance during the López Mateos administration. The stated rationale behind the use of an Inter-American Development Bank loan and state agencies to build the resort city suggests that Ortiz Mena's disciples at the Banco de México were familiar with the issues that had slowed the completion of road infrastructure in Puerto Juárez. By offering credit to developers and even taking partial ownership of hotel facilities, the parastatal organizations Fondo de Promoción e Infraestructura Turística (Fund for Tourism Promotion and Infrastructure) and Fondo Nacional de Fomento al Turismo (National Fund for Tourism Development) mitigated the risks that had dissuaded Mexican capitalists from investing in the Caribbean in the 1950s. Through this, they also sought to address the SOP's concerns about building roads to nowhere. As the original plan noted, the bank's agents sought "to achieve that the development of the selected centers be integral, that is, that the public sector investments in infrastructure and the private investments in hotels, restaurants, golf courses, and other indispensable services be programmed and executed in a coordinated and parallel fashion, to ensure that the centers achieve the optimal state of service and operation as quickly as possible" (Banco de México 1968, 24–25).

In this case, "as quickly as possible" meant that the broader social and economic benefits of the projects would be felt within the span of a few short years, thus avoiding the dissipation of energies and resources that happened when installations remained idle or underused for extended periods. Mexican economists tended to associate this dissipation with a series of undesirable economic effects that I will discuss further in chapter 4. But there was also a political motivation for finishing projects like Cancún quickly. The beginning of a presidential or gubernatorial sexenio is always a dangerous time for projects initiated by previous executives, as incoming officeholders seek to initiate their own signature works. Manuel Ávila Camacho's shifting resources away from the Mérida-Chetumal project to appease his rapacious brother might be an extreme example, but the pet projects and individual predilections of incoming presidents always presented a threat to projects that were inherited from previous sexenios.

By the late 1960s, these contingencies of infrastructural development were familiar to many people living in rural Mayan-speaking communities in the interior of the peninsula, whether or not they were lucky enough to live along the emerging Highway 180 corridor. Many had labored on the road projects, and many more had become aware of this process through various journalistic and oral grapevines. Thus, petitions that were written by rural agriculturalists and urban businessmen reflect a shared anxiety. Every shift in priorities by a new presidential administration carried the threat of inflicting negative infrastructure on other fragile local economies.

The same principles that applied to roads also applied to different forms of state-sponsored development that were enabled by the gradual expansion of modern transport infrastructure. In the next chapter, I will look more closely at a range of agrarian alternatives to the flagging henequen and chicle industries that emerged and collapsed between the 1950s and 1970s. Highly dependent on governmental subsidies, these projects are recalled today as part of a larger narrative about politically motivated waste that is a key component of vernacular neoliberalism. This narrative was shaped by both lived experience and local consumption of critical reporting that circulated in the regional press. As I will also argue, lessons learned during this period informed how Yucatecans born in 1930s, as well as their children and grandchildren, mediated between their own economic interests and the ambitions of urban political elites.

2

**FAILURES OF
DEVELOPMENT**

The Press, Politicians, and
Slow Death of Henequen

I closed chapter 1 by discussing how the slow emergence of three transpeninsular road corridors embodied the potentials and risks of state-sponsored infrastructural development for generations of people in the Yucatán Peninsula. Communities that successfully lobbied for local roadways, or that simply happened to be situated in strategic regions, stood to reap the benefits of greater connection to larger economic spheres. But factors that ranged from landscape conditions to the caprices of members of the political elite could alter the pace and direction of road development. Likewise, a range of technical and political factors influenced which industries received preferential treatment from elected officials. These often-unpredictable changes in development priorities threatened to inflict damaging forms of negative infrastructure on communities that had once anticipated a brighter future.

How did the residents of relatively isolated rural communities inform themselves about the array of characters, practices, and precedents that shaped the regional politics of development? In the first decades of the twentieth century, local political leaders, schoolteachers, and government engineers often served as intermediaries between monolingual Mayan speakers and state officials. This was evidently the case for the teacher Graciano Sánchez, whose advocacy for the residents of several rural communities in central Quintana Roo I discussed in chapter 1. But by the last decades of the twentieth century, with the expansion of literacy and Spanish-Mayan bilingualism, the regional press played a much larger role in the quotidian life of rural communities.

This chapter will look at how the different visions of development that I touched upon in the previous chapter were discussed in the independent regional press. The reporting must be analyzed critically for a number of reasons that I will discuss below. But the specific events that were presented in these media, and the narratives through which they were framed, are essential to understanding the collective store of knowledge that informs the political behavior of people in rural communities. It is also fundamental for understanding the process, more than a generation in the making, which led to the emergence of mainstream political opposition in the Yucatecan countryside. As the first cracks appeared in the hegemony of the Partido Revolucionario Institucional (Institutional Revolutionary Party, or PRI), partisan divisions within the press often mirrored an emerging political diversity in communities that had once been a reliable stronghold for the "official" party. All of these processes contributed to the rise of the discourse of vernacular neoliberalism.

The reporting on which I focus in this chapter is drawn primarily from a single newspaper, the *Diario de Yucatán*, from a period in the early to mid-1970s. This period, and this newspaper, are key to understanding the formation of local opinions about economic development that were explicitly critical of the state and federal governments. Founded by the Cuban Yucatecan intellectual Carlos R. Menéndez, the *Diario* adopted a political stance broadly sympathetic to more elitist factions within the PRI, and later to the right-of-center Partido Acción Nacional (National Action Party, or PAN). It is the paper of record in Yucatán, notwithstanding its fairly transparent political biases. During the period I will discuss in this chapter, its readers could contemplate the prolonged decline of the region's henequen industry, as well as different experiments with alternative forms of commercial agriculture.

By the end of the 1970s, the economic role of henequen and its agrarian alternatives was largely usurped by the creation of Cancún and the subsequent boom in tourism. In this regard, the 1970s present an important period of transition from the agrarian economy that Yucatán inherited from the early Revolutionary era to the tourism that defines its economic fate in the present. In the 1940s and 1950s, rural people in communities like Pisté may have understood that their counterparts in henequen-growing communities were fortunate to inhabit the state's most important economic region. They could take for granted that the depth of state investment in henequen inflicted negative infrastructural effects on other agricultural economies that clamored for the same public resources. But by the 1970s, with tourist sites like Chichén Itzá contributing to a growing industry along the eastern stretch of Highway 180, the disproportionate public expenditure on the henequen zone could seem more difficult to justify.

During this period, the *Diario de Yucatán* was the only widely circulating newspaper in the region that offered frequent and pointed criticism of state and federal policy. The newspaper faced some of the same formal and informal censorship as other outlets in Mexico, and many of its editors and reporters had close relationships with prominent PRI politicians. However, the strength of the Menéndez family's connections among the Mérida power elite allowed them to adopt a far more critical editorial line than quasi-official organs like the contemporaneous *Diario del Sureste*.

Reading archived issues for the *Diario* while researching this book was a source of constant déjà vu for me. Carefully turning the brittle pages, I came across incidents that had been reported to me in interviews and anecdotes for years before I had a clear mental picture of regional politics in the 1970s and 1980s. When I first visited Pisté in 1997, it quickly became clear that newspaper readership was a prominent part of everyday life, and political discussion was a ubiquitous pastime. Walking through town on any given day, I'd see copies of daily papers passed among hotel workers sitting around food stalls in the early morning, and ambulant artisanry vendors spending the afternoon hours between the arrival of tour buses. The same headlines were on the countertop where shop owners would pause in their reading to charge me for snacks or cigarettes. I became used to listening to friends and acquaintances get into passionate discussions about what was for me an unfamiliar cast of characters from the Mérida political elite.

The avid readership that I saw in the late 1990s was generations in the making. Older friends recalled how decades before, when fewer people were literate and there were fewer distractions from television and smartphones, it was common to see groups gather to hear the newspaper read out loud. Many of the dominant political figures in the town, men and women in their sixties and seventies, had long-standing relationships with corresponding journalists to whom they offered insight on local events, and whom they could count on to publish tactically planned political denunciations. Thus, and despite the linguistic, socioeconomic, and educational gulf between the city and the countryside, print news was an established part of the political life of places like Pisté in the second half of the twentieth century.

By the 1990s, newspaper readership was also an embodiment of the political competition and polarization that was becoming more common in rural communities across the state. Though a range of alternative newspapers circulate in Mérida and other urbanized settings, the readership in communities like Pisté gravitates toward the *Diario* and its principal competitor, *¡Por Esto!* Founded in 1991 by a dissident scion of the Menéndez clan (see Smith 2018, 116–17), *¡Por Esto!* follows a more populist editorial line consistent with the traditional nationalism of the PRI. These editorial tendencies are well known in Pisté and other rural communities where I conduct fieldwork, so much so that people refer to the two newspapers as the *Diario de YucaPAN* and *¡PRI Esto!* However, in my experience, newspaper preference doesn't always map neatly onto the partisan orientation of the reader. Many friends and acquaintances prefer the *Diario* even though they identify as Priístas or as sympathizers of left-of-center parties. The heir to a longer editorial tradition, the *Diario* tends to publish more diverse and detailed material from international news services. Many readers also prefer the writing of the *Diario*, notwithstanding its obvious political bias, over the more sensationalistic *amarillismo* (yellow journalism) that they associate with *¡Por Esto!* That said, I also know quite a few people who identify as "priísta de hueso colorado" (red-boned Priístas) and can't tolerate even a few pages of the older newspaper.

This style of news consumption creates a space for political critique, but one that Mexican academics and public intellectuals argue is closely circumscribed around a conservative orthodoxy. Writing in the 1990s, the social scientist and politician Enrique Montalvo Ortega viewed this journalistic bipolarization, and the dominance of the right-of-center *Diario*, as central to the political landscape of modern Yucatán. The *Diario*, as the region's paper of record, tended to tilt general political opinion toward the PAN and to more conservative PRI candidates, while *¡Por Esto!* served as a general apologist for the PRI. Trapped between right-of-center traditionalism and populist authoritarianism, the average literate Yucatecan had virtually no access to the ideology of the independent Left. This, Montalvo Ortega (1996) argued, laid the ideological groundwork for consolidating a conservative bipartisanism that facilitated the neoliberalization of the region's politics, economy, and society. Two decades later, this critique is still common among left-leaning political commentators, bloggers, and intellectuals, who somewhat contemptuously refer to the right-center neoliberal orthodoxy of regional politics with the portmanteau *"prianismo."*

As Benjamin Smith (2018) has documented in a sweeping history of modern Mexican journalism, this kind of orthodoxy was produced by the complicated relationship between the free press and the state in post-Revolutionary Mexico. Cases of violent repression of journalists were not unknown in the mid-twentieth century and have become frighteningly common for Mexican journalists covering the drug war in the past two decades. But the post-Revolutionary state also used an array of nonviolent tools for censorship, from using a parastatal monopoly to manipulate the price of newsprint (Smith 2018, 67–73) to the outright bribery of journalists, commonly known as *el chayote*. In the case of Yucatán's two major newspapers, family ties within the Menéndez clan, and between the Menéndez and other families of the regional elite, invite speculation about the shared interests that limit critique of the dominant socioeconomic system.

If the political critique that appears in newspapers is manipulated by a combination of informal state censorship and the class interest of politically connected publishers, how does it shape the ideology of nonelite consumers of print media? Anthropologist and culture critic Roger Bartra (1987, 2002) famously argued that, whether criticism of Mexico's public policy comes from the political left or right, lowering expectations about the performance of the national leadership tended to reenforce the PRI's political hegemony. This grim assessment of political critique mirrors the effects of the print duopoly discussed by Montalvo Ortega. Consumers of print media are saturated by criticism of the state's failures but exposed to few radical political alternatives. This idea of a "fossilization" of vernacular political ideology in Mexico has become as ubiquitous among many foreign authors as it has among Mexican cultural critics. Writing in the wake of the democratic transition of 2000, US anthropologist Matthew Gutmann (2002) has expounded on the role of vernacular cynicism about political institutions as a form of "compliant defiance" that curtails mass dissent against the ongoing neoliberalization of Mexican society.

Later in this book, I will look more closely at the relationship between vernacular critiques of political institutions and grassroots mobilizations. My own interpretation of events in Yucatán is more hopeful about local-level politics than either Bartra's or Gutmann's. But the formation of political opinion in rural communities *does* seem to reflect a conservative common sense about the best tactics for securing infrastructural projects and other benefits from the Mexican state. This common sense also played a central role in shaping the local discourse that I refer to as vernacular neoliberalism. This vernacular critique of older forms of clientelistic politics has clear roots in press coverage of development during the pivotal 1970s.

ECONOMIC CRISES AND POLITICAL FEUDS

Despite the early expansion of tourism-fueled prosperity in communities along the Highway 180 corridor, the *Diario de Yucatán*'s reporting from the 1970s and early 1980s focuses on the perpetual "crisis" of the state's economy. Struggles over public resources were still dominated by the needs of a failing henequen industry, and dramatized by factional disputes between different groups within the PRI. Those years of economic decline and intra-party feuding created an opening for opposition parties to win elections at the municipal level, leading to further polarization and conflict.

Some of the key dramas that marked this transitional decade emerged from a tense relationship between Mexican president Luis Echeverría Álvarez (1970–76) and Carlos Loret de Mola, the governor of Yucatán. Echeverría had assumed the presidency in a time of nationwide crisis. The killing of dozens of protestors in Tlatelolco's Plaza de la Tres Culturas undermined the legitimacy of the PRI party-state, just as the economic program of Stabilizing Development was showing clear signs of exhaustion (see Ávila 2006; Martí 1985; and Zaid [1987] 2012). Against the prevailing wisdom of some of Mexico's chief economists, Echeverría sought to reestablish the party's prestige by expanding state intervention in vulnerable national industries. This glut of spending lay the foundation for the national financial implosion that would be answered by neoliberalization in the 1980s, as well as for a series of local conflicts associated with a last-ditch expansion of the parastatal henequen sector.

With close ties to the Yucatán's traditional elites, Governor Carlos Loret de Mola embodied the regional "old guard" response to Echeverría's populism. Loret de Mola was a prolific writer, and his memoirs are a good portrait of the ideological and personalistic fragmentation that occurred within the Yucatecan PRI after the 1960s. Though he himself was the consummate PRI "party man," he despised Echeverría, whom he saw as a Mexico City authoritarian who cultivated the loyalty of bad elements in the provincial political class to impose his own will over the Mexican Southeast. Chief among Eche-verría's supporters on the peninsula was Carlos Sansores Pérez, the governor of the neighboring state of Campeche. Echeverría's presidential sexenio also saw the rise of Víctor Cervera Pacheco, a Yucatecan protégé of Sansores Pérez who made Loret de Mola's political life miserable in the 1970s.

Despite their internal feuding, Priístas like Sansores Pérez, Cervera, Loret de Mola, and President Echeverría himself were forced into an uneasy alliance in the early 1970s, as they tried to suppress the rise of the PAN in regional electoral politics. This alliance eventually fractured, and Víctor Cervera survived as the dominant figure of regional politics throughout the 1980s and 1990s. From this position, he would play a central role in implementing the policies that are generally recognized as "neoliberal" in Yucatán and the neighboring state of Quintana Roo.

To understand Cervera's brand of neoliberalization, and the emergence of the PAN as a serious political contender in the state, it is necessary to examine the fracturing of an older political order that was based on simultaneously promoting export-oriented commercial agriculture and the needs of rural communities. This process was critically documented in the reportage and editorial pages of the *Diario*, which shaped how generations of Yucatecans would write and speak about the role of waste, ineptitude, and outright corruption in damaging potentially successful industries. Many of the themes that dominated news coverage in this period still resonate with political critiques that are leveled by rural Yucatecans today. In the 1970s, any discussion of the Mexican state's failed interventions into the Yucatecan economy began with the flagging henequen industry, which will be the focus of the next section.

THE INTERMINABLE DEATH THROES OF HENEQUEN

When President Lázaro Cárdenas (1934–40) granted henequen lands to Yucatecan peasants, the "boom" prices that had generated unprecedented wealth in the nineteenth century were a thing of the past. Though many agrarian communities in the state had received formal ejido grants by the late 1920s, the expropriation and distribution of hacienda lands planted with henequen did not occur on a large scale until 1934–37 (Ortiz Yam 2013, 175–200). Even then, as Ben Fallaw (2001) has described, remnants of the old hacendado class successfully mobilized their own political networks and exploited factional divisions between different groups of rural workers to maintain a degree of control over the land reform process. This pattern repeated itself for a generation, as relatively wealthy private landowners and the workers of newly founded ejidos struggled over the spoils of a steadily shrinking global market.

Between 1937 and 1955, the organization Henequeneros de Yucatán functioned as a state-sanctioned monopoly that set production quotas and controlled prices. This contributed to a restructuring of rural society that was chronicled by the nationally acclaimed journalist Fernando Benítez. A scathing critique of the industry during the period dominated by Henequeneros, Benítez's reporting dwelled at length on the poverty, alcoholism, and sickness that seemed endemic among henequen ejidatarios. Benítez argued that state-sanctioned organizations that controlled defibering and export had essentially assumed the role of Porfirian hacendados and undone the benefits of Cárdenas's distribution of henequen lands to rural workers (see Benítez 1956).

Henequeneros was liquidated under political pressure in 1955, and replaced by a system in which the Banco de Crédito Ejidal (Bank of Ejidal Credit) or Banco Agrario (Agrarian Bank) dealt directly with ejido communities (Escalante 1988).[1] This process of financing was often coordinated by a national agrarian organization, the Confederación Nacional Campesina (National Peasant Confederation) (Escalante 1988, 6; Villanueva 1985, 132–36). Through controlling credits available for different aspects of henequen cultivation, and by offering incentives for raised or lowered levels of production, the banks assumed many of the regulatory roles previously held by Henequeneros de Yucatán (Escalante 1988, 16).

This panorama of managed henequen production was further complicated in the 1960s through the parastatalization of mills that turned raw henequen into finished cordage products. Since the end of the nineteenth century, Yucatecan entrepreneurs had sought to end the state's status as a producer of raw material for the international market by developing an Indigenous cordage industry. Between 1961 and 1964, the federal government took majority ownership of this flagging industry, which was consolidated into the parastatal firm Cordelería de México (Rope Manufacturers of Mexico, or Cordemex). Cordemex joined the Banco de Crédito Ejidal as a stakeholder in state mediation between the global market for hard fiber and local producers in Yucatán.

So, when Luis Echeverría took office as Mexico's president, he inherited a contentious balancing act in which the state mediated between Cordemex's need for cheap raw material, the Banco de Crédito Ejidal's attempt to create a sustainable system of credit, and the livelihood needs of hundreds of thousands of ejidatarios, individual producers, and small-scale hacienda owners (Escalante 1988, 15–18). This heavily subsidized industry turned Yucatán into one of the Mexican states most dependent on federal funding, a condition that bruised the traditional regionalist pride of the state's political elites and was framed as a "perennial problem" by the governing class in Mexico City. Nevertheless, hundreds of thousands of nonelite stakeholders in the henequen industry represented an indispensable reserve of votes for a PRI facing a national crisis of legitimacy.

These tensions generated one of the more memorable encounters between President Echeverría and Yucatecan political figures, a moment recorded in Governor Loret de Mola's writings. During Echeverría's electoral tour of the state in 1970, Loret de Mola arranged a breakfast at the archaeological site of Uxmal, a location that the governor described as "a song in stone to the rain god Chaac," and as an embodiment of the heritage and pride of the Yucatecan people. There, presidential candidate Echeverría was regaled with regional music and laudatory speeches by Fernando Barbachano, a tourism magnate who will figure in later portions of this book (Loret de Mola 1978, 56).

Already irked by some negative press coverage of Cordemex that he had read the night before, Echeverría was visibly perplexed at having to stand when the band played the "national" anthem that had been composed during Yucatán's brief period as an independent nation. This awkward moment was transformed into an "incident" when Barbachano made comments in reference to the "abandonment and oblivion" to which the state had been subjected by Mexico's previous presidents. Echeverría responded angrily, humiliating Barbachano in front of the other dignitaries with a sharp reminder of the seemingly permanent federal subsidy enjoyed by Yucatán's henequen industry. For Loret de Mola (1978, 56–58), this incident came to exemplify the potentially toxic mix of Echeverría's personal insecurities and his prejudice against the provincial societies of Mexico.

Notwithstanding Echeverría's pique at Uxmal, collaboration between him, Loret de Mola, and Yucatecan henequen producers was an inevitable part of economic policy during the sexenio. During the same electoral tour, Echeverría visited the town of Tizimín, in what would become the heart of the state's cattle-raising microregion. This visit was reported in the article "Giro electoral en Yucatán" on the front page of the 2 February 1970 edition of the *Diario de Yucatán*. There, Jorge González Rodríguez, the head of the state's PRI committee and a close ally of Loret de Mola, touted the importance of exploring beef cattle and other alternative industries as a means of inducing rural people to move from overcrowded towns in the hene-quen zone to new agrarian settlements in southeastern Yucatán and central Quintana Roo. But González Rodríguez also underscored the importance of henequen, noting, "[This] proverbial wealth of Yucatán continues to be the primary source of income for the public and the government." Focusing on the importance of this traditional industry for job creation, he proposed that the state expand the acreage of land under henequen cultivation in order to increase the number of work hours available to ejidatarios.

Coverage and assessment of this sort of plan in the *Diario de Yucatán* tended to be equivocal. The Yucatecan economist Rodolfo Canto Sáenz (2001, 103–5) has commented on how the *Diario*'s editorial stance toward the parastatal henequen and cordage industries was consistent with a tradition among the landed elite of blaming state intervention for "ruining" industries that had prospered during the laissez-faire days of the nineteenth century. Just a week after Echeverría's electoral visit, Gabriel Antonio Menéndez, a member of the founding clan of the *Diario* and a longtime contributor, published a note titled "Errors in Planning." There, he cited the collapse of a scheme by the Banco de Crédito Ejidal to foment henequen production in Hecelchakán, a rural municipality in the neighboring state of Campeche. Menéndez observed that, beyond the waste of federal resources and local labor, this project was flawed from its inception. Successful henequen pro-duction in Campeche would have created artificial competition for Yucatán in a time when the global market simply couldn't absorb additional product (*Diario de Yucatán* 1970).

Arguments like these were commonly levied between 1970 and 1976 as a critique of federal intervention in general, and President Echeverría's "populist" agenda in particular. But in truth, it is questionable whether the regional autonomy and laissez-faire capitalism that were idealized by Ga-briel Menéndez would have been viable on the global market. Cheaper and higher-quality hard fibers from Brazil, East Africa, and Southeast Asia, along with the increasing popularity of synthetic fibers, limited the ability of Yu-catán's Henequeneros to compete on the global market. At times, even Cor-demex was forced to import these cheaper alternatives for its cordage plants when native production failed to meet quality standards (see Escalante 1988; Villanueva 1985). In essence, the state and federal government remained committed to an increasingly obsolete agro-industry that employed a large population of rural workers who were reliable PRI voters. This tendency was derided in the editorial pages of the *Diario* through evocations of "parasites in the countryside" (Huchim 1974), or with references to *cuxum luum*—a

Yukatek Maya phrase meaning "moldy soil." This referred to a patch of un-planted land that was needlessly weeded each week so that state-subsidized ejidatarios could bring home a wage (*Diario de Yucatán* 1974d).

This classist and often racist critique of henequen workers would reso-nate beyond the urban readers of the *Diario*. As I read these editorials from the 1970s, I was struck by the degree to which this narrative had filtered into the vernacular speech of Pisté and other communities in the southern and eastern parts of the state, which were historically dominated by traditional maize agriculture. There, many residents distinguish their own work ethic and industriousness from that of rural people in the henequen area, who they say are typically "in their hammock" when they have completed a bare minimum of wage labor (Armstrong-Fumero 2013). This contrast in atti-tudes and lifestyles has also become central to the discourse of vernacular neoliberalism, with which many rural Yucatecans contrast their own entre-preneurialism to the dependency and political docility that they attribute to their agrarian ancestors.

Poor rural proletarians eking out a living in the fields were not the only focus of the *Diario*'s criticism in the 1970s. Writers for the paper observed, for example, that relatively wealthy "small property owners" had been the primary beneficiaries of the increased prices and purchase quotas of 1974, leaving the far larger masses of ejidal planters mired in their decades-long stagnation (Correa Rachó 1975). On 15 June of the same year, they called at-tention to seemingly inexplicable practices, like Cordemex's purchase of tons of low-grade and damaged fiber from the state of Tamaulipas, when there seemed to be a surplus in local ejidos. Throughout that summer, reporters and columnists like Pedro Góngora Paz (1974) couldn't keep themselves from inserting mentions of the helicopter that had been purchased by Cordemex executives at the price of 2 million pesos for reasons that were not entirely clear. And, as always, there were questions about the lack of transparency regarding the fate of payroll tax deductions, and the apparent graft of millions of pesos in loans destined for ejidal organizations.

Not all of the news and opinion pieces on henequen were so negative in the 1970s. After all, many of the elite families whose views were represented in the *Diario* still had very substantial investments in the industry. It is note-worthy, however, that the newspaper's more hopeful reporting on henequen focused more on changes in global market conditions than on improvements that could be brought about by government intervention.

For example, readers would have found optimistic assessments of the henequen industry in 1973 and 1974, after production declines in competitor nations. Similar optimism appeared when the reduction in global oil output during the embargo by the Organization of Petroleum Exporting Countries eased some of the price competition from synthetic fibers and allowed Cordemex to expand its purchases of locally produced henequen. An extensive report from 29 March 1974 foresaw a promising future for national fiber production. Noting a 14 percent increase in sales in the Mexican market, one official was quoted as extrapolating that the 50,000 tons consumed in Mexico implied a ratio of one kilogram of henequen consumption per Mexican citizen per annum. Based on then-current rates of growth in the national population, this would mean that Mexicans could consume the entirety of a 150,000-ton annual production by 2000, thus guaranteeing the viability of a tariff-protected national industry into the twenty-first century. Two weeks earlier, on 16 June, another Cordemex official was quoted as citing a 50 percent increase in raw fiber prices and noting that "men who refuse to lose faith are the ones who make Mexico great."

For readers of the *Diario* in the 1970s, the dissonance between glowing projections for the revival of henequen and more skeptical assessments of the current state of the industry created the image of promising resource that was plagued by the inefficiency inherent in state-run projects. In truth, hundreds of thousands of Yucatecans were dependent on production that operated on a scale simply unsustainable in the global market, tariff protections notwithstanding. The industry survived on the life support provided by a mixed state and federal bureaucracy that was rife with inefficiency and corruption. Fatally flawed but politically indispensable, the henequen industry lumbered on into the 1990s, inflicting negative infrastructural effects on alternative agrarian economies that competed for the same funds and government intervention.

DUBIOUS ALTERNATIVES

In chapter 1, I discussed alternative agrarian economies, ranging from cattle, to sugar, to modernized maize production, that had been imagined by economists and entrepreneurs since the 1940s. The maize zone of southern and eastern Yucatán, like the "tribal" area of central Quintana Roo, were the geographical key to these plans. In the 1970s, after the completion of the often-delayed Mérida-Chetumal and Escárcega-Chetumal road corridors, these projects were still largely speculative. An article from 10 October 1970 joyfully proclaimed that "the era of chicle [had] been overcome" in Quintana Roo, more than thirty years after President Cárdenas had been confronted with the scathing criticisms made by the Secretaría de Obras Públicas (Secretariat of Public Works) of the industry and its management by Francisco May Pech. The headline of an editorial from 7 March of the same year referred to a "sleeping wealth" of new agricultural potential in eastern Yucatán and central Quintana Roo, which had apparently never been awakened in the decades since the road network opened those regions for development.

Despite optimistic assessments like these, the *Diario*'s editorial coverage of state-sponsored agrarian development during the overlapping Loret de Mola and Echeverría sexenios tended to be framed in the same critical terms as discussions of the henequen industry. I will touch on three types of projects that were reported on between 1970 and 1976, and that are consistent with the alternatives to henequen that had been imagined since the 1940s. Sugar mills, irrigation, and mechanizations schemes for mixed fruit and maize cultivation, and cattle husbandry are all iconic of the perceived potentials of new agro-industrial frontiers. In the *Diario*'s editorial pages, each was also an example of the perceived limitations of state-subsidized production.

The sugar industry was, in some respects, a relic from an earlier period of the peninsula's history. The expansion of land-hungry sugar plantations in the years before the Caste War of 1847 has been interpreted by some authors as one of the catalysts for the generations-long conflict (Rugeley 1996, 13–14). When Yucatecan and foreign entrepreneurs reestablished the industry in the later nineteenth century, it existed on the periphery of a regional economy dominated by henequen. Though these producers initially found a ready regional market for sweeteners and liquor, Yucatecan sugar entered a period of decline in the 1940s (*Diario de Yucatán* 1975h).

As the most significant source of rural employment in the state, the henequen industry absorbed the lion's share of federal funding, and its continuing development was perceived as exercising negative infrastructure against the sugar region. Projects to construct a state-supported refinery facility in Pucté during the presidential sexenio of Adolfo López Mateo (1958–64) never materialized. Loret de Mola recalled making requests for the revival of this project, or the development of similar facilities in other parts of the state, to a skeptical President Echeverría (Loret de Mola 1978, 110). In the end, Echeverría seems to have warmed to Loret de Mola's suggestions, adding Yucatecan sugar to the orgy of parastatalization that marked the final years of his sexenio. On 15 March 1975, the *Diario* featured a long article detailing construction on a major refining facility that would begin operation by 1977 near the historical sugar region of Catmis in the south of the state of Yucatán.

Columnists and letters to the editor questioned the very principles behind the parastatalization of the sugar industry. Writing in late June, Eduardo Escalante Trejo recalled a time at the beginning of the century when the *ingenios* of Catmis and Kakalná met the entire consumption needs of the state under the stewardship of private entrepreneurs. This brief flourishing ended when the Banco Agrario ceased providing credits for private landowners in the region in the 1940s, and when overregulation of alcohol sales made the industry as a whole less profitable (*Diario de Yucatán* 1975h). This call for fostering private investment and reducing industry regulation was echoed a week later on 7 July, in an editorial by Gustavo Rodríguez, who argued that the high price of sugar on the global market would prove attractive to private entrepreneurs were it not for the governmental strategy of artificially depressing prices for the sake of national consumers. Arguments like these echoed an ongoing debate between national business organizations and then–presidential candidate José López Portillo, who saw the nationalization of sugar as a necessity (*Diario de Yucatán* 1975b, 1975c). Coming from Yucatecan authors, arguments favoring private enterprise over further parastatalization echo the narrative in which state intervention "ruined" the once-thriving henequen industry.

Other reporting in the *Diario* seemed to draw a parallel between the inefficiency, corruption, and labor unrest that characterized contemporary henequen production and the parastatal sugar sector. Throughout 1975, front-page articles detailed labor unrest in parastatal sugar operations in the Mexican states of Veracruz and Morelos (*Diario de Yucatán* 1975d) and the burning of fields by disgruntled workers in Orizaba (*Diario de Yucatán* 1975a). An article from 12 March of the same year reported on the more than 60,000 sugarcane workers who were inactive in Oaxaca and Veracruz, echoing the frequent critiques of "moldy soil" and "rural parasites" in the inefficient state-operated henequen industry.

A similar critical narrative, focusing on the administrative inefficiency of parastatals and the ills of rural workers, was applied to schemes focused on modernizing the production of traditional Indigenous cultivars. One such project, funded by the Banco Agrario, turned the former Hacienda Tabi over to ejidatarios from the municipality of Oxkutzcab in order to develop mechanized cultivation of maize, tomato, watermelon, and other traditional crops. This project was subjected to a scathing editorial by Gaspar Antonio Xiu Cachón. A native of Oxkutzcab who traced his ancestry to the conquest-era Maya ruler Ah Tutul Xiu, Xiu Cachón was an ally of Loret de Mola's nemesis Víctor Cervera Pacheco (see Castillo Cocom 2005). Positioning himself as a speaker for peasants from the south of the state, he noted that the ejidatarios of Oxkutzcab were thoroughly uninformed regarding the realities of this project, which would bypass their local agrarian committee and essentially reduce them to poorly paid employees on their own lands (Xiu Cachón 1974b). This, he argued, would doom the Tabi project to the same failure as similar schemes in Dzonot Carretero and Maxcanú.[2] An official from the Banco Agrario published a note the following day rebutting Xiu Cachón's arguments about the project's structure, framing the project as an expansion of an already-successful irrigation scheme in Oxkutzcab (*Diario de Yucatán* 1974a). Nevertheless, Xiu Cachón's original letter framed the project within a familiar critical narrative by highlighting both the inefficiency of state interventions and laborers.

One final and much-touted solution to Yucatán's henequen woes involved expanding cattle production. Cattle raising offered different potentials, and different problems, when compared to other forms of commercial agriculture. Unlike sugar and irrigated agriculture, cattle husbandry can occur on a range of scales, from the well-capitalized rancher raising herds on private lands to the individual peasant grazing one or two animals in a house plot or the bush of an ejido. This diversity of scale was also the cause for conflicts between small-scale producers and the Loret de Mola administration. The kind of cattle husbandry that was imagined by development boosters functioned on a large scale, whether it be managed collectively by ejido communities or by well-capitalized entrepreneurs. For example, one 1974 project involved having Cordemex purchase cattle to provide an alternative income source that would wean underproducing ejidos in the state's north from their henequen dependence (*Diario de Yucatán* 1974b).

These projects, bolstered by new regulatory laws, represented a devastating negative infrastructure for many former cattle keepers I have met through my ethnographic work in the eastern parts of the state. There, small-scale cattle production had provided an important source of cash income for generations of maize agriculturalists who let their animals graze in the bush. Laws published in the 1940s had sought to enforce fencing requirements and the registration of livestock, but these were largely unenforceable. However, the old cattle herders whom I interviewed in the early 2000s considered layers of enforcement and regulation that were imposed in the 1970s to have been especially destructive to their style of production. A bitter lament I heard repeatedly was that Loret de Mola and like-minded elitists in the PRI had sacrificed small-scale production to favor wealthy ranchers in Tizimín and cooperative ejidatarios in the henequen zone. Adding insult to injury, these were the same groups that had already benefited from generous credits from the Banco Agrario (Armstrong-Fumero 2013, 123).

Journalistic reporting on alternatives to henequen, like the lived experience of small-scale cattle herders in the east of the state, embody the same conundrum of development in the 1970s. Faithfully reported statements from political figures like Loret de Mola underscored the importance of federal funding to the development of the peninsula's "sleeping wealth." Yet simultaneously published opinion pieces framed state intervention as a potential disaster for both moneyed capitalists and peasant communities. Many of these critiques resonated with the lived experience of people like the cattle owners of Pisté and neighboring communities. Like the negative infrastructures that emerge from road construction, laws and funds meant to foment the cattle industry in targeted regions turned small-scale producers in other parts of the state into "losers" in the game of development.

YUCATÁN'S DIRTY WAR: MORAL PANIC AND YOUTHFUL REBELLION

Given that the editorial line of the *Diario* stressed "less" government intervention as a solution to the state's economic ills, it should come as no surprise that contributors took an even stronger stand against various socialist alternatives being promoted by students and labor activists. Readers of the newspaper during the middle years of the Loret de Mola sexenio would have gotten a sense that communist subversion was an epidemic across the Western world. Front-page reporting detailed bombings in Monterrey, the actions of the radical teacher and agrarian activist Lucio Cabañas, and the strange story of the kidnapping and radicalization of Patty Hearst. Editorials and cultural pages wrote against the dangers of miniskirts and Marxist literature, praised the Spanish dictator Francisco Franco, and ran weekly excerpts from the work of Aleksandr Solzhenitsyn.

When it came to the far less violent radicalism of students on the peninsula, the conservatism of the *Diario*'s editorial line was just as evident. Notwithstanding their constant criticism of the financial waste and clientelism of the state-run industry, staff authors were dismissive of direct action from student and grassroots groups. In this regard, the newspaper was complicit in a series of paradoxical effects that Montalvo Ortega (1996) attributes to the politics of the Loret de Mola sexenio. General discontent with organizations affiliated with the Confederación de Trabajadores de México (Confederation of Mexican Workers) and the Confederación Nacional Campesina, along with prominent acts of political repression, fanned the flames of independent mobilizations throughout Mexico. The post-Tlatelolco ethos of reconciliation led presidential administrations to appease dissenting groups by strategically incorporating leaders into different government positions. But as left-leaning activists in the state would note a generation later, this appropriation of dissent, along with a disdain in the mainstream press toward "terrorists" and "radicals," prevented the consolidation of lasting, autonomous civil society organizations (Montalvo Ortega 1996, 95–96).

Given this editorial line, it is somewhat surprising that the *Diario* would help to publicize some incidents that would inspire student and left-of-center activism generations later. The short career, death, and commemoration of the student labor activist Efraín Calderón Lara, known popularly as El Charras, would be an important rallying point for generations of opposition leaders. A law student, Calderón Lara advised labor unions ranging from shoe factory workers in the town of Ticul to urban transit workers in Mérida. A staunch opponent of the clientelism of the Confederación de Trabajadores de México, he was associated with direct actions that marked the rise of a limited independent labor movement in the state. By the winter of 1974, the protests, blockades, and labor stoppages associated with this movement had become a thorn in the side of Governor Loret de Mola, who later intimated that El Charras was being manipulated by his Campeche-based rival, Carlos Sansores Pérez (Loret de Mola 1978, 204–7). Though the details are still debated (see Lara Zavala 2007), conversations between the governor and several representatives of state security forces led to the kidnapping of Calderón Lara by plainclothes police officers on 13 February 1974. His body was discovered five days later near the road between Felipe Carrillo Puerto and Chetumal.

The aftermath of the killing marked some of the tensest weeks of the Loret de Mola sexenio. Although the governor was able to preserve his position and remain above official suspicion in the murder, the chief of the regional security forces, his immediate subordinate, and five officers implicated in the kidnapping and murder were ultimately tried and jailed. These gestures did little to appease the politicized student body of the Universidad Autónoma de Yucatán (Autonomous University of Yucatán), and massive protests and road blockages rocked Mérida for months to come.

Throughout this process, the *Diario de Yucatán* was consistently critical of student activists, even as it reported on the investigation of Calderon Lara's death with a level of detail that did little to help Loret de Mola's position. Before his death, El Charras had appeared several times in the pages of the

Diario, and always in a less than positive light. Especially derisive was the description of his role in an attempted takeover of a shoe factory in Ticul, which ended abruptly when El Charras and his handful of independent unionists were run out of town by members of the local Confederación de Trabajadores de México affiliate and scores of their friends and relatives (*Diario de Yucatán* 1974e). Even as protests erupted a month later in the wake of his disappearance and death, the editorial page of the *Diario* railed against student agitators and their fellow travelers. They published a 19 February 1974 letter titled "La colectividad silente" by the intellectual Ernesto Romano, who noted that the youthful addiction to "exotic" political theories—read, Marxism—could only lead to the rise of "totalitarianism."

Coverage of the Charras affair had lasting effects on public opinion, which in some ways undermined the larger ideological position of the *Diario*. While the paper's staff writers had been less than generous to El Charras and other student protestors, their detailed reporting of his death to mainstream audiences amplified and legitimated an oppositional narrative that circulated within ephemeral student newspapers and the oral history of academic institutions. I first encountered this counternarrative during my own ethnographic research in 2002, long before I had a personal interest in the politics of the 1970s. At some point that summer, I had bought a copy of a short biography that Loret de Mola had written of the Reform-era hero Cepeda Peraza. I happened to have it in my hand when I met a friend from Pisté named Rubén Dzul for a breakfast of *cochinita pibil* at a local taco stand. Looking at the cover, Rubén narrowed his eyes a bit and asked why I was reading it. When I responded truthfully—that I had run out of things to read and the book was cheap—he laughed and dug into his breakfast. But when Rubén ordered his second round of tacos, he said, "You do know that's the governor who killed El Charras, right?"

More than a decade later, I reminded Rubén about his comment, and he told me about his experience with the larger implications of the El Charras affair. In 1974 he had been a teenage student at a residential vocational school on the border between the states of Quintana Roo and Yucatán. As he recalls, the police discovered El Charras's body within a few miles of the school, and some of the local students tried unsuccessfully to find the crime scene after reading some of the details in the newspaper. In the weeks that followed, the culture of student protests that had been decried for months in the *Diario* found echoes among the young rural residents of Rubén's school. He remembers a general sense of "hatred" toward Loret de Mola in the school, expressed in chants like

Chicle de Menta!	Mint chewing gum!
Chicle de bola!	Gumballs!
Chinga tu madre,	Fuck you,
Loret de Mola!	Loret de Mola!

The youthful rebellion in the technical school soon went beyond insulting cheers. Rubén recalls that the events in Mérida inspired his cohorts to oust an elderly school director they considered to be a poor manager. Chief among their complaints was the lack of variety in the food, which they summed up in sign they posted in the halls:

DESAYUNO: Frijol	BREAKFAST: Beans
ALMUERZO: Frijol con huevo	LUNCH: Beans and eggs
CENA: Frijol, a huevo	DINNER: Beans (damn straight!)

Like the university students in Mérida, the teens at Rubén's rural technical school built a barricade and closed the local road, essentially pinching off access from the state of Yucatán to inland central Quintana Roo. The gambit was successful. The superintendent of their school was changed, the food improved, and some of the students even found themselves invited to political events in Mérida. Like many young people during Luis Echeverría's sexenio, they learned that this sort of direct action was risky but might be embraced by a state hungry for populist redemption.

Although the name of El Charras is rarely invoked in protests by rural people in Yucatán today, the events of 1974 echoed far beyond the initial round of civil disturbances. Rubén Dzul remembers his youthful experience blocking roads in protest as a precursor to direct actions that he would help organize later in his life. By the 1990s and early 2000s, protests in Pisté would often lead to residents' closing the roads in and out of town, and in so doing blocking entry to Chichén Itzá and transit on Highway 180. Antiradical reporting in the *Diario de Yucatán* did little to curtail what would become a favorite political strategy of many of its readers.

EVERYDAY LEVERAGE AND A SHIFTING BALANCE

While a teenage Rubén Dzul was exploring new and brazen styles of political protest, older politicians in his home community were engaged in more traditional forms of negotiation and contestation with the governing regime. As an independent medium for reporting complaints against the government, the *Diario de Yucatán* (1974c) played a key role in those strategies. On

8 February 1974, the *Diario* reported on one of Governor Loret de Mola's official tours of Pisté. There, he met publicly with the *comisario municipal* José Cituk to discuss work that needed to be done on the local municipal hall and plaza. They also discussed the problem of collecting property and utility taxes from local hotels. An avid reader of the *Diario de Yucatán*, Cituk was familiar with the tone and content of the reporting on development in various regions of the state. It's therefore unsurprising that he took up a familiar narrative formula and commented to the governor about Pisté's chronic "abandonment" by the state authorities. This wording seems to have struck a nerve in Loret de Mola, and the *Diario* reported that he publicly chided Cituk. The governor stated that, while it was good for communities to make requests of their leaders, it was inappropriate to claim "abandonment," especially given the investments in road infrastructure and electrification that Pisté had already received.

It's impossible to say whether the irony of this exchange was lost on Loret de Mola. He had, in essence, embarrassed Cituk with the same prickly response that President Echeverría had offered to Fernando Barbachano at that breakfast in Uxmal two years earlier. In any case, the encounter doesn't seem to have had a lasting effect on the comisario. When I met an elderly Cituk in the early 2000s, he had nothing but positive recollections of the former governor. Cituk may have recognized that there is no such thing as bad press for a rural community seeking the attention of politicians.

Soon after he met the governor in person, Cituk's demands were empowered by the same newspaper that had reported on Loret de Mola's rebuke. The *Diario*'s reporting on state-sponsored projects in Pisté during Cituk's tenure drew on interviews with the comisario and his allies, and tended to be laced with a strong sense of impatience. The restoration of the roof of Pisté's municipal building was delayed repeatedly after having started in December 1974, and Cituk was not shy about noting that the state and federal contributions to the project had not yet arrived (*Diario de Yucatán* 1974d). Throughout the spring and summer of 1975, he took advantage of the spending glut at the end of the sexenio to report on delays in receiving equipment for the electrification of parts of the town (*Diario de Yucatán* 1975e). Later that year, he contributed to reporting on the awful state of the plumbing in the town's municipal offices (*Diario de Yucatán* 1975f). The public shaming of slow government interventions might have worked. On 1 December 1975, an article simply titled "Pisté" reported that the municipal building had been completed (*Diario de Yucatán* 1975g). The same article noted that speed bumps had "finally" been installed at a dangerous intersection in downtown Pisté, after the governor's "swift intervention" following a traffic death.

José Cituk's successful use of the *Diario* to leverage action by the governor hints at larger anxieties that plagued members of the political elite in the 1970s. Representations of a monolithically stable *pax priísta* tend to gloss over the fact that municipal and even gubernatorial elections were competitive in Mexico for decades before the democratic transition of 2000. Politicians like Loret de Mola were very aware that rural residents consumed media coverage that often dwelled on "failed" government investments. Given the prevalence of this mainstream political skepticism, responsiveness to the demands of rural leaders like Cituk was crucial in cultivating the PRI's traditional "voter reserve." This would become particularly important in the turbulent 1980s and 1990s, as the right-of-center Partido Acción Nacional emerged as a power in the state.

This strategy of appeasement was further complicated by feuding between factions within the PRI elite that came to a head in the early 1980s. Loret de Mola was succeeded as governor by Francisco Luna Kan, the representative of a different, though occasionally allied, faction within the party. That alliance became stronger as their chief rival, Víctor Cervera Pacheco, gained prominence. Luna Kan and Loret de Mola lobbied strenuously against him to anyone within their party who would listen. Notwithstanding the growing *panista* threat, they claimed, the representative of the PRI should be "cualquier menos Cervera" (anyone but Cervera). But by the presidency of Miguel de la Madrid Hurtado (1982–88), the luck of the more traditionalist Yucatecan Priístas had run out.[3]

In the next chapter, I will look more closely at the social, economic, and political impacts of the neoliberal reforms implanted in Yucatán by the Cerveristas. One of the features of *cerverismo* as a political phenomenon was a strategic blending of populist traditions with neoliberal reforms that brought a definitive end to the state-subsidized henequen industry. Ultimately, these transformations cost the Cerveristas the unwavering support of the PRI's traditional rural voters. But for over a decade, Cervera and his allies seemed to succeed in concealing the neoliberal transformation being developed in elite policy circles behind a veneer of continuity with an older political order. This blurring of ideological boundaries would influence the equally heterodox forms of vernacular neoliberalism with which rural residents made sense of these transformations.

The press coverage of pre-Cervera *priísmo* that was at the substantive heart of this chapter is another important component of these vernacular critiques. People who recalled the process of constructing the transpeninsular road corridors were already familiar with the game of positive and negative infrastructure that went with large-scale development projects. The critique of specific political actors and projects that appeared in the pages of the *Diario* filled in a series of conceptual gaps by highlighting the calculations that led decision-makers to generate benefit for some communities at the expense of others. Editorialists and staff writers also sought to explain why these projects were doomed to fail, compounding the cost to the general good. Returning to Adam Kotsko's phrase, many of the "demons" that populate vernacular neoliberal discourse on development have their roots in this reporting. In particular, unproductive agriculturalists who reliably vote for PRI candidates in exchange for wasteful government programs continue to be a common feature in my friends and informants' critiques of local politics, even decades after the final liquidation of the parastatal henequen industry.

On its surface, this bleak view of development politics seems consistent with the limited expectations that Bartra (1987) sees as integral to the cultural legitimation of the Mexican state, or with the "compliant defiance" that Matthew Gutmann (2002) finds in popular protest. But the critical reportage of the 1970s provided an important means of agency and leverage for "mainstream" politicians like José Cituk. It also provided models of direct action for young students like Rubén Dzul, who would apply these lessons to later conflicts and crises.

3

THE NEOLIBERAL POPULISM (OR POPULIST NEOLIBERALISM) OF VÍCTOR CERVERA PACHECO

When I began conducting ethnographic research in 1997, many of the people I met in Pisté celebrated a recent collective "awakening" (*despertar* in Spanish; *ajlil* in Mayan) from the political subservience that they attributed to state-dependent agriculturalists. For many local families, critiques of the failures of parastatal agriculture in the 1970s dovetailed with the lived experience of prosperity from the tourism economy. This perspective shaped a discourse that I refer to as vernacular neoliberalism, which continues to inform contemporary engagements with the politics of development. The next two chapters will shift emphasis slightly from the shared history of experiences with positive and negative infrastructure to the changing political landscape that gave rise to these new local subjectivities.

Mexico's "neoliberal transition" often looks ambiguous, and less than complete, in the vernacular discourse of the communities where I have conducted fieldwork. This reflects the fact that a radical economic change that began with Cancún had roots in the early 1970s, preceding and overlapping with the first phases of the postcrisis reforms of the 1980s. This blurred boundary within the peninsula's experience of neoliberalism also reflects ambivalences in the narratives that politicians and many of their constituents use to frame the events of the 1980s and 1990s. During those decades, many policymakers stressed continuities between projects that furthered free market priorities and the traditional developmentalist mandates of the Revolutionary state. Furthermore, changes in national policy priorities tended to be hidden behind continuities in forms of electioneering that involved sexenio-end spending sprees on social programs, particularly targeting the rural voters of the Partido Revolucionario Institucional (Institutional Revolutionary Party, or PRI).

In some respects, Mexico's tradition of personalist politics and a quasi-monarchical presidency provided neoliberal reformers with a valuable rhetorical tool through the discourse of "moral renovation" (*renovación moral*). The string of economic crises that began in 1982 had been fueled in large part by the glut of government spending during the "populist" Echeverría and López Portillo sexenios. For many international commentators, as for some members of Mexico's political elite, this was clear evidence of the unsustainability of state-directed development that hinged on deficit spending (see Aguilar Camín and Meyer 1993; Gracida 2004). But the dominant systemic critique employed during the de la Madrid administration, which was forced to deal with the most immediate fallout of economic collapse, was a call for "moral renovation" (see Krauze 2013). From this official perspective, the fault for the collapse was not on the model of development per se but on opportunities that were "lost" as corrupt leaders squandered or stole public monies. As some critical authors suggested, this emphasis on the moral failings of individual political figures tended to deflect criticism from inequalities that were inherent in the Mexican economy and political system (Montalvo Ortega 1996). Just as important, tying the crises to the personal failings of former presidents allowed de la Madrid and his successors to frame reforms that would undermine existing social safety nets as "emergency" measures meant to save cherished institutions from the effects of immoral sexenios.

In Yucatán, this mix of privatizations, populist styles of electioneering, and ambiguous demands for "moral" reform developed against the backdrop of Víctor Cervera Pacheco's uncontested dominance in regional politics. Having effectively sidelined his rivals in the state's PRI, Cervera served as interim governor between 1984 and 1988 before assuming an influential national position as secretary of agrarian reform during the sexenio of Carlos Salinas de Gortari. Even during his six-year absence from his native state, he exercised considerable informal influence and was considered a kingmaker in the peninsula's politics. After the close of the Salinas administration, Cervera returned home to run a controversial campaign for a second gubernatorial term between 1995 and 2001. Not done with Yucatecan politics, he ran unsuccessfully to become mayor of Mérida, dying of a massive heart attack shortly after his 2004 defeat.

The period when Cervera reached the height of his official and informal powers saw a significant shift in state investment in various regional industries, and in the development of related infrastructure. These changes included a definitive shift from agrarian-focused development, the consolidation of a new economy dominated by tourism, and the emergence of *maquila* production as an important adjacent sector. In many respects, Yucatán's neoliberal transition mirrors Cervera's own political evolution. Early in his political career, he cultivated networks among regional representatives of the Confederación Nacional Campesina (National Peasant Confederation) and other traditional rural constituencies of the PRI. However, during his tenure as the secretary of agrarian reform, he oversaw the implementation of constitutional reforms that led many agrarian communities throughout the country to sell their collective landholdings. Through his web of influence and political patronage, he also played a role in the ultimate demise of state-sponsored henequen production. Finally, Cervera was an important innovator in developing the maquiladora industry in Yucatán. In essence, he oversaw the decline of an older agrarian economy and the consolidation of tourism and other sectors that were seen as more "competitive" in a post-NAFTA reality.

Much of Cervera's success as a politician resided in his ability to reconcile these transformations with the traditionally populist image of the PRI (Morales Ramírez 2006). Neoliberal policies devastated the local economies of the henequen zone, but the Cerveristas managed to cultivate a loyal following in the countryside until the very end of the 1990s. Many commentators argue that this became possible through the crassest forms of political manipulation, particularly the unchecked distribution of bicycles, sewing machines, farm tools, and other gifts in rural communities during election cycles. While this sort of electioneering was an important factor, I would argue that

Cervera and his circle also benefited from an ambiguity regarding the true nature of the national "transition" that had been taking place since the 1980s.

In later sections of this chapter, I will look more closely at the rearrangement of elite factions and rural political activists that took place over the course of the *cerverato*, as Cervera sought to bolster his own power base amid the death throes of the political order that had maintained the henequen industry and other parastatals. Though this strategy proved successful in forging new ties between the regional PRI and the prime movers in tourism and other emergent industries, it ultimately undermined the traditional pact between the party and rural citizens. An unintended consequence of this shift was the development of local oppositional networks that led the right-of-center Partido Acción Nacional (National Action Party, or PAN) to a number of electoral successes over the course of the 1990s. Some of the communities where I have conducted ethnographic research saw an expansion of competitive municipal elections during this period.

Before examining these regional and local phenomena, I will look more closely at some of the larger, national-level processes that defined the field of possibilities for the Cerveristas, their clients, and their constituents. One was a strategic rewriting of national history that framed neoliberal reform as an extension or "renovation" of older institutions and development projects. Though this rhetorical maneuver proved successful in some cases, it often collided with the reality of economic crises that impacted the livelihoods and savings of Mexicans across the socioeconomic spectrum. The experience of this dual phenomenon in Yucatán contributed to the initial success and eventual downfall of *cerverismo*. For many people in rural communities, it is also at the heart of the collective memories that coalesce in the phenomenon of vernacular neoliberalism.

CANCÚN AND CRISIS

In 1992, Miguel Mancera (1992), then director of the Banco de México, received an award from Cancún's Consejo de Promoción Turística (Council of Tourist Promotion) in recognition of the bank's central role in creating the urban and logistical infrastructure of the resort city. In his acceptance speech, Mancera framed the Cancún's successes as bridging the older traditions of Stabilizing Development and the more contemporary terrain of globalization and open markets. Drawing from the perspective of his mentor, the finance minister and development economist Antonio Ortiz Mena, Mancera observed that maintaining the price stability was the "primordial responsibility" of all central banks. This fact had often frustrated the older strategy of import substitution industrialization, which led to a reliance on imported technology and materials. This tendency tilted the balance of trade in favor of Europe and the United States and potentially devalued the peso. In this delicate context, tourism showed particular promise. As an infinitely renewable "export," it could help maintain a balance of trade, which had direct consequences for exchange rates and ultimately monetary pressures.

This, Mancera observed, created a paradoxical situation. Spearheading a vast infrastructural program like Cancún, the bank found itself participating in the kinds of state investment and borrowing that had played a central role in the crises of the 1980s, notwithstanding its "primordial responsibility" to maintain a stable currency. To justify this paradox, Mancera invited those in attendance to join him in a thought experiment in which the site of Cancún functioned like a nation. The imaginary nation of Cancún had inflows and outflows of goods, services, and money. Before investment by federal agencies turned the largely empty stretch of coast into a resort city, its balance of payments would have been essentially neutral. After the investment, the balance of trade fell quickly on the side of "imports," a condition whose effects were dreaded by responsible bankers. But, Mancera argued, this particular risk was entirely worthwhile. Some of Cancún's "imports" disappeared through consumption of overpriced goods and services by the architects and construction workers who built the hotels. However, many more pesos left a permanent footprint on the physical structures and infrastructures of the new tourist city. What would have happened, Mancera asked, if the central bankers of the country of Cancún had been so terrified of trade imbalance that they had refused the Inter-American Development Bank loan? In that case, he concluded, a good balance of payment would have been attained at the cost of Cancún's never having been built.

The point, Mancera argued, was to strike a balance between price stability and avoiding the protectionism that limited Mexico's access to larger global markets. In this respect, he viewed the neoliberal reforms of the de la Madrid and Salinas administrations, including the ongoing negotiations for NAFTA, as a positive revision of Stabilizing Development. Cancún was born of a project created during the golden age of protectionism, and, Mancera noted, had received the enthusiastic support of the Ortiz Mena himself (see also Ortiz Mena 1969). But, by its very nature, the Cancún project was destined to transcend the protectionism that had marked the early phases of the Stabilizing Development era. Mancera noted that the tourism sector has "in all times . . . acted within a tacit free trade pact with all of the world." Implicit here is the idea that foreign dividends brought by tourism could free Mexico from the limits of its older protectionist economy in which limited federal funds were essential to the survival of inefficient national industries. Free trade could end the dependence on public funds in which selected sectors and regions could only develop at the expense of others.

When I first read it in 2017, what struck me about Mancera's speech was how it proposes a history of tourism and neoliberalism that blurs the boundaries between the free market policy of the late 1980s and early 1990s and its developmentalist predecessor. In this regard, it runs against assertions made by some of Mancera's predecessors at the Banco de México. Ortiz Mena *did* enthusiastically embrace the Cancún project, but he did so in a far more "orthodox" developmentalist way. In presentations made in 1969, he cited tourism as the most important new front in the decades-long battle to improve the balance of trade with the United States by providing an influx of foreign expenditure. However, he explicitly framed an increase of touristic "exports" as a complement to policies that limited expenditures on imports among Mexicans at home and abroad (Ortiz Mena 1969, 36–37). That is, Cancún tourism emerged as a part of a larger import substitution project that was antithetical to the notions of free trade that Mancera would tout in 1992.

The fact that Mancera was able to reframe a massive experiment in state-supported capitalism as a precursor to free trade globalization is, in fact, consistent with a broader heterodoxy in thinking about development in Mexico toward the end of the twentieth century. In an insightful study of Mexican economists trained since the 1950s, Sarah Babb (2001) contrasted the professional theses of graduates of the Universidad Nacional Autónoma de México (National Autonomous University of Mexico), a department associated with Marxist and developmentalist economics, with those produced by graduates from the Instituto Tecnológico Autónomo de México (Autonomous Technological Institute of Mexico), which is more associated with liberal and neoliberal traditions. Though she found a limited tendency among graduates of the Instituto Tecnológico Autónomo to cite more classical economists, and for their contemporaries at the Universidad Nacional Autónoma to have more of an affinity to Marxism, neither camp was particularly orthodox. This blurred boundary between neoliberal political economy and its predecessor mirrors a broader tendency that Amy Offner (2019, 16) has observed throughout the Americas, in which the tools applied to free market reforms in the 1970s and 1980s "came from the repertoire of mid-century state-building itself."

In essence, the intellectual and social contexts that produced Mexican economists seem to have created fertile ground for the pragmatic ambivalence that is evident in Mancera's speech.

The hindsight of several decades may have hardened the perspective of Ortiz Mena's closest disciples, some of whom became explicit critics of the new neoliberal order. Toward the end of his life, Carlos Enríquez Sauvignac, who played a central role in the planning and creation of Cancún, vehemently asserted an identity as a "development economist" in the mold of the 1960s (Pedro Moncada Jiménez, pers. comm., 12 July 2018). While he might have agreed with the first half of the argument that Mancera made in 1992, he sought to distance himself from the globalizing, free market logic that seems to have become its ultimate justification.

This latter-day critique of the neoliberal project by one of the creators of Cancún would resonate with many of the rural Yucatecans who have prospered in the tourism sector. When Mancera delivered his acceptance speech in Cancún, he was already a player in the negotiations that led to the North American Free Trade Agreement (Salinas de Gortari 2017), a treaty whose adoption was the immediate catalyst for the Zapatista uprising that would become iconic of Indigenous resistance to neoliberalism. Though this kind of grassroots uprising has been rare in Yucatán, the Zapatistas, their charismatic leader, and their anti-neoliberal rhetoric have been invoked in protest of policies that are perceived as economically harmful to rural participants in the tourism trade (see Armstrong-Fumero 2013, 170–71). This is notwithstanding the tendency for many of these same rural Mayan speakers to appropriate discourses of entrepreneurialism that resonate with neoliberal ideology. The heterodox political cultures of Mexico tend to cast aspersion on the failures and extremes of economic ideologies, even as they embrace some of their more quotidian expressions.

As the head of the Banco de México, Mancera also played a role in the famous "December Mistake" of 1994. What began as a series of monetary adjustments that were meant to facilitate the implementation of NAFTA ultimately resulted in a catastrophic devaluation of the peso. Though the cheaper peso proved a temporary boon to tourism and the maquila industry (Ramírez Carrillo 2004, 130), it impacted working-class incomes and the savings of a generation of middle-class Mexicans, including many successful handicraft merchants in communities where I have conducted research. This frustration with national economic policy was one driver for the emergence of grassroots political opposition that began to turn rural municipalities into electoral "swing" districts. I will return to these rural defections from the PRI at the end of this chapter. First, I will discuss how parallel forms of discord emerged within elite political factions in the Yucatán Peninsula, where the Cerveristas sought to establish a balance between their agrarian past and their globalized future.

THE CERVERATO

As I have noted, Víctor Cervera Pacheco's role in legitimating the neoliberal project of the late 1980s and 1990s is somewhat ironic, given his earlier association with agrarian protest, the populism of Luis Echeverría, and the undermining of the traditionalist PRI factions represented by Carlos Loret de Mola. But as the PRI's "indispensable man in Yucatán" during the de la Madrid, Salinas, and Zedillo sexenios, he was intimately tied to reforms on the national and regional scale. As I described above, Cervera completed his period as interim governor in 1988, then moved to Mexico City to serve in a national-level cabinet position as Salinas's secretary of agrarian reform. From that position, he contributed directly to the implementation of the 1991 constitutional amendment that permitted the privatization and sale of the collectively held ejido lands of rural communities.

This association of the aging populist with neoliberal reform was not lost on his critics, members of traditionalist PRI factions associated with Loret de Mola. Víctor Manzanilla Schaffer (1998b), whose term as governor was cut short in 1991 amid Cerverista machinations, wrote at length about the betrayal of the Revolutionary state's political legacy, contrasting neoliberalism to the "humanism" with which earlier regimes had sought a just and socially responsible development. Where Luis Echeverría was the presidential villain of Loret de Mola's autobiographical oeuvre, Manzanilla Schaffer (1998a) blamed his own political catastrophes on Carlos Salinas de Gortari, who ultimately forced his resignation when the governor refused to intervene illegally to undermine the electoral prospects of the Yucatecan PAN. Víctor Cervera is a common thread in the narratives of both Loret de Mola and Manzanilla Schaffer, having been first the Yucatecan enabler of the populist Echeverría and later of the neoliberal Salinas.

If anything, Cervera was richly rewarded for his neoliberal "evolution." In 1995, he launched a successful bid for a second period in the governor's palace in Yucatán, a move that was widely decried as a violation of the strict six-year limit on executive office enshrined in the Mexican Constitution. But over the course of the Salinas years, the Cerveristas had consolidated their hold over the party at the state level, which made them equally indispensable to incoming president Ernesto Zedillo. By some accounts, after the retirement of his old mentor Carlos Sansores Pérez, Cervera's tutelary role extended across the peninsula to influence Priísta candidates in the neighboring states of Campeche and Quintana Roo (*La Revista Peninsular* 1998). Bonds within this informal political network would be strengthened through the spoils of coastal real estate developments that Cervera facilitated during his tenure at the Secretaría de la Reforma Agraria (Secretariat of Agrarian Reform).

Until the very end of the 1990s, it seemed that the anti-Cervera grumbles of Mérida-based political elites had few echoes in the countryside. As I noted in chapter 2, Carlos Loret de Mola became a highly unpopular figure in the wake of the El Charras affair and due to the restrictions that he placed on cattle husbandry. With strong links to student organizations and the Confederación Nacional Campesina, Cervera had an almost legendary prestige in rural areas. In the 1980s and early 1990s, before "neoliberalism" had become a watchword of oppositional politics, the populist performances that framed his political and economic reforms seemed to resonate with the ethos of "moral renovation" popularized by de la Madrid. Deeply invested in traditional displays of political largesse, the Cerveristas' mastery of the art of lavish gift-giving during election season led the press to refer to their campaign caravans as a "mobile hardware store" (Bonfil Gómez 2004). These campaigns drew heavily on the classic iconography of rural populism. In the 1990s, for example, Cervera attended conferences on national history with an honor guard of rural men dressed as Cruzo'ob rebels (Ben Fallaw, pers. comm., 2018).

The presence of this performative political largesse was quite tangible in rural communities when I began my ethnographic research. Between 1999 and 2001, I spent a number of weeks teaching English and conducting oral history interviews in Popolá, a village of 200 people in the municipality of Yaxcabá. At the time, most families in Popolá lived in traditional pole-walled, thatch-roofed houses. Between 1993 and 1996, most of these families had been beneficiaries of a state-level program that poured a cement floor for each pole-walled house. Each and every one of these floors included a roughly one-by-two-foot rectangle of text molded into the cement that commemorated the program executed under the mandate of Víctor Cervera Pacheco. I remember musing that most of the 200 residents of Popolá woke up each morning to a reminder of the governor's largesse the moment that they stepped down from their hammocks.

These populist performances may have helped cement Cervera's rural "voter reserve," but the governor's most innovative politicking involved urban business elites who would be the primary beneficiaries of the coming waves of privatization and market liberalization. During his two periods in the statehouse, he consolidated two influential groups of Yucatecan business magnates into formal cabinet positions and advisory councils. During his first period (1984–88), this group consisted of capitalists who emerged from Mérida's traditional elite. Alliances had shifted somewhat during the period when he moved to Mexico City to serve in Salinas's cabinet, so his second period as governor saw him turn to "new money" that included powerful Lebanese Yucatecan retail entrepreneurs. In effect, the regional capitalists who rounded out Cervera's court reflected his transformation during the Salinas sexenio from a "traditional" rural populist committed to the old order of state-sponsored henequen to a promoter of a more NAFTA-friendly economy based on tourism, maquila production, and the service sector. Cervera's favored business magnates enjoyed preferential access to contracts for the maquiladora sector that expanded to an unprecedented degree in the late 1980s and 1990s, and to valuable real estate that became available for development after the privatization of ejido land on the periphery of the capital of Mérida (Canto Sáenz 2001; Córdoba Azcárate 2020; Montalvo Ortega 1996; Pacheco Bailón 2007; Ramírez Carrillo 2004).

Cervera's affiliates in the business community would also play a key role in developments across the state border in Quintana Roo, and in the rise of the coastal tourist attractions that would eventually be branded as the Riviera Maya. Mario Villanueva Madrid, the governor of Quintana Roo from 1993 to 1999, was mentioned in the political press as Cervera's political "godson" (*Proceso* 1998), much as Cervera himself had been seen as a "godson" of Carlos Sansores Pérez. During Villanueva's tenure, many of the key land purchases in the coastal region south of Cancún were made official. Among the purchasers were major national hotel chains as well as individual investors who ranged from members of Cervera's informal cabinet, to former presidents of Mexico, to Carlos Hank González (*Proceso* 1998), the reputed founder of the political network known as the Atlacomulco Group.

During the process of forming the Riviera Maya, particular favor was given to Francisco Córdova Lira, president of the Xcaret Group, which would come to dominate tourism throughout the peninsula by the 2000s. The site that is currently the flagship ecopark Xcaret was developed in the mid-1980s through a collaboration between the Mexico City–based designer Miguel Quintana Pali and associates of Ritco, a construction firm that had played a role in the initial development of Cancún (Checa-Artasu 2009). Opening its doors in 1992, Xcaret developed a successful model of all-inclusive "experience" tourism with a self-proclaimed ecological sensibility.

Mario Villanueva Madrid's tenure as governor of Quintana Roo was crucial for the expansion of Xcaret's empire, which added the coastal properties that would become the partner parks of Xel-Ha and Garrafón on Isla Mujeres (Medina 2014; *Proceso* 1998). These properties lay the groundwork for further expansion, and by the 2000s Xcaret was seeking to control inland tourism circuits. This inland expansion contributed to a series of disputes that will form the central dramas of the later chapters of this book.

Reporting in the political magazines *La Revista Peninsular* and *Proceso* suggested that Cervera aided the Xcaret Group and Villanueva Madrid throughout this process. A 1998 article suggested that the sale of coastal land that had previously been part of the Sian Ka'an biosphere reserve had been facilitated by Cervera during his tenure as the national secretary of agrarian reform (*Proceso* 1998). This suggests that Cervera's tenure in the national secretariat involved working as an agent for a regional political network that would redefine the touristic and economic landscape of the entire peninsula in the last two decades of the twentieth century.

By the end of Cervera's second term as governor, the fractures that would eventually create new political openings for opposition parties had become evident. Business magnates who had enjoyed the cacique's favor during his first term as governor and felt "betrayed" as he shifted patronage to upstart groups began to defect to the PAN (Montalvo 1996; Pacheco Bailón 2007). The strategies adopted by the Xcaret Group itself hint at the changing political realities of the later years of the Cerverato. Listing the group's governing board members as of 2007, the geographer Martín Checa-Artasu highlights the diverse affiliations of kinship and political activism that allowed them to weather the changing realities of the turn of the millennium. The three brothers who helped found the original ecopark as co-owners of the Ritco construction group are blood cousins of the Tabasco politician, national PRI party leader, and unsuccessful 2006 presidential candidate Roberto Madrazo. Xcaret executive director Francisco Córdova Lira was another cousin of the Madrazo brothers. But he was also a founding member of the "Amigos de Fox," a political organization created in 1999 to facilitate the election of Panista Vicente Fox to the presidency (Checa-Artasu 2009, 52). Although the Xcaret Group would eventually return to the good graces of the Yucatecan PRI, their late embrace of *panismo* reflects the changing political tides on the peninsula. Similar processes were occurring in the countryside, where Cervera least expected them.

In March 2001, on the eve of the election that would bring Panista Patricio Patrón Laviada to the Yucatecan statehouse, the political magazine *Proceso* reported on a series of unprecedented fractures among the state's prominent Priístas (Mora and Santana 2001). The defection of some of Cervera's old associates from the business world had been chronicled for years, but journalists Martín Mora and Rosa Santana noted that the mass exodus of agrarian leaders to the PAN struck the aging cacique "where it hurt the most." These included leaders of the state's Confederación Nacional Campesina affiliates, which Cervera had played a prominent role in since the late 1960s. Another prominent defector was his old friend Gaspar Xiu Cachón, who had been a frequent and very public detractor of Carlos Loret de Mola and other establishment Priístas who had tried to stall Cervera's rise in the 1970s and 1980s (see Castillo Cocom 2005). Mora and Santana quoted some of the key defectors as citing the excesses of Cervera's decades-long *cacicazgo* as a primary motive for their sudden switch in party alliances. Despite Cervera's powerful charisma, the liquidation of the henequen sector, the general retreat of the state from agrarian reform, and the post-1994 economic crisis damaged his prestige in the countryside. Many of my friends and informants in Pisté assert that this dissent was brewing below the surface of the apparent pliability of rural voters for decades before the dramatic 2001 election. One story in particular hints at the dissent that was hidden behind some of Cervera's most apparently successful populist performances.

Reading the *Diario de Yucatán* and other major regional newspapers, it seems like no political visit to a rural community would be complete without a row of pretty young women in traditional dress handing flowers, linking arms, or kissing the VIP. These girls appear like nameless embodiments of feminized rural Indigeneity receiving the largesse of virile political patriarchs. Mariana Chuc, a lifelong Panista whom I interviewed in 2015, had taken part in one such reception for Cervera in the 1980s. She was in her early teens at the time and remembers coming home from secondary school to find her excited father telling her that she needed to change out of her uniform and into a huipil in order to greet Governor Cervera Pacheco.

Mariana remembers being flustered and even a little scared. In those days, she said, meeting a governor was like "meeting a God or the Prince of Wales." She was given a bouquet of roses to hand to Cervera, and was ushered to the front of the receiving line, which was to be populated by "the most humble, the most Maya girls, for the photos in the newspaper." As Mariana recounted these details in 2015, I remember that her teenage son and niece, who had never heard the story, started to laugh incredulously from the corner of the kitchen. They were even more amused as Mariana recalled how her father and the other local politicians made her and the other girls kiss the governor on the cheek. Laughing with her hands pressed against her eyes, she said, "What was I thinking when I kissed that man?"

That kiss would be particularly ironic given the radical transformation of Mariana and her family's political horizons just a few years later. Her father, the same man who had press-ganged her into Cervera's reception, converted to Panismo in the 1990s. She recalls that class tensions within the community, and the dominance of a few wealthy families with connections in Mérida, led to his disillusionment with the "official" party. Just a few years after he had been a "red-boned" Priísta, she remembered, her father began complaining that Priístas were "thieves, pigs, everything that is dirty. They have no heart. They would kill their own brother. All that they are interested in is money and power." He even named his dog Priísta, so that he could heap verbal abuse on it at his leisure.

The dramatic transformation in the political horizons of Mariana Chuc's family reflects a series of local processes that took place in parallel to the expansion of competitive elections during the Cerverato. Writing in the 1990s, Quetzil Castañeda (1996) documented conflicts within Pisté and other communities in the municipality of Tinum that swirled around the former town's attempts to secure its status as an independent municipality. Tensions between power brokers tied to the PRI and a growing community of self-identified Panistas played a central role. More than two decades later, Pisté is still a comisaría or municipal dependency of Tinum. But the rupture of the PRI's monopoly on local politics has left lasting imprints on the political culture of the municipality. This is reflected in the partisan behavior of people during local elections, as well as in the more ambiguous discursive terrain through which they make sense of political developments they encounter in ¡Por Esto! and Diario de Yucatán.

Rubén Dzul, whose teenage rebellion during the Loret de Mola years I described in chapter 2, observed this process from its origins in the 1980s and 1990s. He recalls that the "pioneers" of the PAN in Pisté were not more than twenty or so people, consisting of five original "luchadores sociales" (social reformers) and their close kin. They had become important actors in local politics by the end of the 1980s, despite being vastly outnumbered in the municipality.

Although the Panistas of Pisté scored some early electoral victories at the level of the local comisaría, conflicts with Priísta municipal presidents in Tinum often resulted in the satellite community's being denied federal funds that were administered from the municipal seat (see Castañeda 1996). As if tensions within the municipality were not enough, the early Panistas of Pisté also struggled with the distinctive organizational structure of their own party. Unlike the PRI, which has a history of mass membership coordinated through corporatist institutions like the Confederación Nacional Campesina and Confederación de Trabajadores de México, the PAN has been identified as a "party of notables" with a far more restricted membership (see Mizrahi 2003, 56–57). Thus, during the first decades of their existence as a more or less organized group, the rank-and-file Panistas of Pisté had virtually no contact with party leadership in Mérida. As late as 2015, after well over a decade during which PAN voters formed a formidable bloc in much of rural Yucatán, there were no official registered members in the municipality.

By the 1990s, on the eve of PAN victories in the Yucatecan statehouse and Mexican presidency, the Pisté activists had built enough of a constituency to field successful comisario candidates and challenge the PRI at the municipal presidency level. At this point, the local Panistas faced a serious internal challenge as they tried to forge more democratic conduits linking the party leadership and the local grassroots. Sometimes, self-identified PAN militants temporarily abandoned the formal party structures to field candidates through minor parties like Convergencia Nacional. But despite these momentary defections, a core of activists and voters who identified as Panistas grew steadily in Pisté and some other corners of the municipality of Tinum. By 2010, after a few developments that I will discuss in chapter 4, the importance of Tinum as a "swing" municipality brought the state PAN leadership into a much closer relationship with local activists.

Besides creating precedents for competitive multiparty elections, the first decades of Panismo in Pisté helped to diffuse a vernacular political critique that focused on the PRI's long history of manipulating rural people through corrupt and inefficient government programs. This drew heavily on the discourse of "moral renovation" that had begun within the neoliberalized PRI itself. For Rubén Dzul and many dedicated Panistas with whom I have discussed these topics, moral renovation is closely tied to their party's official rhetoric of eliminating personalism and clientelism through liberalism that strives for "the common good" (Martínez Valle 2000; Mizrahi 2003, 22–24). Other components of vernacular Panismo in communities like Pisté seem to draw on critiques that were widely reported in the Diario de Yucatán since the

1970s. As I will describe further in the next chapter, I have heard many local Panistas criticize the ideological complacency, economic inefficiency, and welfare dependency of traditional agriculturalists, echoing elitist characterizations of "rural parasites" engaged in an obsolete henequen industry. Given the transformation of the *Diario* into a more or less transparent advocate for Panismo by the 1990s, this line of critique can be read as a common bond between rural and urban members of the party.

Still, other aspects of rural Panismo contrast with its more established urban and elitist counterpart. Though the Catholic Right has been an important component of Panismo—especially in Mérida—many Panistas in Pisté are devoted Protestants and often critical of the establishment religion that was central to the party's early development. For many of the political "pioneers" in the community, the ideological essence of Panismo lay in the stridency of its calls for "moral renovation" in politics rather than in the party's more traditional religious conservatism. This emphasis might lead some rural Panistas to downplay their party's national affiliation with right-of-center politics. I was not surprised, for example, by Rubén Dzul's response when I pressed him on whether he considered the PAN to be a right or left party. At first, he politely dismissed the terms of my question, observing that the national-level PAN had a history of "working with" the PRI and occupied a similar space on the political spectrum. But a moment later, he said that the Panistas of Pisté had a history of struggling against stronger opponents for a fairer distribution of resources, which he considered made them a solidly "leftist" party.

Rubén's "leftist" characterization of the PAN underscores an aspect of rural party politics that is often unspoken by urban political leaders. Rural communities that have traditionally been characterized as part of a homogeneous PRI-leaning constituency are, in reality, economically stratified. The "stronger opponents" to which Rubén referred above consist of a coalition between entrepreneurs from the west and north of the state who had relocated to Pisté and relatively wealthy local families that wielded significant informal power over poorer employees, relatives, and neighbors. Like other Panistas in Pisté, he suggests that the resentments that led to mass defections from the PRI had as much to do with the behavior of the official party's local representatives as it did with ideology or policy decisions at the state or national level.

Mariana Chuc explained the homegrown sources of this resentment to me with an anecdote about her father-in-law Don Beto, a poor maize agriculturalist who raised pigs as his main source of cash income. At the time, a powerful cacique named Eliazar Cupul was comisario municipal of Pisté and the head of the local PRI committee. He also happened to be a successful merchant, and the only person in town who bought pigs for transport and sale in Valladolid. Don Eliazar's wealth and local connections made him invaluable to the PRI during election season. The party, in turn, looked the other way as he allegedly skimmed cash from the town's already meager funds.

Mariana recalls as a young girl seeing her future father-in-law make repeated trips to visit Don Eliazar, only to be left waiting for hours in front of the comisario's house. After a few days, when a family member's sickness or children's school expenses had made Don Beto truly desperate, Don Eliazar would offer an embarrassingly small sum for the fattened pig. And, Mariana noted, Don Beto would accept the sum gratefully!

Mariana cited this story as a good example of the attitude that was exploited for generations by the PRI. Poverty compelled local people to gratefully accept assistance from political leaders, even when this defied the logic of fair business and obliged them to humiliating acts of obeisance. But with few options outside of agricultural work, most people born before the 1970s had little choice but to play along. These personalistic relationships blurred the boundaries between business and politics, so that poor Don Beto could be relied upon to vote for the PRI as readily as he sold his pigs for a pittance. Cervera's gifts of bicycles and sewing machines, like federal programs that offered cash payments to agriculturalists, were just larger-scale examples of the same structure of paternalism and subservience.

For Mariana Chuc, as for many self-identified Panistas I know in Pisté, the change in social class and occupation that came in the wake of the tourist boom did more to transform local attitudes than the ideology of the opposition party. One of the central themes of my previous research was the emergence of what I referred to as a "postpeasant" identity when families used income from the tourist industry to expand their personal capital and finance education for their children (see Armstrong-Fumero 2013, 128–33). My choice of the term "postpeasant" came directly from how this social status was articulated by my friends and informants. As Mariana herself observed, "Campesinos are dependent on the government. But those of us who work in Chichén [Itzá], do you think we would prefer having a boss over working for ourselves?" For many people with whom I've spoken in Pisté, the roots of competitive elections in the municipality stem from the political freedom and "awakening" afforded by postpeasant lifestyles.

"Moral renovation" meant different things to different political operators in 1980s and 1990s Mexico. Just as Mancera's acceptance speech attempted to graft the legitimacy of nationalistic development onto a new economic paradigm, Cervera's management of alliances and political performance sought to work a similar magic act on the electoral terrain of the peninsula. He and his followers were successful in doing so until the end of the 1990s, when *cerverismo* ultimately succumbed to some of the same pressures that created electoral openings for opposition parties across Mexico. In the case of the Yucatán Peninsula, this decay of traditional alliances was punctuated by the disillusionment of elite factions that had fallen out of the governor's favor during his second administration. As parallel discontents germinated in the countryside, Cervera's own cacicazgo became a target for "moral renovation" by a newly empowered opposition.

The stories told by my friends and informants in Pisté hint at other local factors that shaped these rural defections from *cerverismo* and *priísmo*. While the Catholic conservatism of the PAN made this a natural home for many in Mérida's urban middle class, some rural people gravitated to the party with less ideological or religious orthodoxy. The fact that rural Panistas built local networks, and scored more and more electoral wins, without official membership in the "party of notables" suggests that this was largely a marriage of convenience. However, through its association with the rejection of PRI authoritarianism and a social demand for "moral regeneration," a pragmatic Panismo gained a symbolic importance that transcended explicit party ideology. For people like Mariana Chuc, Rubén Dzul, and other activists whose stories I will discuss in the next chapter, it was an expression of personal economic autonomy that their parents could hardly have dreamed of.

This autonomy, bought largely with the prosperity brought by the tourist trade, brings me back to Miguel Mancera's 1992 acceptance speech. Mancera apocryphally traced the roots of free trade to the classic figures of Stabilizing Development and hoped that this continuity would grant legitimacy to current neoliberal policies. People whom I have interviewed in Pisté and neighboring communities offer a different chronology, and one that is far less flattering toward the PRI of the 1980s and 1990s. Their local economy changed dramatically—and for the better—since the 1970s. Income from tourism allowed local families to navigate the crises of the later 1980s and early 1990s from a somewhat better position than their contemporaries in other parts of the country. The new lifestyles and aspirations that were enabled by this relative prosperity contributed to the development of "postpeasant" identities that many people in Pisté associate with a broader political awakening.

The rise of these postpeasant identities presented an important check on the Cerveristas' assumption that neoliberal reforms could be legitimated through association with more traditional ways of doing politics. For many rural families that had prospered in the tourist industry, the "traveling hardware store" that accompanied Cervera's electoral caravans had lost much of its appeal by the 1990s. Direct cash transfer programs known as Progresa and Oportunidades would be very important in rural communities in the last decades of the twentieth century, and will be discussed in more detail in chapter 5. But PAN "pioneers" like Rubén Dzul and party stalwarts like Mariana Chuc often cite the tourism prosperity that emerged during the same period as reducing their dependence on government programs and election-year gifts that were geared specifically toward agriculturalists. This in turn enabled them to air grievances against members of an older local elite. These opposition activists recognize that many families in Pisté, and many more in the communities that surround it, are still receptive to traditional practices of PRI electioneering. But by the end of the 1990s, they had consolidated enough of an opposition network to break the monopoly of older local leaders, and tilt many elections. The fact that this political identity is connected to changes in lifestyles and aspirations brought about by tourism development hints at broader cultural changes in rural communities. In the next chapter, I will examine how the close ties between tourism development and political autonomy have shaped some rural Yucatecans' sense of their status as Mexican citizens and self-identified Maya people.

4

PESOS, DOLLARS, AND MAYA IDENTITY

As I discussed in the previous chapters, many of my friends and informants in Pisté associate their political "awakening" with changes in local perspectives that came with the tourism industry. At the heart of this was a rejection of clientelistic relationships and dependency that they associate with the peasant agriculturalists who were the most faithful Partido Revolucionario Institucional (Institutional Revolutionary Party, or PRI) voters. Many aspects of this "awakening" also parallel what Adam Kotsko characterized as a political theology of neoliberalism, turning certain capitalist logics into fundamental principles of material and moral life. Many Pisteños state that values learned in the commodity market "opened their eyes" (*abrieron sus ojos* in Spanish; *p'il u yiich* in Mayan) to the tricks and deceptions that had successfully bought the votes of their peasant grandparents. Still, elements of this vernacular neoliberalism often coexist in everyday speech with a commitment to maintaining the town's ejido landholdings, respect for traditional rural lifeways, and older narratives of regional identity. In this regard, the vernacular neoliberalism of rural Yucatán is as heterodox as the political strategies employed by the Cerveristas in the 1980s and 1990s.

In this chapter, I will approach several aspects of the social identity of people in Pisté and neighboring communities through five historical and ethnographic vignettes. First, however, I will give a brief summary of some of the ways monetary and fiscal policy figured in the origins of the Cancún project, and how these aspects of policy were experienced in the everyday lives of rural Yucatecans. As I will show, phenomena like inflation and currency devaluation figure prominently in local memories of the 1980s and 1990s, as do different uses of the dollar bills that arrived in the pockets of foreign tourists. Dollars, pesos, and different ways of using them figure both in characterizations of the town's changing lifestyle and in critiques of politicians whose economic mismanagement has inflicted pain on generations of Mexicans. These local financial practices and memories of the failures of elite politicians converge in the entrepreneurial ideals that are at the heart of vernacular neoliberalism.

DEFENDING THE PESO

In the 1992 speech that I discussed at length in chapter 3, Miguel Mancera characterized the strength and stability of the national currency as the "primordial" responsibility of the national bank, whose agents planned and orchestrated the Cancún project. In the late 1960s, Mexican economists believed that foreign tourists spending dollars in Cancún and similar resort areas could reduce Mexico's chronic trade deficits and in turn bolster the value of the peso in relation to foreign currencies (see Espinosa-Coria 2013; and Martí 1985). Building the infrastructure of those resorts in an "integrated" and timely manner also avoided the local inflationary effects of the starts and stops that marked the decades-long development of the Highway 180 corridor. That is, the vast swaths of rural countryside and barren coasts that would become Cancún would not be flooded with cash wages until there was adequate infrastructure to bring in enough consumer goods to establish an affordable price equilibrium. Thus, the Cancún project embodied a vision of state intervention that combined monetary protectionism with measures that kept basic consumer goods affordable for rural and working-class urban families. By extension, the failure to maintain price stability—either through devaluation or inflation—was construed as a fundamental failure of a national administration.

In this regard, President José López Portillo (1976–82) presented a sort of cautionary tale for subsequent Mexican politicians. In the face of a looming financial crisis toward the end of his sexenio, he vowed to "defend the peso like a dog." This folksy turn of phrase would haunt him as the peso crashed, notwithstanding his highly unpopular decision to nationalize Mexico's private banks. Journalists reported angry citizens barking loudly at López Portillo's public appearances. In the later 1980s and 1990s, when the failures of his administration became the primary target of calls for "moral renovation," ironic references to the "canine fidelity" of venal political leaders became common in the writing of Mexico's political pundits (Cruz and Durán 2017, 74; Krauze 2013, 430). So, Mancera's claim about the "primordial responsibility" of a national banking system touches on something that was as much of a point of anxiety for the political class as it was for the purchasing public.

Though the de la Madrid administration tended to focus on López Portillo's "moral" failings as a president, the final collapse of Stabilizing Development also had much to do with the macroeconomic dynamics of state-driven industrialization. As I discussed in chapter 3, Antonio Ortiz Mena and his disciples were deeply committed to both currency stability and parastatal economic development. They assumed that state intervention was necessary to protect both the markets that consumed native industry and the purchasing power of Mexico's national currency. But many Mexican and foreign observers argued that this policy was ultimately counterproductive to industrial development, since the "overvalued" peso had the potential to drive capital out of the country (Gracida 2004). The idea that trade imbalances were actually exacerbated when an overvalued peso drove Mexicans to consume more imported goods also gained traction among economists in the late 1960s. These persistent imbalances raised the price tag of both monetary and commercial protectionism, threatening the long-term sustainability of both policies. This greatly increased the likelihood of simultaneous economic stagnation and runaway inflation, the dreaded "stagflation" of the 1970s (Martí 1985).

An emerging consensus about the exhaustion of the Stabilizing Development paradigm was what drove Ortiz Mena's disciples at the national bank to explore tourism. Given the limitations of "traditional" industrial production in Mexico, the status of tourism as a locally staged *export* sector presented an ideal solution. Tropical beach attractions with nearby Maya ruins could be marketed transnationally to tourist-consumers, who then transported *themselves* to the goods, services, and experiences that they wished to pay for. Bringing dollars directly to the regional and ultimately national economy, tourism contributed to a positive long-term balance of payment without requiring the unsustainable protective measures that had defined industries like henequen (see Clancy 2001).

These perceived benefits to Mexico's balance of trade allowed the bankers to overcome prejudices against tourism development that had been common among intellectual and political elites in the first half of the twentieth century (Babb 2011, 92–98). Though tourism was already a significant industry in Mexico in the 1930s and 1940s, political elites were reluctant to embrace it as a route to national prosperity. The expansion of the road network linking Southern California to the Mexican Northwest in the early twentieth century was viewed on both sides of the border as opening this region to touristic development and foreign investment (Kim 2015; Núñez Tapía and Méndez Reyes 2018). However, throughout this period, some intellectuals and political leaders in Mexico raised concerns that ranged from a distaste for the gambling- and booze-fueled tourism that marred border cities like Tijuana (Gruel Sández 2017; Schantz 2010) to more generalized moral panics about the impact of gringo values and entertainment on the national culture (see Berger 2006, 1–25). This resistance receded toward the end of the 1960s amid growing fears about the future of industries that could not function without a significant degree of public subsidy.

By the 2000s, it was evident that tourism development had less of an impact on balance of trade and currency stability than the bankers had anticipated, particularly when compared with the somewhat later development of the maquila industry (see Espinosa-Coria 2013). But in the 1970s, the success of tourism and the stability of Mexico's currency were closely tied in the public justifications for promoting this industry. For example, in 1976, following the first major devaluation of the peso since the 1950s, the Secretariat of Tourism published a note in its newsletter regarding the monetary importance of the industry. The newsletter stated that it was "the duty of all Mexicans" to defend the new trade equilibrium that would become possible now that the peso was no longer "artificially" overvalued. The note observed that tourism, as an export activity that helped create demand for Mexican goods and currency, was a crucial part of this "defense," since it bolstered the national currency while other industries adjusted to the new possibilities of the international market.[1]

Currency fluctuations had a very immediate and tangible effect on the lived experience of millions of families, lending credibility to the patriotic value of "defending" a new monetary equilibrium. However, the specific monetary argument of the Secretariat of Tourism's note would likely have been lost on many rural consumers, for whom local inflationary effects could have the same impact on the price of consumer goods. Still, there seems to be a distinction in how many of my informants perceive price increases that came with the prosperity of the local economy and those associated with financial collapses that reflect the failure of the state. The first two vignettes that I will present here illustrate this contrast.

"IF YOU CAN'T MAKE MONEY, YOU'RE LAZY": INFLATION AMID PROSPERITY

A constant feature of my early interviews about the history of Pisté and neighboring communities was just how much prices had changed, for better or for worse, since the early 1960s. Elderly people took special delight in asking me to guess how much a sack of corn sold for forty years ago, or how much a woman could earn with a day's housekeeping during the first years in which local hotels operated. They hoped to stun me with the pitiable amounts that were earned in the past, or with how "given away" (*regalado* in Spanish; *réegaláadobil* in Mayan) certain items had once been. Though some of these stories were framed in terms of the hardship of making ends meet in the twenty-first century, many of these elders correlate the rise in prices to a concurrent increase in the earning power of local people.

Don Javier Maas was in his late sixties when I interviewed him in 2001. He had been a major figure in municipal politics as an "old guard" Priísta from the late 1960s to the 1990s, and he had made a significant sum of money through the development of businesses that catered to tourists. Thinking back to his youth in the 1950s, he recalled a cash-poor community of people with few opportunities for labor outside of agriculture. Prices for maize and other crops were pitiably low in the nearby markets of Valladolid and Dzitas, and sales of cattle or pigs involved risky transactions with often-unscrupulous middlemen. Worse still, young men and women entered the workforce with the same basic skill set as their neighbors, further depressing the price of locally hired labor. Don Javier recalled that, as a teenager, he would make charcoal on his family's plot and carry it, two sacks at a time, to the town's *k'iiwik* (square) to sell. At the end of a successful day, he might earn just a little more than the four or five daily pesos that other boys made by weeding people's yards and milpas. As he put it, "It made you sad to see it."

Don Javier observed that paid work in road construction was one of the few sources of "outside" cash in the 1950s and 1960s, and therefore highly desirable. This reflects a common phenomenon in mid-twentieth-century rural Mexico where the income generated from roadwork was as important to local communities as the expansion of infrastructure itself (Bess 2017; Waters 1998). These brief infusions of cash were too few and far between to make much of a difference in Pisté until the completion of Highway 180 in the late 1950s and early 1960s. By then, the influx of cash did not all disappear into scarce and overvalued consumer goods. Rather, it allowed local penny capitalists to invest in the production of handicrafts or the preparation of food that they could sell to tourists who trickled in from Mérida.

Other elderly people to whom I've spoken refer to Volkswagen buses, known locally as *aak'o'ob* (turtles), that arrived daily from the early 1960s on. In those days, Don Javier recalls that it took about five or more hours for a bus to arrive from Mérida. This meant that most tourists spent at least one night in Pisté, in hotels staffed by local workers, where they became easy targets for handicraft vendors. The scale of the tourism was tiny compared to what would arrive decades later from Cancún, but the "turtles" came reliably and established a predictable rhythm of investment and sale for local capitalists.

By the dawn of the 1970s, when Cancún entered into operation, a vastly larger flow of tourists arrived from the eastern expansion of the 180 corridor (see also Castañeda 1996; Castellanos 2010; and Córdoba Azcárate 2020). The influx of tourists, along with the injections of cash prompted by seasonal labor migration to and from the resort city, had an undeniable inflationary effect on prices. Don Javier seemed to view this as a positive thing, as the rise in the price of goods was accompanied by an even greater increase in the price of labor. He noted that it cost him at least a hundred pesos to hire someone to weed a small plot where he planted watermelons, roughly ten or eleven US dollars in 2001. Compare this to the five "old" pesos, or somewhat less than fifty US cents that he quoted as the going rate for a day of such labor in the early 1960s. Adjusted for inflation and the transition from "old" to "new" pesos, this anecdotal comparison amounts to a difference between five dollars in 1960 and more than twice as much in 2001.

Don Javier conceded that this rise in prices was a burden to many local consumers, but he also implied that it was largely offset by the overall increase in tourist-fueled prosperity. He observed that people on the lowest rungs of the socioeconomic ladder, who took menial jobs like weeding others' house plots, drew particular benefit from the rising price of such services. As Don Javier put it, "Now, if you can't make money here, it's because you're lazy."

Anecdotal accounts like Don Javier's suggest that rural people who prospered through the tourism industry observed some of the local inflationary effects that informed the national bankers' rationale for "integral" development. But as Mancera argued in his 1992 thought experiment about the imaginary "country" of Cancún, trade imbalances and inflationary pressures could be justified if they created income flows that trickled down the social strata. This also seems consistent with the moral of Don Javier's narrative. Today, prosperity is distributed unevenly in Pisté and surrounding communities, and many people in the lower economic strata still struggle to make ends meet. But successful capitalists like Don Javier created new local demand for labor from agrarian communities whose residents were traditionally dependent on federal safety nets or migration to distant urban centers like Cancún or Mérida (see Castellanos 2010). The young men who weeded Don Javier's watermelon patch may have entered the tourist economy too late to become wealthy themselves, but they share the same potential to earn cash close to home and imagine postpeasant lifestyles that were unavailable to their parents.

"THERE ARE DOLLARS HERE!" OR, HOW TO CRISIS-PROOF A HOUSEHOLD

The stated monetary goal of the Cancún project, the stabilization of the peso by improving the balance of trade, is probably obscure to many people in Pisté, as it would be to the vast majority of tourists who pass through there. However, increased access to dollar bills, and their frequent use in local exchanges, can prompt a series of vernacular reflections on the turbulent history of Mexico's currency. The peso crisis of the 1980s, compounded by the effects of the December Mistake a decade later, taught a generation of Mexicans that savings and investments kept in pesos could be quite fragile. For rural Yucatecans who participate in the tourist market, the solution to this fragility sometimes lies in the possession and judicious use of dollar bills.

When I asked a local friend in her forties why she claimed that people in Pisté were more cosmopolitan and forward thinking than most of their contemporaries in the city of Mérida, she laughed and responded, "Because there are dollars here!" She elaborated that these "dollars" came attached to foreign tourists from whom the people of Pisté acquired new ideas, fashions, and tastes (see Armstrong-Fumero 2013, 130). Pisteños are far from unique in attributing this kind of symbolic value to currency (Maurer 2006). In an article about engagements between the Kandha tribal minority and the Indian development state, Pinky Hota (2019) discusses the diverse ways Kandha people use the conspicuous manipulation of money to combat primitivist stereotypes and assert their status as citizens of a modern, market-oriented society. The fact that my friend referred specifically to dollars, versus pesos, brings an added wrinkle to these monetized performances of modernity. Writing about the physical form of dollars sent home by Chinese migrants from Fujian, Julie Chu (2010, 174, 203–5) notes that the possession and exchange of foreign currency serves as a marker of self-consciously cosmopolitan identities and market-oriented values. A parallel process takes place in Pisté and other communities on the tourism circuit, where dollars are a physically tangible marker of contact with the lucrative tourism market. But unlike the Fujianese villagers Chu studied, and unlike the millions of Mexicans whose livelihoods depend on remittances from migrant relatives, many residents of Pisté see themselves as enjoying the relative privilege of working in an economy that generates dollars in their own backyards.

Besides serving as a metonym for a distinctly local form of prosperity and lifestyle, dollars are prestigious possessions whose stability in relation to the Mexican peso grants them a series of additional functions in local exchanges. This homespun currency exchange works through an informal logic that is distinct from institutional finance and formal exchange markets. Nevertheless, it has contributed to a series of vernacular practices that give tangible local form to the intended monetary impacts of Cancún.

For as long as I have been going to Yucatán, there have been tourists who run out of pesos and use foreign currency to purchase food, services, or handicrafts. This was particularly common in the early years of the 2000s, when there was a significant movement of tourists through downtown Pisté but no ATM machines and few formal exchange booths. After they were used to purchase food or handicrafts, foreign bills would cut a circuitous path in local exchanges before ending up in a state-sanctioned exchange booth or bank. In these informal exchanges, dollars are referred to as being "grabbed" (*agarrados* in Spanish; *ch'a'abi* in Mayan) from tourists, a phrasing that implies a different form of transaction from the simple exchange of goods for currency. Unlike prices that are quoted and negotiated in pesos, payment in dollars involves informal exchange rates which are rounded up or down to the nearest ten, entailing an additional layer of calculated loss or gain.

I've never employed quantitative tools to create a formal model of the community's monetary flows, given that the quasi-legal nature of many of the transactions would make formal data gathering on this topic complicated. However, I have observed hundreds, if not thousands, of "grabbing" exchanges over the course of more than two decades, and can offer some broad outlines. One interesting factor in "grabbing" exchanges is the way they have related to the periodic devaluation of the peso in relation to the dollar. In the late 1990s, when the summer exchange rate at public booths in Yucatán tended to fluctuate between nine and twelve pesos to the dollar, the going value of a "grabbed" dollar was ten pesos. This meant that, in some cases, local sellers were able to cancel out the effects of a peso depreciation by forcing tourists to spend their dollars at a fixed rate of ten pesos. In the later 2010s, when depreciation of the peso led to formal local exchange rates of seventeen to twenty pesos to the dollar, a "grabbed" dollar in Pisté usually seemed to go for twenty pesos. This suggests that, while paying with dollars often meant sacrificing a few pesos in the late 1990s, "grabbers" of dollars took a small loss on each exchange twenty years later.

Given the amount of haggling that often accompanies handicraft sales (see Castañeda 1996), a seller's willingness to sacrifice a few pesos by "grabbing" dollars at a one-to-twenty exchange rate is probably a sound strategy for closing a deal. But it also reflects the desirability of dollars as a stable store of value. I have known families of artisanry vendors that try to hoard "grabbed" dollars to exchange at the bank during periods that offer an advantageous rate, which often coincide with the lean months after the end of the tourist season.

The idea that dollars are a more reliable store of value than the peso reflects the experience of generations of Mexicans who faced brutal setbacks to their own savings and finances after the monetary crashes of the 1980s and 1990s. For some rural Yucatecans that I have known for many years, these monetary horror stories bring an ironic twist to a genre of "lost treasure" tales that were once commonly told in those communities. In the past, it was common for Maya agriculturalists to hide clay pots, glass jars, or old tins full of hoarded silver coins in the bush where they farmed. There are stories of old men who died before revealing the resting place of their hoard to their children, and of "lost" pots or jars of coins that are occasionally found in the bush. Supernatural powers are imputed to these hidden hoards, which can disappear and reappear of their own spectral volition. Other stories suggest that the hoards are haunted by ghosts that take the form of snow-white roosters or bulls, perhaps the angry souls of their original owners (see Armstrong-Fumero 2014).

Currency fluctuations add a twist to this tradition. In a number of stories I have heard, the hoards unearthed in the bush consist of rolls of cash that were carefully bundled in plastic bags before being sealed in glass jars or cans. By the time that they were unearthed, after the collapse of the early 1980s and the subsequent introduction of the "new" peso in 1994, they were essentially worthless. Not surprisingly, these jars and cracker cans full of devalued bills are not usually considered to be haunted.

Where the Mexican peso is capricious enough to spoil a buried treasure, many rural Yucatecans that I know refer to dollars as if they were a store of value that exists outside of the social and political order that corrupts Mexican currency. These stories add an interesting twist to George Foster's classic analysis of the idea of limited good in the Michoacán community of Tzintzuntzan. Foster characterized Tzintzuntzeños as believing that all good things, from wealth to honor to bountiful harvests, exist in a finite and contested supply. Benefits gained by one individual or family inevitably came with a concomitant loss to others. The two exceptions, Foster (1967, 143–52) observed, were tales of buried gold that appeared in milpas and caves, and remittances sent by relatives working in the United States. Both exceptions consisted in forms of wealth that originated outside of the closed world of contemporary Tzintzuntzan and entered people's pockets independently of the zero-sum game that normally governed local economic life.

A half century later and hundreds of miles away in rural Yucatán, buried treasures have been compromised by the currency fluctuations of the 1980s and 1990s. But dollars play one role similar to what they did in the cosmology of 1950s Tzintzuntzan, insofar as they represent a stream of wealth generated far beyond the boundaries of the local contexts of agriculture and other traditional forms of labor. The moral value of the dollar in Foster's Tzintzuntzan was its ability to transcend the context of scarcity that turned any individual's profit into a source of resentment and social disharmony. In contrast, my own interlocutors in 2000s Yucatán often framed the value of the dollar as residing in the stability of a foreign power that provides a foil for the incompetence of Mexico's leaders. The transcendence of the dollar owes less to its externality to the closed system of labor in a rural community and more to its independence from the machinations of politicians who created a generation of crises.

The two vignettes I have presented so far offer a contrast between perceptions of "good" inflation that lets the prosperity of rich merchants trickle down and "bad" devaluations that can erase years of profit and hard work in a flash of technocratic incompetence. They reflect some of the ways the local transition from an agrarian to a touristic economy shaped people's perception of the value of currency. In both cases, fluctuations in the value of the peso have political and moral implications, for both the local workers who are offered new opportunities for profit and the nonlocal politicians whose legitimacy hinges on the purchasing power of citizens. Most local people don't frame their history with Cancún-based tourism in the same terms as the bankers who originated the project. But there is a clear vernacular consciousness of the intersections between state-sponsored infrastructural or development projects and the "bottom line" of local families. Seen against the failures of various schemes of agricultural development in the 1970s, the construction of Cancún is a seemingly unique development project that gave tourism workers a modicum of stability during a protracted period of economic crisis. Furthermore, the dollars that flow inland and westward from Cancún are a metonym for a stable purchasing power that has proved elusive in Mexico's troubled financial policies. For all its flaws and inequalities, the tourism economy offers local families a range of strategies that makes them less vulnerable to economic change than their agrarian ancestors and neighbors.

Given that the venality and incompetence of political elites is so central to this vernacular consciousness, it's not surprising that many people in Pisté believe that they themselves could do a better job of stewarding the nation's resources. However, many of the grievances that are aired in local political discourse focus on how Mayan-speaking entrepreneurs are marginalized in the processes of decision-making that have such large impacts on their everyday lives. The next two ethnographic vignettes will examine these grievances, which offer some surprising insights into local interpretations of the classist and racist forms of exclusion faced by millions of Indigenous Mexicans.

"WE ARE JOB CREATORS": IGNORED ENTREPRENEURS

At the heart of the "Cancún Model" is the idea that the private investors that retained control of the city's hotels after the withdrawal of the federal entities that initially financed the project would continue to serve as "generadores de empleos" (job creators). The 1968 memorandum that first articulated the Cancún project gives a broad sketch of a "multiplier effect" that was to be the engine of this ongoing growth. The authors of the memo observed that, during the period of initial investment, the creation of each hotel room provided employment for construction workers, electricians, plumbers, architects, and also for agriculturalists who fed this army of workers. Every year after its completion, each room would attract a sequence of tourists who provided direct employment for service workers in the hotel, but also indirect employment for a range of food producers.

Based on data from 1960, the bankers estimated that an initial investment of 300 million pesos would lead to the construction of 1,000 rooms, which would generate 1 billion pesos (US$80 million at 1968 exchange rates) in tourist spending annually. When the respective "multipliers" were applied,

construction work on the initial thousand rooms would create 11,819 permanent jobs, while subsequent expenditures by the tourists lodged in those
same rooms would generate as many as 48,384 additional jobs.[2]

The idea that government-funded development projects had a multiplier
effect in generating employment was not original to the Cancún project. In
Yucatán, it figured in the rationale for propping up the languishing parastatal
henequen sector, for the development of a sugar industry, and for the other
agrarian schemes discussed in chapters 2 and 3. Where Cancún differed was
in the successful way that the role of maintaining these projects was transferred to the private sector. During the Echeverría and López Portillo sexenios, industries like henequen and sugar required ever-increasing degrees of
state investment, as epitomized by the government purchase of all private
cordage firms and the nationalization of sugar mills at Catmis and Kakalná.
Neither of these parastatal industries survived the neoliberal reforms of the
later 1980s and 1990s. In contrast, the hotels that had been constructed
under the mandate of the Fondo de Promoción e Infraestructura Turística
had passed into private ownership, and a new generation of hoteliers and
restauranteurs expanded tourist offerings for decades to come (see Clancy
2001; and Martí 1985).

In this respect, the Cancún project anticipated the privatizing ideals of the
neoliberal reforms of the late 1980 and 1990s, notwithstanding some of the
bankers' insistence that they themselves were dyed-in-the-wool development
economists. In Yucatán, particularly during the *cerverato*, the successes of
the Cancún model intersected with an emergent neoliberal political culture
through the unprecedented presence of private businessmen in high-profile
political positions. Some of the early investors in Cancún, like the prominent Mérida-based businessman José Chapur, were part of several groups
of Yucatecan capitalists who gained political influence as cabinet members
and informal associates of Governor Cervera Pacheco (see Ramírez Carrillo
2004, 246).

Writing about the coalitions between the governor and businessmen like
Chapur during the Cerverato, the political scientist Luis Alfonso Ramírez
Carrillo notes that new kinds of political legitimation had entered vernacular
discourse. Terms like "neoliberalism, productive restructuring, decentralization, and state reform" were often cited as keys to securing a prosperous
and democratic future for Mexico (Ramírez Carrillo 2004, 102). Along with
civil society at large, nongovernmental organizations (NGOs) and business
confederations were now framed as the most prominent actors in national
political life. And, as Ramírez Carrillo (2004, 103) observes, "The most

participative and conspicuous actor [in this time] was the individual businessman [*empresario individual*]. . . . Their private benefit is now openly seen
as public benefit."

The image of the heroic entrepreneur has a distinctive place in the capitalist cosmology of rural communities on the tourism circuit. The expansion of tourism into the interior of the peninsula formed a new generation
of local capitalists, including small-scale restaurant owners and handicraft
vendors. Although their own risks, investments, and profits differ vastly in
scale and impact from those of wealthy national and regional developers,
many of these local capitalists have attempted to appropriate the identity of
the "heroic" entrepreneur.

The convergence of Indigenous peoples, Indigenous identities and the
moral economy of neoliberalism has been a topic of a number of academic
discussions. These analyses range from different efforts by ethnic capitalists to brand and market Indigenous cultures (Brown 2004; Comaroff and
Comaroff 2009), to the touristic marketing of the explicitly "anti-neoliberal"
Ejército Zapatista de Liberación Nacional (Zapatista National Liberation
Army) (Babb 2011, 99–104), to the "ethnic entrepreneurship" of Guatemalan
Mayas and diasporic Latinos discussed by Monica Dehart (2010). But these
intersections between indigeneity and entrepreneurship seem to be far less
intelligible within public discourse on tourism development in Yucatán. As
far as mainstream media outlets like the *Diario de Yucatán* are concerned,
rural entrepreneurs like the handicraft vendors of Pisté embody the evils of
the "informal" economy and have not assumed this aura of public benefac-
tors. This attitude is echoed in the work of various government agencies. In
previous research, I noted a pervasive double-standard applied to artisanry
projects originating in small communities. State and federal agencies geared
toward development in rural Maya communities tend to promote projects
that are organized as cooperative, community-based associations. However,
well-off rural entrepreneurs from the same places who have tried to partner
with these organizations in different capacities are often snubbed as profit-driven caciques without a valid social mandate in their own communities.
The press is similarly dismissive of the positive social impacts of these local
capitalists, particularly when their activities are framed as "disruptive" to
large-scale tourism at archaeological sites (see Castañeda 1996, 1997).

For some people in communities like Pisté, this snub of local Maya capitalists is not only racist but explicitly political. In an interview that I conducted in 2015, thirty-five-year-old Rafael Pech referred to the handicraft
vendors of Chichén Itzá—many of them his relatives and neighbors—as

"generadores de empleos" (job creators). When I asked him to elaborate, he noted,

> There's no doubt that [they] create jobs. They have the people who carry their merchandise to the archaeological zone for them, and people who paint figures for them. Usually, the people who carve [the figures] are not from Pisté but from other villages. It's a chain. If the government were intelligent, it would support the artisans. Each artisan financially maintains [*mantiene*] ten families or so. Because of that, those families don't depend on the state [*el Estado*]. But the state wants those families to depend on them [and therefore doesn't support the local merchants].

Born in a rural community in the mid-1980s, Rafael observed the paradox of the same neoliberal state that has embraced urban entrepreneurs like Chapur and the Xcaret Group fostering more traditional types of paternalism among many of his neighbors. This is, in fact, the formula that defined the politics of the most successful years of the Cerverato: traditional clientelism in the countryside and probusiness privatization in the city. But like many of his contemporaries who began their working life in the tourism industry, Rafael seems to prefer policies that would allow him and his neighbors to assume the capitalist mantle of their urban peers rather than a restoration of the older social pact between agriculturalists and the Revolutionary state.

In chapter 3, I discussed how many committed Panistas in Pisté associate mass defections from the PRI with the "awakening" of people liberated from traditional forms of rural clientelism. The root of this transformation in local politics is the economic independence afforded by the tourist market. Rafael's comments here suggest that this goes beyond explaining the choices of individual voters to enabling forms of leadership that hinge on the ability of local capitalists to generate employment for their less well-off neighbors.

Interestingly, this explicit association of local leadership with success in contemporary capitalism is not necessarily viewed as irreconcilable with the traditional lifestyles and values of Maya people. Rafael's comments about local job creation were part of a longer conversation in which he critiqued a Priísta governor's sometimes-violent intervention in the municipal politics of Pisté. As a remedy, he has suggested using contemporary legal experiments in enforcing *usos y costumbres* (customary law) in Indigenous communities. By re-creating the traditional institution of *tatich* (community headman), he proposed a way of establishing autonomous local governance that could resist pressure from whichever party dominated the state government. The cultural autonomy that he seems to imagine, in which self-identified Maya capitalists contribute to the livelihood of local workers and artisans, is consistent with the image of the heroic entrepreneur that was popularized by the neoliberal transformation that began during the Cerverato. In Rafael's vision, however, the fundamental injustice of labor exploitation is mitigated by the fact that the capitalists share a range of traditional bonds and obligations with the workers from whom they derive their profits. Protecting local autonomy and access to Chichén Itzá, the primary cash cow of the regional economy, could be a collective endeavor that promotes unity across socioeconomic groups.

In this regard, Rafael Pech articulates a vision of leadership that parallels the "ethnic entrepreneurship" whose role in the Guatemalan Indigenous organization Cooperación para el Desarrollo Rural de Occidente (Cooperation for the Rural Development of Eastern Guatemala) was discussed by Monica Dehart. As Dehart noted, the concept of "ethnodevelopment" emerged within post–Cold War development discourses that stressed free trade, political decentralization, and the promotion of human rights. Grassroots organizations that were embedded in local communities, and had deep familiarity with local sensibilities, were seen as more legitimate partners for global donors and development banks than more centralized state bureaucracies (Dehart 2010, 29–31). This in turn motivated grassroots organizations to develop organizational strategies and models of local development that were compatible with the decentralizing, free market vision of their translocal collaborators (Dehart 2010, 39).

Though this kind of ethnic entrepreneurialism was touted as highly successful in late 1990s Guatemala, it's difficult to imagine Yucatecan policymakers or tourism developers taking such a positive view of Rafael Pech's vision of a market-oriented Indigenous autonomy. This unintelligibility of politically autonomous Maya entrepreneurs mirrors the exclusionary vision of markets that Hota documented in her ethnography of development institutions working in Kandha tribal communities. As she noted, development discourse in India has a historical tendency to characterize authentic Indigeneity and participation in modern markets as mutually irreconcilable (Hota 2019).

Given the degree to which different forms of ethnic entrepreneurship thrived in Guatemala and other parts of Latin America, the resistance to self-identified Maya entrepreneurs like Rafael Pech could be attributed to the competition and realpolitik of tourism development in the Yucatán Peninsula. Many Pisteños hope to carve out a space in a heavily saturated tourist industry over which powerful private firms that are closely allied with the state seek to expand their control. An expansion of public education to wean rural Maya communities from the informal tourism economy has been a common feature of regional development discourse. This reflects a history in which highly disruptive confrontations between local communities and state and federal agencies have punctuated struggles over key tourist sites.

Equally unpalatable for regional political and business elites is the fact that the ethnic autonomy envisioned by Rafael Pech is seamlessly woven into contemporary party politics. Part of the appeal of the Cooperación para el Desarrollo Rural de Occidente, the Maya organization on which Dehart's (2010, 31) study focused, was the fact that it positioned itself as explicitly apolitical in the broader context of Guatemala's postwar elections. In contrast, the twenty-first-century *tatich* posited by Rafael Pech would be engaged in highly partisan municipal politics that fray the bonds between towns, villages, and the state government with each election cycle. In this sense, for all of the similarities between Rafael's imagined communitarian government and some successful grassroots organizations, the description that he gave me seems more aspirational than realistic. Nevertheless, it provides a coherent portrait of how to turn Maya cultural heritage into the basis for prosperity in a contemporary globalized market.

These claims of ethnic rights to profit from archaeological sites brings me to a set of grievances that often dovetails with complaints about the marginalization of local capitalists. Specifically, this is the idea that the geographic extent of ancient Maya culture provides the basis for a regional identity that has been undermined by territorial divisions and a political geography imposed by the modern Mexican state. In the next vignette, I will trace the history of some of the narratives through which people in communities like Pisté instantiate this identity. These narratives reflect a complex intersection of deep-seated local experiences, texts borrowed from urban literary traditions, and the collective experience of the tourism economy.

MAYAS OF THE CARIBBEAN AND THE COBÁ CONNECTION

One of the truisms of the Yucatecan historiography is the state's frequent assertions of cultural and even political autonomy from the larger Mexican Republic. This often takes the form of a series of historical grievances. For close to a decade in the mid-nineteenth century, the state of Yucatán—which then included the current entities of Campeche and Quintana Roo—successfully defended its independence from Antonio López de Santa Anna's

Mexico. In 1847, under the existential threat posed by the Caste War, Yucatecan elites were forced to reintegrate into the Mexican Republic under humiliating terms. Adding insult to injury, feuding between elites in Campeche and Mérida led the former to secede and form a new state in 1863. A further territorial loss came in 1902, when the lands occupied by former Caste War rebels were designated as the Federal Territory of Quintana Roo.

This history of shared grievance over the "loss" of territory is deeply enmeshed with the construction of Cancún, which was followed by the designation of Quintana Roo as a constitutionally independent state in 1974. Besides cementing the loss of a historical portion of Yucatán, this process of designating Quintana Roo as a state triggered discussions about the historical boundaries of the old federal territory, and threatened to further reduce Yucatán's territorial base.[3] For months, the *Diario de Yucatán* published dozens of reports and angry editorials that demonstrated a rare cross-party consensus against further *desmembramiento* (dismemberment) of the state (Romano 1974; Xiu Cachón 1974d, 1974a). This dramatic term evokes a long essay by the beloved regional poet Antonio Mediz Bolio, which defined the "authentic" Yucatán as being contiguous with the pre-Hispanic entity known as the Mayab. The hypothetical borders of Mediz Bolio's Mayab corresponded to the traditional territory of speakers of Yukatek Maya and related languages, and encompassed the entirety of the Mexican states of Quintana Roo, Yucatán, and Campeche as well as much of the nation-state of Belize and the Petén department of Guatemala (see Mediz Bolio 1974).

Mediz Bolio's essays seem to be the inspiration for a number of editorials published in the *Diario de Yucatán* in 1974 and 1975 as a response to the readjustment of the state's borders (for example, Romano 1974). As one author argued, Yucatán had already been robbed of tax revenue from the "coastal goldmine" where Cancún was rapidly taking shape, while peasants in the henequen zone were being robbed of the "natural migration" to and from lands that had been the home of their ancestors. In his own statement on the border controversy, Governor Loret de Mola questioned the constitutionality of the federal executive's presumption to redraw borders that had been established in state constitutions. Beyond that, he stated, "The person who thinks that the economic problems of Yucatán can be resolved by depopulating the state falls into the same error as the doctor who tries to cure an anemic patient by causing a hemorrhage" (Loret de Mola 1974). In a rare show of cross-factional solidarity, Gaspar Antonio Xiu Cachón, the Cerverista activist who published frequent criticisms of the governor's policies, enthusiastically supported Loret de Mola's position (Xiu Cachón 1974c).

This idea of a larger Maya territory that is "dismembered" through modern political boundaries emerged in a number of everyday conversations during my fieldwork.[4] In many cases, the extent of this vernacular Mayab is defined more by archaeological sites that have a tangible presence in the lives of rural communities than by the kind of literary vision associated with authors like Mediz Bolio. In 2015, I had a conversation with Rubén Dzul about the research I was then conducting. He became especially animated when I turned to the impacts of beach tourism in Cancún, and the degree to which Pisté and nearby communities had changed from being an agrarian periphery of Mérida to being satellites of a touristic economy rooted in the Caribbean. He said, "That's how it is! I was thinking about this the other day. Yaxunah is just twenty kilometers south of here, and it has a *sacbé* [raised causeway] that leads all the way to Cobá in Quintana Roo. Because for the [ancient] Maya, this place was always connected to Quintana Roo, not to Mérida."

Rubén was referring to the famed *sacbeo'ob* (raised causeways) of the Classic Period archaeological site of Cobá in Quintana Roo, about two hours' drive to the southeast from Pisté. The best known of these is an impressive piece of ancient engineering that stretches sixty-two miles westward to the site of Yaxunah, rising three meters above the forest floor at its highest point. Other sacbeo'ob that radiate from Cobá head eastward and have been associated with various sites on the Caribbean coast.

I knew that Rubén's invocation of the "Cobá connection" was consistent with his own life experience. Already familiar with central Quintana Roo from his years at a residential school there, he took a number of jobs in trucking and food delivery associated with the development of the tourist corridor between Cancún and Yucatán. He invested those earnings in the various handicraft and food service businesses that he ran after returning to his hometown of Pisté. So, his personal finances, like his own education, followed the eastward path of Cobá's sacbeo'ob. Also, in 2015, suggesting that Pisté and its neighboring communities had more of a connection with Quintana Roo than with Mérida was probably a commentary on contemporary politics. In those years, the town was enmeshed in an ongoing conflict with "Mérida" as embodied by the gubernatorial administration of Priísta Rolando Zapata Bello.

At the time, I assumed that Rubén's tracing the history of these Caribbean connections to the causeways of Cobá was an association that was made on the spot by someone who spoke about archaeological sites daily with his customers. Years later, however, I came across a string of texts that anticipated the logic of his comment. Cobá's causeways have a longer history in imaginings of the unified infrastructural modernization and economic prosperity of the various political entities that make up the Yucatán Peninsula.

In 1972, Mexico's Instituto Nacional de Antropología e Historia (National Institute of Anthropology and History) began the first large-scale project of excavation and consolidation of architecture at Cobá. This massive project was planned and funded explicitly to complement the development of Cancún. The planners' intent was to encourage tourism to a cash-starved region of inland Quintana Roo (Graham 2004). But decades before then, Cobá and its sacbeo'ob were well established in Mayanist archaeology and regional literature.[5] The Yucatecan anthropologist Alfonso Villa Rojas, who traveled the full course of the sacbé in 1933, noted that he was motivated to do so by "picturesque legends" regarding the road that he had heard during his ethnographic fieldwork in Chan Kom. He suggested that ceremonies performed by villagers on the periphery of the roads, along with stories they told to explain their origin, reflected an ancestral memory of pre-Hispanic life (Villa Rojas 1934). This characterization of the road as an almost mystical artifact of the Indigenous past fit well with themes in romantic regional literature on the Mayab. Authors like Antonio Mediz Bolio and Luis Rosado Vega popularized highly stylized Spanish translations of Maya folktales that referenced vast underground rivers or the supernatural "living rope" (*kuxa'an suum*) that had linked Indigenous cities in antiquity. The archaeological sacbeo'ob instantiated these mystical corridors in physical reality.

In the years before and after the creation of Cancún, the romance of Cobá's causeways was also recruited for the more secular ends of tourist infrastructure. In April 1966, a Yucatecan teacher named Evelio Díaz Sierra wrote to the private secretary of President Gustavo Díaz Ordaz to reiterate an earlier request to be appointed as inspector of archaeological monuments in the state of Yucatán.[6] He included an example of a self-published newsletter titled *Turismo y Comercio*, which included the article "New Routes for Tourism." Paradoxically, this article on "new" routes opened with a map and description of the network of sacbeo'ob radiating from the ruins of Cobá. In describing the site, *Turismo y Comercio* made clear parallels between the ancient sacbeo'ob and the then-emergent corridors linking the center of the Yucatán Peninsula and the Caribbean.[7]

Almost a decade later, the ancient roadways of Cobá seem to have still been a common device for giving contemporary infrastructural developments a longer historical pedigree. A 1972 thesis from the Mexico City's Escuela de Ingenería Municipal (School of Municipal Engineering) detailed the infrastructure that had been constructed in Cancún since 1968. It made projections for the expansion of integrally planned tourism inland and along the coast, including the impacts of the project that was currently being developed at Cobá. In the description of Cobá's future potential for tourism development, the sacbeo'ob are described as one of several potential lines for linking the site to existing road infrastructure, as if these were still transitable in 1972 (Rojas Ubaldo 1972, 5).

What the 1972 thesis also underscores is the fact that Cobá was more than just another destination developed for tourists from Cancún. Its opening to archaeological work and eventual tourism was part of a larger process of expanding the Cancún model beyond the original resort city to encompass the entire Yucatán Peninsula.[8] The site's ancient roadways also perform important symbolic work for tourism development, by positing an organic historical link between contemporary road infrastructure and the roads used by the ancient society whose ruins are the region's most profitable commodity.

These connections have important implications for people like Rubén Dzul who have an ancestral link to the builders of that ancient regional infrastructure. On the surface, his reference to historical links between Pisté and the state of Quintana Roo was an assertion of the ethnic and linguistic unity of the Yukatek Maya people, mirroring the claims that Xiu Cachón had used in his critiques of the border disputes of 1974. But the Cobá-Yaxunah causeway, and the particular role that it played in the modernizing visions of regional developers, also grounds Rubén's assertion in a more specific historical moment marked by the economic and political transformations of the last third of the twentieth century.

This attribution of ancient pedigree to more modern political geographies adds an interesting wrinkle to discussion of identity politics that have been at the center of Mayanist research in the past several decades. In his highly influential works on colonial-era Yucatán, Matthew Restall (1997) demonstrated that the individual community or *kaj* was the fundamental unit of belonging for Indigenous people on the peninsula, usually trumping larger identity categories like "Indian" or "Maya." Similar observations have been made for the modern period by authors like Juan Castillo Cocom (2005; see also Castillo Cocom with Luviano 2012), Peter Hervik (2002), Quetzil Castañeda (2004), Wolfgang Gabbert (2004), and Paul Eiss (2010). The regional unity invoked by Rubén Dzul in 2015, like the unity of Maya agriculturalists that Gaspar Xiu Cachón asserted in 1974, is difficult to reconcile with this historical record of dozens of independent microregional and communitarian identities. Instead, Dzul and Xiu Cachón both draw on narratives with a distinctly modern genealogy, narratives that blend romantic visions of the Mayab with late-twentieth century-aspirations for integrated regional development.

This kind of appropriation of Westernized literature and economic development in no way delegitimizes the solidarities that can be constituted around a shared language, cosmology, and customs. But it does ground these collective identities in the same social processes and political moments that gave rise to the discourses that I refer to as vernacular neoliberalism. In the case of the Cobá connection, it is a phase of Yucatecan and Mexican modernity that saw the decline of an older developmentalist and populist order and a range of adaptations to the distinct realities of the neoliberal twenty-first century.

"THE MAYA PESO": MILLENNIALS IN THE TOURISM INDUSTRY

The generation of Mexicans born in the 1980s spent their childhoods weathering the various economic crises that undid the economic progress their parents had enjoyed during the waning years of Stabilizing Development. For those born in communities like Pisté, childhood was somewhat different, and the monetary impacts of the peso crises were partially mitigated by the expanding prosperity of the regional tourist economy. For these Maya millennials, the confluence of money, entrepreneurship, and local identity that I have traced above was a pervasive fact of life. Their generational perspective will be the focus of this concluding ethnographic vignette, and will be explored in more depth in the chapter 5.

When I first visited Pisté as a college freshman in 1997, I befriended a number of teenagers who spent their summers working as ambulant handicraft vendors on the sidewalks and streets in front of the town's restaurants. This practice was called "doing *tiich'*," a reference to the Maya verb for raising an object above one's head (see Armstrong-Fumero 2013, 109). Through much of the late 1990s and 2000s, state and federal authorities were successful in keeping handicraft vendors outside of the actual archaeological zone. With stalls in the state-sanctioned market adjacent to the zone in high demand, doing tiich' was the only access enterprising teens had to the tourist dollars that poured through their town. It offered a means of helping their families, of earning a bit of pocket money, and of spending the days with friends away from adult supervision.

Ambulant sales by minors have always been controversial, though much of this controversy is based on a series of willful misconceptions and moral panics. For years, a sign outside of the Hotel Mayaland warned visitors not to purchase from children who had been pulled from schools in order to sell handicrafts on the street. Though I knew of a number of youngsters who dropped out of secondary school after seeing what they could earn on the street, I knew quite a few others who limited tiich' to a summertime or after-school activity and successfully completed their mandatory years of education. In their thirties now, many recall ambulant selling as a very useful activity through which they learned a bit of English, French, and Italian and developed a confidence that serves them well in their current jobs in the tourist sector.

I remember a common sales pitch and gag among these young artisanry vendors as being the *peso maya*. This is a variation of the classic "one dollar" bait-and-switch, in which a seller attracts a customer to a fancy carving with cries of "one dollar," only to reveal that that price referred to the simple keychains that they held in their other hand. The tricked tourist might walk off in annoyance, or they may give the seller an opening by asking just how much the nicer craft item costs.

In the *peso maya* pitch, teenagers would name the price of the item as being "one Maya peso." When the tourist offered a peso coin, the vendor would laugh, "Not a *Mexican* peso! A *Maya* peso is worth more!" Just how much more varied. Sometimes, the Maya peso was a dollar, between nine and twelve Mexican pesos. Sometimes it was 20 or 400 pesos, increasing at intervals that reflected the base-twenty counting system of the ancient Maya. Like the "one dollar" pitch, the *peso maya* risked annoying the customer. But it tended to unfold through a more explicit and self-conscious verbal game that revolved around the tourist's and vendor's shared familiarity with Maya culture.

Today, it's rare to see people doing tiich' on the main drag of Pisté. Since the 2003 reoccupation of the zone by vendors, adult merchants have participated in a slightly more formalized system that restricts them to individual stalls and prohibits the presence of minors. Other factors have made ambulant sales in town less attractive to the teens who are excluded from the archaeological zone. The most important is perhaps the expansion of restaurants and handicraft markets to the east of Chichén Itzá, which "capture" tourists by paying commissions to guides who herd in their charges before they even arrive at the archaeological zone. Xcaret's model of captive tourism was the last nail in the coffin of any kind of handicraft sales on the streets of Pisté, where the few remaining brick-and-mortar shops make most of their money by wholesaling to vendors who occupy stalls within the archaeological zone.

Still, for a generation of millennials, the years they spent doing tiich' were a formative experience in a regional market that was created during the waning years of the Stabilizing Development era, and that allowed them and their parents to weather the storm of economic crises and neoliberalization in comparative prosperity. The *peso maya* figures in some of their recollections of this era. One reading is that the pitch is a humorous acknowledgment of the marketization of culture, the fact that Mayanness had become so much of a commercial good that it was indistinguishable from money itself. Such self-conscious and ironic performances of commercialism are a mainstay of the ethnographic literature on the sale of souvenirs and ethnic art across the world (Castañeda 1996; Nicks 1999; Steiner 1994). But the *peso maya* also embodies the possibilities that became imaginable for those fortunate enough to have direct access to tourists. Its value was flexible and subject to massive expansion because it was being requested by a Maya person who held more power over their economic destiny than other Mexicans, who could only hope to be paid in "regular" pesos.

In this chapter, I have used moments like these from my ethnographic research to trace the broader historical and social contexts that shape vernacular discourse on culture, politics, and economics in Pisté. While these narratives about the economics of Maya-themed tourism differ in logic and content from the explicit rationale of Mexico City bankers and politicians, there are perceptible continuities between policies imposed from the top down and the political identities of rural, nonelite citizens. As I observed above, these local political identities are marked as much by grievance regarding different forms of exclusion as they are by acknowledgment of the tangible benefits that have emerged from the more successful instances of state-guided development. But aggrieved or not, most of my interlocutors in Pisté seem to be both economically and culturally invested in the system that evolved in tandem with Mexico's neoliberal transformation. This investment has contributed to the emergence of the discourse and common sense that I term vernacular neoliberalism, which informs contemporary experiences ranging from household planning, to education, to political participation.

One of the most striking aspects of this dual investment is the degree to which vernacular neoliberal notions permeate local identity discourse, even if people rarely refer to "neoliberalism" as a specific ideology. Critiques of older agrarian lifestyles that depend on government assistance defy the common conflation of Indigenous and agrarian politics in Latin America. But these critiques are consistent with media narratives that were consumed by rural newspaper readers in the years leading to the economic crises of the 1980s. The frequent conflation of Maya identity and ethnic autonomy with capitalistic values appropriates the image of the "heroic" entrepreneur that was popularized during the Cerverato. Many of the grievances expressed by rural tourism workers reflect inequalities that were deepened by the privatizations and free market reforms of the last four decades. But neoliberalism is such a polyvalent and heterodox discourse that it also provides the narrative tool with which rural Mayan speakers articulate their hopes for political agency and a prosperous future.

5

THE PROMISES AND PITFALLS OF HIGHER EDUCATION

Rural Yucatecans fortunate enough to live near major tourist corridors were able to weather a generation of financial crises, and many appropriated some key elements of neoliberal discourse into the articulation of ethnic identity. But, as the experience of rural capitalists who are maligned by development institutions shows, prejudice and elite realpolitik continue to marginalize Yucatán's Mayan speakers within the very industry upon which they depend. As I will discuss in this chapter, the "education" that is touted by those who wish to stamp out the informal tourism economy offers limited professional alternatives for many of the individuals who seek it out. In this regard, artisanry merchants in Pisté and neighboring communities share an experience that is common to tourism workers across the Yucatán Peninsula. Matilde Córdoba Azcárate (2020) has referred to Yucatán's tourism as a "sticky" industry, which brings prosperity to different communities at the cost of a range of social, economic, and environmental harms that become an endemic part of local reality. Within the larger argument of *this* book, what Córdoba Azcárate refers to as "stickiness" can be viewed as a kind of negative infrastructure that heavy public and private investment in Yucatán's tourism industry imposes on the development of alternative economic sectors.

This "stickiness" of tourism is particularly evident in the professional outcomes of rural people who have attained more education than their parents. An expansion of secondary, tertiary, and higher education during Mexico's neoliberal era was presented to the national public as a means of democratizing access to prestigious careers and higher-paying jobs. Given their relative potential for upward mobility, many families in communities like Pisté were well positioned to take advantage of these opportunities. Education is, in fact, an important component of the vernacular narratives of neoliberal transcendence that I discussed in chapter 4. But as many recent graduates learn, the tourism industry that has created millions of lower-level service jobs and a thriving informal handicraft sector hasn't generated nearly as many opportunities for university-trained professionals. This lack of professional alternatives contributes to a series of local conflicts that will be at the heart of the final chapters of this book.

In some respects, schools were the first element of federal infrastructure that was encountered on a massive scale by rural people in Yucatán. Writing about the 1930s and 1940s in the Morelos community of Tepoztlán, Wendy Waters (1998) observed that the "modernizing" effects of the first public school emerged in tandem with the completion of a major roadway that linked the village to the "outside world." During this same period, the three road corridors decreed by Lázaro Cárdenas remained largely speculative for most Yucatecans. Many of the first teachers who traveled to rural communities in the state did so on horseback down narrow bush trails (Armstrong-Fumero 2013). There, in relative isolation from Mérida and other major cities, they orchestrated the construction of hundreds of schoolhouses and related structures, and implemented an ambitious plan for expanding literacy and bilingualism in Spanish (Dawson 2001; Eiss 2004; Fallaw 2004; Quintanilla and Vaughan 2003).

By the time I began my fieldwork in the late 1990s, many rural Yucatecan families were contemplating even broader educational horizons for their children. Although it has received relatively little attention from academic historians and anthropologists (see Levinson 2001), the expansion of higher education at the end of the twentieth century is the subject of a large body of policy literature by Mexican educators and their international interlocutors. In many respects, Mexico followed international trends in the post–Cold War era, when a constellation of NGOs, private investors, state institutions, and international development banks contributed to the rapid expansion of higher education in the Global South. This trend has continued through the first decades of the twenty-first century (see Marginson 2016).

The secondary and tertiary schools that are stepping-stones to universities are one of the few components of Mexico's public sector that expanded significantly under the country's neoliberal transition.[1] During the negotiations for what would become NAFTA, Mexican policymakers sought to promote educational parity with the United States and Canada in order to maintain a degree of competitiveness within an increasingly transnational labor market (Varela Petito 2008, 32–35). The impacts of this expansion of education were evident during my own fieldwork. By the early 2000s, I often heard parents who had entered the workforce with no more than a few years of formal schooling reminding their teenage children that they couldn't expect to find a job as a waiter or cashier without at least their secondary school diploma. During this period, two national poverty-alleviation programs known as Progresa (Programa de Educación, Salud y Alimentación, or Education, Health, and Nutrition Program) and Oportunidades offered conditional direct cash transfers to hundreds of households in Pisté, providing them with a financial cushion against fluctuations in the local tourism market. The fact that keeping children in school through the compulsory years of secondary education was one condition for receiving these payments significantly increased the average years of educational attainment in the community.

Some members of Mexico's policy elite have hailed this expansion of educational options as a sign of the nation's transformation into a "middle-class society" (Castañeda 2011). However, other academics and public intellectuals have characterized the country's higher education as developing in a context of perpetual "crisis" (see Guevara Niebla 1981). By the 2000s, many looked warily at the "massification" of public education during the previous decade (see Gama Tejada 2017, 63–65), and observed persistent disparities in quality across states and communities. Furthermore, changes in labor markets meant that the graduates of these new institutions had fewer viable professional outlets for their newly acquired expertise (González Casanova 2001; Navarro Leal and Contreras Ocegueda 2014; Ornelas Delgado 2002, 15–24; Suárez Zozaya 2010; Varela Petito 2008, 32).

In this unfortunate regard, Mexico seems to mirror a common theme of recent ethnographic studies of uneven professional outcomes and frustrated ambitions. One consequence of the rapid expansion of higher education in the Global South has been the saturation of regional job markets with degree holders, many of whom face bleak prospects. In contemporary ethnographic literature, these structurally unemployed students and recent graduates often become associated with different ills of neoliberal modernity. Craig Jeffrey (2010), for example, documents the social suffering of young male students in northern India, for whom the experience of "passing the time" without gainful employment becomes a grinding reminder of precarity and downward mobility. Jocelyn Chua (2014, 172–76) has documented similar anxieties and negative career outcomes among young professionals in southern India, where frustrated achievement is often associated with a regional mental health crisis. In his ethnography of everyday experiences of corruption in Nigeria, Daniel Smith (2010, 33–38) interviewed various university students and professionals who found participating in email scams to be their only viable source of income, turning them into purveyors of the very forms of informal employment and outright illegality that they had hoped to escape through education. As I will discuss in this chapter, the terrain of higher education in Yucatán is fraught with a similar sense of precarity and futility. For many families in communities like Pisté, it is also associated with a range of novel psychological and social pathologies that present their children with more risk than promise.

In the next section of this chapter, I will trace the development of educational infrastructure in the Yucatecan countryside during the 1990s and 2000s to provide a broader framework for understanding the history of these new opportunities and disparities. Then I will provide a series of ethnographic vignettes of the ways federal direct-transfer programs changed the pattern of family life in the 1990s, increasing demand for higher education. For some students, travel to high schools and universities in the nearby city of Valladolid proved a transformative experience, in terms of both their education and exposure to more cosmopolitan lifestyles. However, as I will also show, mixed educational outcomes and negative press coverage of local universities has fed a series of moral panics that cast doubt on the overall value of higher education. Along with particular dynamics of the local economy, these doubts tend to reinforce dependence on types of tourism-related labor that have generated repeated conflicts between local workers, regional tourism magnates, and the state government.

THE RISE OF HIGHER EDUCATION IN EASTERN YUCATÁN

When I began fieldwork in 1997, communities in the east of Yucatán were in the midst of an expansion of secondary and preparatory schools beyond the small city of Valladolid and into the towns and villages of its rural periphery

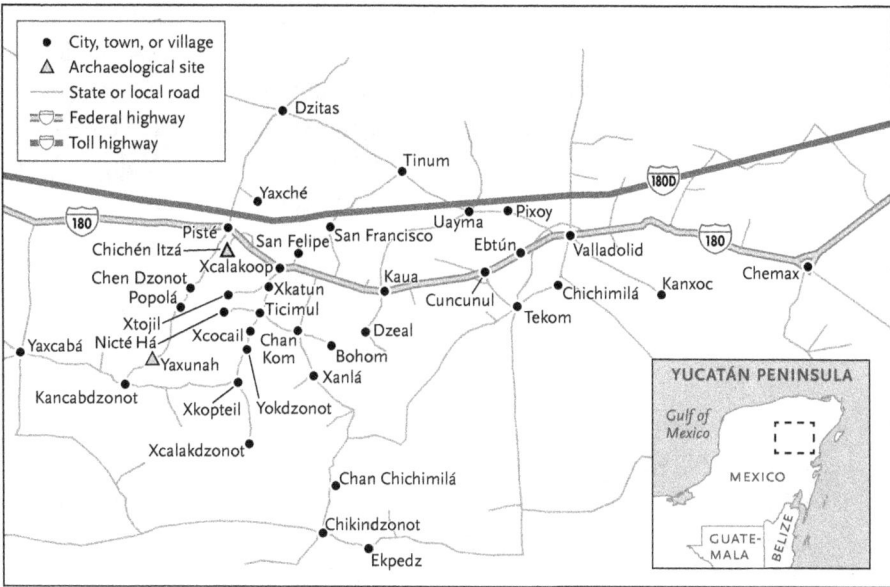

Map 5.1. Valladolid and its peripheries.
*Map created by Nicolás Reyes, Heather Rosenfeld, and Kalaʻi Ellis
at the Spatial Analysis Lab, Smith College, Northampton, MA.*

(see map 5.1). At the close of the 1970s, students in these municipalities had few options other than making a significant investment to commute to one of several secondary and preparatory institutions in Valladolid.[2] Over the course of the 1980s, secondary schools were founded in the municipal seats of Chemax, Chichimilá, and Tinum, as well as in the heavily populated comisarías of Pisté and Xcan. In the 1990s, particularly in the years immediately following the ratification of NAFTA, at least thirty new secondary schools were founded in over two dozen communities that ranged in population from several thousand to just a few hundred residents. These were the first such institutions in the municipal seats of Chan Kom, Kaua, and Yaxcabá. Between 2000 and 2019, several dozen additional institutions, many of them employing alternative formats ranging from adult-focused education to the televised delivery of pedagogical content, further expanded these offerings.

This expansion of options, however, entails new hierarchies of quality and access. A common observation of many parents in communities like Pisté and its neighbor Xcalakoop is that the attainment of students from rural public schools is consistently lower than that of their urban counterparts. This in turn makes them less competitive in the market for higher education.[3] Parents of secondary-school-age students have offered me one consistent explanation for this academic underperformance: underqualified rural teachers. Historically, Mexican public school teachers have enjoyed a form of tenure through the conferral of permanent posts or *plazas* by the federal Secretaría de Educación Pública (Secretariat of Public Education, SEP). Informal or outright illegal means of buying or selling plazas plagued the system for much of the twentieth century, leading to a series of controversial reform attempts in the 2010s (see Arriaga Lemus 2015). These reforms have been gradually implemented, but many parents that I know say that the "traditional" forms of corruption are alive and well in rural schools, which tend to receive far less oversight than their urban counterparts.[4]

Even the majority of teachers who attain their post "by the books" and make good-faith efforts to provide quality educational content can be hindered by the level of resources available to them. The question of resources is particularly acute in areas where the relatively low population of students leads to the implementation of alternative models of teaching. The most prominent of these tiers is the *telesecundaria* (televised secondary school). Though different models have been implemented over the decades, basic telesecundaria education involves recorded lectures being beamed onto a screen through satellite television or, more recently, cellular connections. Students are assisted by several trained proctors. The first large-scale experiments with telesecundaria education began in the late 1960s, though they were expanded radically in the 1990s (Dorantes Carrión 2019). Official data from the state Secretariat of Public Education list around 150 schools founded in Tinum and neighboring municipalities since the 1990s. Of these, forty that were built in communities of a thousand or fewer residents employ digital transmission of course content. Another forty are based on the *secundaria comunitaria* model employed in communities of fewer than twenty-nine students and offer more limited curricula.[5]

Telesecundarias and other alternative rural schools are a controversial topic in many of the communities where I have conducted research. In Popolá, an isolated village of 200 where I taught English and recorded oral history narratives between 1999 and 2001, secondary education became accessible in 1995 after the foundation of a telesecundaria in the neighboring village of Yaxunah. Before that, the only local teenagers who completed secundaria were those who had family in larger communities or could find part-time work and relocate to Pisté, eighteen kilometers to the north. Many rural families in similar situations find telesecundarias to be the only financially viable option for their children. I have heard some parents in Popolá and other communities repeat the common SEP talking point that the presence of several proctors at a telesecundaria means that students receive more personal attention than they would at a traditional school. Other parents seemed to find this less than convincing and went to considerable lengths to send their children to traditional institutions in Pisté or in the municipal seat of Yaxcabá. This attitude seems consistent with large-scale survey data, which show significantly lower levels of educational achievement and a much higher dropout rate in telesecundarias across Mexico (Mantilla Gálvez 2018; Suárez Zozaya 2010, 104–12).

For those who could afford it in the 1990s and early 2000s, the highest-quality educational options were the competitive public secondary schools in Valladolid, or one of several private institutions in that city. In the 1990s, when I started conducting fieldwork, I knew of only three people in Pisté and Xcalakoop, out of a combined population of around 7,000, who were close to completing a university education at the prestigious flagship Universidad Autónoma de Yucatán. All had been exceptionally high achievers in primary school. But, perhaps more important, all three had parents who were willing and able to incur significant expense by sending them to secondary and preparatory school in Valladolid.

One phenomenon associated with the increase in minimum years of schooling is a concurrent rise in demand for higher education options. By the 2000s, the role of Valladolid as an education destination had expanded to include universities that emerged to serve young people who lacked the funds to relocate to Mérida. In 2005, the public Universidad del Oriente was founded in Valladolid as a means of making higher education accessible to students from the rural, largely Indigenous municipalities on the periphery of the city (see Reyes-Foster 2019). It was joined a decade later by a public intercultural teachers' college. Besides these two public options, much of the "unmet demand" for higher education in the region around Valladolid is addressed by private institutions, all of which were founded as secondary and preparatory schools before adding higher degrees in the late 1990s and 2000s.[6] The largest of these is the institution currently known as the Centro Universitario Valladolid (Valladolid University Center), which was founded in the 1990s as the postsecondary Bachillerato Francisco Montejo.[7] It has since grown into the largest private institution in the city, offering a dozen different degrees in design, healthcare, tourism, and business administration to over 3,000 students.

The expansion of this type of private university in Mexico has been accompanied by considerable controversy regarding quality and processes of certification.[8] Education scholars rank private institutions as possessing a higher or lower *perfil* (profile) based on factors such as the presence of adequate data infrastructure, a teaching staff dominated by individuals with postgraduate degrees, and entrance standards more or less equivalent to those of more prestigious public institutions. Lower profile institutions often bear the public stigma of being referred to as *escuelas patitos* (little duck schools). Escuelas patitos are often characterized in the press as preying upon the large population of college-bound students who lack the grades to enter public institutions or the economic resources for "high-profile" private ones (Cuevas-Cajiga 2015, 59–60; *Perfiles Educativos* 2002, 137).

Overall, the large-scale surveys that are available suggest mixed results in educational attainment after these decades of expansion in secondary, preparatory, and university options. In a 2015 government survey, Yucatán ranked twenty-fourth out of Mexico's thirty-two states in terms of the average years of schooling of its citizens.[9] But if overall numbers are low in comparison to more industrialized states in the north and center of the republic, the same statistics suggest that residents of the peninsula states have greater access to education than people in other heavily rural states with comparably large populations of Indigenous-language speakers.[10] Studies conducted in 2017 ranked Yucatán's secondary and preparatory education as the strongest in the Mexican Southeast, with results in language and mathematics that are comparable with those of more industrialized states such as Jalisco, Querétaro, and Aguascalientes (*La Jornada Maya* 2017).

On the surface, unemployment data also suggest that Yucatán and its neighboring states are fertile ground for newly minted professionals. Due in large part to the tourist industry and related service sectors, Yucatán and neighboring Quintana Roo both enjoyed particularly low levels of unemployment in comparison with other states in Mexico through the 2010s (Chan 2019; *Palco Quintanarroense* 2019). However, this correlation can be deceiving, as the precarity that existed in the regional job market was disproportionately shouldered by professionals. A 2018 study found that Yucatán and Quintana Roo topped the list of Mexican states with the highest levels of unemployment among residents who completed *preparatoria* and university education. In 2000, the percentage of unemployed high school and college graduates in Yucatán and Quintana Roo was 22 and 28 percent, respectively. By 2017, those figures had leaped to a bleak 56 and 50 percent, even as overall rates of unemployment for those states remained among the lowest in Mexico (*Unión Yucatán* 2018).

In late 2019, I had the opportunity to speak with a colleague at a major US university who had worked extensively with the Vicente Fox administration as a consultant on the educational reforms of the early 2000s. Familiar with the plight of recent college graduates in states like Yucatán, I asked him about the role of career outcomes in gauging the successes and failures of different programs in Mexico. He replied that, though this was a factor in most evaluations, it was important to remember that the rationale that had guided the development of universities in Europe and the United States should still be applied to countries like Mexico. That is, a university education adds value to an individual's life by providing general knowledge and thinking skills that would be useful outside of any particular career trajectory.

As a liberal arts professor myself, I had to agree with the sentiment behind his comments. However, I left that conversation thinking that that argument would be a tough sell to many of the Yucatecan families that I had seen make sacrifices to secure a *profesionista* future for their children. This was not to say that people from rural communities do not value knowledge for its own sake. But the ambivalent outcomes experienced by those who pursue advanced education often seem like a poor return on the transformation of household economies and habits that was involved in supporting children through extended schooling. These mixed outcomes are also difficult to reconcile with the dangers that many rural families associate with higher education settings. In the following sections, I will explore the local lived experiences and popular and media discourses that contribute to the ambivalence with which many rural Yucatecans view higher education.

FAMILY LIFE AND EDUCATION SINCE THE 1990S

Higher education has been a constant topic in my conversations with friends in Pisté, particularly when I answered questions about my own life and future plans. I had just finished my freshman year in college when I first participated in an ethnographic field school in town. For close to a decade after that, as I finished an undergraduate degree and a doctorate, I still identified myself as a student. Given what must have seemed like an endless academic career in a community where only a handful of people attended college, I often found myself a point of reference in families' conversations about the professional trajectories of their adolescent and young adult children. In many cases, these conversations ended with my tutoring teenagers on a variety of academic topics and offering advice about the skill sets needed for different career paths. Often, though, I just found myself in the uncomfortable position of being loudly praised for my ability to "dedicate myself" to study by parents who sought to shame children who had recently dropped out of preparatory school.

Many parents who prospered in the tourist industry derive pride and social prestige from funding their children's completion of more years of formal schooling than they themselves were able to attain. This sacrifice is especially poignant insofar as "extra" years of education prevent adolescents from helping their parents in their labors or diving into the tourist market themselves. By the 1990s, this abstention from the adult economy was also motivated by the Progresa/Oportunidades family of programs (see Gálvez 2018, 137–42; and Levy 2006). Besides incentivizing the completion of secondary school, these programs also involved other components meant to transform the livelihood and lifestyle of entire families. Progresa or Oportunidades payments were tied to childhood nutritional support, parental compliance with regular medical checkups, and occasional attendance at classes or workshops on public health. Since mothers are considered by the state to be the primary caregivers of children, they were the direct recipients of the cash payments and attendees at events staged in tandem with the program.

This conditionality increased local compliance with preventative healthcare and transformed the gender dynamics of participation in government programs in significant ways. During the early years of my research, I knew that, once every month or so, families in Pisté planned their morning around a "meeting of ladies" (junta de señoras in Spanish; U juunta koolelo'ob / nojoch maamao'ob in Mayan) that took place in the municipal building. There, mothers attended lectures by government health promoters and were informed about new program conditions with which they might be expected to comply. The monthly meetings also provided an opportunity to smooth out any irregularities in their own or the local government's records of their children's schooling and medical visits. Some of my friends characterized this as the feminine counterpart of the meetings traditionally held for male ejidatarios. As several participating mothers told me, the federal government now recognized women's contribution to rural households and had invented Progresa as "the ladies" counterpart to Procampo, another direct assistance program that targeted maize agriculturalists.

Some of my academic colleagues at various Mexican universities have praised the Progresa and Oportunidades programs as one of very few major federal interventions of the neoliberal era that have brought tangible and lasting benefits to rural people. Some of them, Gen Xers and millennials from rural communities, see the positive effects of direct payment programs in their own early education. At least in terms of increasing the average level of educational attainment, these transformations have been evident during my time as an ethnographer, particularly with larger families. For example, a couple that I will refer to as Benigna Ucán and her husband Esteban Ek are parents of seven, and were in their early fifties when I first met them in the late 1990s. Though they lived fairly comfortably from selling handicrafts and the products of Don Esteban's milpa, direct cash payments from Oportunidades and Progresa helped offset the cost of hiring household help that freed up the time of their school-age children. By then, their oldest children were in their twenties and had entered the handicraft trade without completing secondary school. Their middle children, however, all graduated from at least the secundaria, just as their youngest siblings were beginning primary school with expectations of a similar, if not longer, educational trajectory.

Still, compliance with Progresa and Oportunidades was not without its annoyances. I remember that Don Estaban always chafed at the fact that Doña Benigna had to attend courses on children's health taught by a twenty-something nurse, which he saw as a lack of respect toward the *nojoch mama* (household matriarch). One morning, as he saw her off to one of the classes, he repeated, "You've already raised my little ones! What's *she* going to teach *you* about raising children?" Doña Benigna laughed at his grousing but continued on her way. The courses never seemed to bother her, but she did become very frustrated at some of the policy changes that marked the transition from Progresa to Oportunidades in 2002. These included household inspections in which promoters made sure that families were not raising free-range poultry in their yard, which recipients were told could spread salmonella to children. The price of store-bought eggs would cut into the benefit payments, to say nothing of the fact that Doña Benigna would have to give up the dozen turkeys she had been raising for a granddaughter's baptism celebration.

Besides forcing changes in Doña Benigna's household economy, the educational mandate that came with Oportunidades gave her children a very different series of skills and expectations from those with which she herself was raised. As in other parts of Mexico, the extension of adolescence through education exacerbated a series of generational tensions (Pérez Islas 2010). Baby boomers in rural Yucatán worked alongside their parents and relatives from their early teens onward and developed manual labor skills and a work ethic under the close supervision of older relatives and intimate acquaintances. Their children, born in the late 1980s and raised during the implementation of Progresa and Oportunidades, spent far more time in formal educational institutions. As with Indigenous communities throughout Mexico, extended periods of schooling and preparation for participation in the formal wage economy meant the loss of much traditional knowledge of agriculture, bushcraft, cookery, and household artisanry (Gálvez 2018, 135–58; Pacheco Ladrón de Guevara 2010). Thus, while Don Esteban and Doña Benigna's older sons were able to help their aging father plant and harvest his milpa, their younger siblings were fairly incompetent at agricultural work.

Another result of this extended adolescence was that these rural students participated in various regional and national youth cultures in a way that would have been impossible for their parents (Armstrong-Fumero 2019; Taylor 2018). This kind of generation gap was not without precedent in rural Mexico, as Wendy Waters (1998) notes in her discussion of the foundation of public schools in mid-twentieth-century Tepoztlán. But where the latter tended to manifest through young people leaving their home village for the city, the generation gap that I observed in the 1990s and 2000s dovetailed with new possibilities for local prosperity fueled by tourism. For many parents, this immersion in a poorly supervised community of age-mates, many of whom had their own income derived from handicraft sales, brought risks like drug use and inappropriate sexual activity. Even "good" sons and daughters developed expectations that were difficult to reconcile with their parents' plans. People born in the 1960s recall getting to know their future spouses through traditional forms of supervised courtship, which involved months of visits, negotiations, and gift exchange between the families of the bride and groom before the marriage ceremony and eventual cohabitation. In contrast, their children and grandchildren develop intense emotional and often physical relationships in the streets, food stalls, and parks where they hang out on the walks between home and school. When these youngsters decided to marry or cohabitate, parents often found it impossible to convince them to do so according to the slower traditional process.

Perhaps the greatest irony for many parents who benefited from direct cash transfers through Progresa and Oportunidades is that their adult children often remain in occupations similar to their own. For people employed in the tourism industry who are now in their fifties and sixties, the expansion of education through these programs offered their children an opportunity to escape that volatile market. But this rationale for escaping the risky industry into a white-collar profession can be a tough sell to love-struck youngsters who are eager to begin married life. During their summer recess from secondary and preparatory school, many teens in the communities where I have conducted research help their parents sell handicrafts or set up small informal stalls of their own. During a good day in the high tourist season, a handicraft vendor in Chichén Itzá could net 1,000 or even 2,000 pesos, many times the 2018 daily minimum wage of just over 100 pesos. Besides offering fast money, participation in the informal tourism economy offers the much-coveted condition of being one's own *patrón* (boss). The dual freedom of working without a *patrón* and of establishing an independent household is often far more appealing than the institutional career paths offered by teacher's colleges, technical institutes, and universities. I have known many families that endured the strictures of Progresa and Oportunidades requirements, and then spent thousands of pesos trying to turn their children into *profesionistas*, only to have them drop out, marry, and sell handicrafts. Years of study and expense lead back to the career that their parents had adopted with nothing more than a primary school education.

THE COLLEGE EXPERIENCE IN VALLADOLID

For students from rural communities who *do* choose to complete preparatory education, the ultimate aspiration is often to earn a university degree. Though it is still less common for students from Pisté and neighboring communities to gain admission into the prestigious Universidad Autónoma de Yucatán, various public and private options in Valladolid have significantly expanded access to the college experience. But, for many parents from rural communities, these opportunities bring risks associated with forms of youth culture that have been the subject of recent moral panics disseminated through the popular media.

Just as it is in the United States, sociality is a central part of the Mexican college experience. Historically, it's far more common for university students in Mexico to live with their parents as they complete their studies than it is for their North American peers. Nevertheless, extracurricular activities associated with preparatory schools and universities are central to the formation of professional, artistic, and literary associations. Known simply as *grupos* (groups) these peer cohorts figure prominently in the literature on the "informal networks" that play a central role in the organization of politics and business in Mexico (see Ai Camp 1985 and 2002; and Levinson 2001). The changing scene of higher education at the turn of the millennium has democratized this experience, allowing people outside of traditional urban elites to form their own professional grupos.

For rural students, travel is at the heart of postsecondary education. Some of the most positive memories that friends have shared regarding their education involve becoming accustomed to moving between the sleepy communities where they were born and raised to the more urban setting of Valladolid. When I first interviewed him in 2014, Rafael Pech was a recently graduated accountant. Like many of his relatively well-off peers in Pisté, he had completed preparatory school in Valladolid, returning years later to study at a private university. The experience, he recalls, was as much a political awakening as an intellectual one. He noted that during the years that they studied in Pisté, he and his peers remained in the same local space as their parents, where they were relatively sheltered from the harsh realities of the formal economy. There, he observed, it was easy to accept the traditionally paternalistic relationship between the Mexican state and its rural citizens. He argued that, like their parents, teenagers who remained in their native towns and villages could be easily convinced that the election-year distribution of goods and infrastructural projects were largesse through which political leaders earned voters' loyalty.

This perspective changed for Rafael and his classmates through their daily commute to Valladolid, where he completed preparatoria and later university studies. Through that, he learned that errors in the management of Mexico's state-run oil monopoly could significantly change the price of his daily travels. Spending money in the city, where merchants were more likely to provide him with a detailed printed receipt, taught him about the sales tax and the fact that the "gifts" that were distributed during election years had been purchased with tax revenue derived from Mexican citizens. Just as important, these were experiences that he shared with classmates who came from a dozen other rural communities and the town of Valladolid itself. This diverse group of peers now forms part of an enduring network that provides mutual aid in business and occasional political activism.

Rafael is in his late thirties now, and his first trips to Valladolid took place when he was a teenager in the 1990s. Since then, the landscape has changed significantly for young people from rural municipalities who travel to Valladolid. First, there is the fact that many young people seem to be beginning university studies at a younger age. Rafael began college in his late twenties, after working for nearly a decade at various tourism-related jobs. But some of his younger cousins, like dozens of other young people born in Pisté in the late 1990s, explore higher education opportunities immediately or very soon after completing the preparatoria at the age of eighteen or nineteen.

Since the mid-2000s, they have also done so with a range of local choices that would have been impossible just a decade earlier.

Different options bring different benefits, and different perceived risks, to prospective students. In contrast to the United States, private universities in Mexico are often perceived as having lower academic standards than their public counterparts. However, private institutions probably benefit from the perception that their public counterparts are hotbeds of unrest, where radicalized students, pejoratively referred to as *chairos*, spend more time engaging in far-left protest than in completing their studies. This has been a common theme in many criticisms of Mexico's universities since the 1960s and has been revived periodically in the national media. It is also an explicit selling point of the private institutions like the Universidad Anáhuac Mayab, whose vision statement included contrasts between its own educational values and the "unlimited" freedom of expression found in public universities.[11] Implicit in that statement is the assumption that private school students benefit from an education that is relatively undisturbed by protest and conflict.

The Universidad del Oriente, the first and largest public university in Valladolid, faced its own student protests through much of the 2010s. These received extensive coverage in the mainstream news media, with the attending damage to the school's reputation (*Diario de Yucatán* 2018c). Just six years after its foundation in 2005, the Universidad del Oriente faced a mobilization of students demanding the removal of a director. The alleged "irregularities" of her tenure ranged from unexplained staff turnover, to faculty teaching in fields for which they had no formal training, to abuse of institutional vehicles. The most damning accusations involved the administrators coercing students to attend political rallies in Valladolid. A second round of protests in 2014 demanded better classroom infrastructure and higher-quality instruction (*NotiRASA* 2014).

In my own conversations with Universidad del Oriente staff and alums, it seems clear that the university provides an academic home for dedicated students with few economically viable alternatives. The protests reflected very real institutional and staffing problems that stem from the university's unique organizational structure.[12] But friends in Pisté have cited coverage of these protests as one motive for their choice to attend more expensive private institutions, even though their own community is situated within the geographical zone meant to be served by the affordable public university.

Private institutions of higher education have the reputation of being far less politically volatile. This reputation accounts, at least in part, for the success and rapid expansion of the Centro Universitario Valladolid. Residential college even became a reality in eastern Yucatán after the construction of hundreds of dormitory rooms by the Centro Universitario Valladolid in the early 2000s. However, though the school is not known for specifically "political" disturbances, other aspects of its student life have been subjected to damaging media narratives. Four of the university's students took their own lives within a few months of each other in 2019, resulting in extensive coverage in the *Diario de Yucatán* and *¡Por Esto!* The ensuing panic prompted state health authorities to designate the local student community as a "suicide hotspot" (*foco rojo*) in need of emergency intervention (*Diario de Yucatán* 2019c, 2019a; *¡Por Esto!* 2019a).

These seemingly connected tragedies speak directly to anxieties that have deep historical roots in Yucatán. Many Yucatecan journalists—and even some academics—characterize suicide by hanging as a cultural predilection of Yukatek Maya people, referencing causes ranging from the historical trauma of debt peonage to the sinister influences of the pre-Hispanic goddess Ix Tab.[13] Most clinicians reject this culturalist and potentially racist narrative, and link "hotspots" like those of 2019 to economic precarity (see Reyes-Foster 2019). But given that the state's health authorities have designated suicide as a regional crisis, this remains a prominent topic for sensationalistic journalistic narratives that tend to foment moral panics about cultural issues rather than careful consideration of the precarity faced by Yucatán's youth (*Diario de Yucatán* 2019b, 2019c; *¡Por Esto!* 2019a).

What struck me most about press coverage of the 2019 tragedies was the virtual absence of any discussion of college students' diminishing postgraduate prospects, and the emphasis instead on the emotional damage caused by student life itself. *¡Por Esto!*'s reporting on the first of the suicides concluded with the observation that "among students of the CUV [Centro Universitario Valladolid] it is mentioned that on the same campus there are two groups: the popular partiers and the ones who are just there to study. Obviously, the first *ejerce bullying* [bullies] the second on not a few occasions" (*¡Por Esto!* 2019a)

This association of student life with "bullying" homes in on another moral panic that has gained prominence in the national and regional press in the mid-2010s (*La Jornada* 2014). I had never heard the anglicism *bullying* used in Spanish until the mid-2000s, when it suddenly seemed to be on the lips of every parent that I knew in Pisté.[14] In many conversations I have had with people from rural Yucatán, bullying and suicide tend to be cited as signs of a larger moral crisis affecting Mexico's youth, casting a pall over the much-celebrated expansion of education across the republic.

These entwined moral panics have brought much-needed attention to mental health in a country where psychotherapy has historically been stigmatized (see Reyes-Foster 2019). But they also tend to deflect the causes of political discontent and personal anxiety from the economy to different aspects of the youth culture associated with higher education. The association of suicide with bullying in private universities, like the characterization of public university students as volatile chairos, gives frightening form to a generation cultural gap separating rural youths born since the 1990s from their parents. While the primary schools that first taught Spanish and reading in the 1930s form a cherished collective memory, the new educational horizons that emerged at the end of the millennium are often associated with psychological and moral dangers that have few precedents in the life of rural communities.

WHAT MAKES A BETTER FUTURE?

Of the chapters that make up this book, this one presented me with a particularly pointed series of personal doubts and questions. As a liberal arts professor, I have built a part of my professional identity around the defense of a traditional model of teaching and learning that values the construction of knowledge and critical thinking for their own sake. As I mentioned earlier, this vision of education seems like a tough sell to families that struggle to convince their children that professional training is preferable to the fast but unpredictable income of the tourist market. Parental anxieties about the psychological impacts of bullying, like persistent doubts about the marketability of degrees, can compound this skepticism. While adding valuable skill sets to one's personal portfolio is consistent with the vernacular neoliberalism that informs many rural Yucatecans' view of money and politics, it has not tended to generate tangible results for many once-hopeful families.

Some rural residents, like Rafael Pech, reflect on their years of higher education as a positively transformative experience. But however positive or negative the college experience is, the large-scale survey data seem clear. University graduates in Yucatán have relatively few viable outlets beyond tourism for the education that has become increasingly accessible in the past twenty years. Seen from a longer historical perspective, the degree of state and private investment in the development of tourism has inflicted negative infrastructure on alternative economic sectors that could accommodate more recently graduated professionals.

The sociologist María Suárez Zozaya has gone so far as to argue that positive career outcomes were never the primary purpose of many of the low-quality institutions of secondary and higher education that have developed in Mexico since the 1990s. Instead, she suggests, these emerged as a means of "containing" a population of rural and poor urban youth who are excluded from the neoliberal economy and viewed as potentially dangerous by the state (Suárez Zozaya 2010, 102–3). In much media discourse, these disenfranchised adolescents are pejoratively referred to as *ni-nis* (neither-nors). That is, as youngsters who neither work nor study and participate in petty crime and pseudo-political disturbances while living rent-free with their parents (see Castañeda 2011). Like the "welfare queen" of Reaganite North America, the ni-ni occupies the "demonic" role of Adam Kotsko's (2018) neoliberal political theology. "Dangerous" dropouts instantiate the moral values associated with the contemporary economy through their apparent refusal to take full advantage of opportunities for intellectual and professional growth. This moral panic about alienated youth is sometimes cited in defense of flaws in Mexico's educational system. As an alternative to populating the streets with a generation of ni-nis, underperforming schools seem like a lesser evil.

The demonization of youth who refuse both higher education and work in the formal sector has especially complicated implications in communities like Pisté. Following Quetzil Castañeda (1996, 1997), several authors conducting research near Chichén Itzá have documented the ways local handicraft vendors have been vilified in the discourse of politicians and urban journalists (see also Breglia 2006). In chapter 4, I described the experience of the teenagers who were part of this community of vendors in the late 1990s. During this period, a major hotel posted a large sign that begged tourists not to buy handicrafts from these children, who it implied had been pulled from school by their parents. As the sign stated in several languages, those children "deserve a better future."

This sign misrepresented what was most often a side hustle for students to earn some cash after school and during vacations. But perhaps more important, the sign posited education as a means of exiting the informal economy, and "real" careers as irreconcilable with the ambulant vending that supplemented the incomes of hundreds of local families. The "better life" that the sign attributed to education never materialized for many of those teenage handicraft vendors. But from the perspective of the hotel, it's likely that institutions of secondary and higher education were just a convenient means of "containing" the youthful entrepreneurs who competed for the attention of tourists. In this regard, higher education substitutes for more aggressive forms of policing that tend to marginalize local residents in major tourist sites across the developing world (Carrier-Moisan 2020; Hodge and Little 2014; Kennelly 2015).

This demonization of handicraft vendors figured prominently in conflicts that defined the political life of Pisté and its neighboring communities in the 2010s. The relative lack of nontouristic employment in the region all but guarantees continued tension between local communities, state and federal agencies, and large-scale tourism operators. In the next two chapters, I will discuss key local conflicts that emerged in the 2010s. These conflicts reflect historical continuities in struggles over vital economic resources and state-sponsored infrastructure that I have discussed throughout this book. They also demonstrate how forms of political ideology and collective action that have deep roots in these communities have been adapted to new styles of political campaigning, new modes of tourism, and new media technologies.

6

A CANCELED MAYA DISNEYLAND

Struggles for Access in an Age of Captive Tourism

In the previous chapter, I discussed how business elites and politicians use the "need" for higher education as a thinly veiled denigration of rural Yucatecans' participation in informal markets connected to tourism. As Quetzil Castañeda (1996), Lisa Breglia (2006), and others have documented, state and federal agencies have clashed for decades with rural residents of Pisté and neighboring communities over the selling of handicrafts at Chichén Itzá. In the mid-2000s, this generation-long conflict over access to tourist dollars entered a new phase. This involved a series of innovations in "captive" tourism, and in how state institutions partnered with key private firms. From the perspective of many rural community members, these changing dynamics of tourist traffic undermined the flow of customers and dollars on which their families had relied for generations.

The goal of this chapter is twofold. In the first two sections, I will trace some changes in the global and regional tourism industry in the past two decades, and how these have coincided with new development strategies adopted by state and federal governments. The twenty-first century has seen the steady growth of a model of "captive tourism" in which a small number of firms with their own transportation fleets seek to move clients between multiple sites as part of a single branded package. The state government of Yucatán was particularly invested in promoting this model of tourism through a renewed emphasis on what it termed "cultural infrastructure." Broadly stated, this term refers to large-scale planning for the development of resources like museums and performance spaces, which emphasizes the means of bringing consumers to attractions as much as the management of cultural sites (see Rosenstein 2018). The resulting integration of state-operated cultural sites, public road infrastructure, and private capital became the signature policies of several gubernatorial administrations of the 2000s and 2010s.

The final three sections of this chapter will turn to forms of local resistance against this collusion between private capital and public infrastructure. I will focus on conflicts that ultimately derailed a 2012 project that the press referred to as a "Maya Disneyland." This project became a target of municipal-level politicians in Pisté when it became clear that it would inflict significant negative infrastructure on businesses in town. This popular resentment was likely exacerbated by a multigenerational conflict with people from a neighboring municipality who would have benefited significantly from the completion of the project.

Political leaders in Pisté launched a successful attack against the Maya Disneyland by asserting local control of collective landholdings, their ejido, that had been legally formalized by the agrarian reform of the Mexican Revolution. Mexico's 1917 Constitution established ejido lands as inalienable federal territories that are farmed and managed collectively by members of a given community. The 1991 constitutional reform that led many communities to liquidate their collective landholdings has not been an attractive proposition in Pisté, where the high real estate value of land near Chichén Itzá provides an ongoing motive for collective stewardship (Armstrong-Fumero 2013, 175–77). This locally repurposed agrarian institution provided one legal bulwark against projects that threatened to inflict negative infrastructure on the town and its residents.

When the state government retaliated against Pisté's dominant political faction in 2015, locals turned to the time-tested practice of blocking Highway

180 in protest. Even after a series of defeats, this faction was able to turn local discontent with the state government into an effective electoral coalition. Thus, for all of the innovation behind state-sponsored cultural infrastructure in the twenty-first century, people in communities like Pisté found strength in a much older toolkit of agrarian institution and direct action. The success of these strategies embodies those elements of older political legacies that have survived and been redeployed within the heterodox political logic of vernacular neoliberalism.

XCARET AND THE RISE OF VECTORIAL TOURISM

As an ethnographer, I gradually became aware of the evolution of "captive" tourism through subtle changes in the everyday landscape of Pisté and Chichén Itzá. Between 1997 and 2002, I became accustomed to seeing the parking lot behind the main entrance of the site crowded with buses. Besides the ADO transit buses that would drop off tourists and work commuters every hour, the parking lot was packed with a dozen or more variously colored vehicles affiliated with different tour companies. In the 2010s, the parking lot tended to be just as crowded but far less colorful. Nine out of ten of the buses were operated by the Xcaret Group—massive, sleekly styled black vehicles with a feathered serpent emblem painted on the side.

This tourism conglomerate played a central role in a wave of collaborations between private enterprise and the state government that emerged amid the neoliberal reforms of the *cerverato*. After decades of expansion, the Xcaret Group's dominance over tourism in the peninsula is a question not simply of volume but also of branding. The ubiquity of their buses on the roads, of their billboards beside the roads, and their guides in tourist sites makes it difficult to avoid the company's distinct ways of framing the regional landscape. Perhaps the most recognizable gimmick is the letter *X*, which is pronounced "sh" in Yukatek Maya and provides an initial taste of phonetic exoticism for anglophone tourists: "It's pronounced *shcaret*, not *zcaret*." The back of the signature black buses is decorated with a double-columned list of the different "eXperiencias Xcaret" (Xcaret eXperiences) offered by the company, all of which begin with an on-brand *X*. These include the 1990s stalwart Xel-Ha, Xochimilco (a simulacrum of the famous central Mexican canals built in Cancún), and an "adventure park" named Xplor. The various cenotes that the buses visit are referred to as "Xenotes." And, much to the indignation of many archaeologists and Yukatek Maya speakers who live on the edge of Chichén Itzá, the name of the site is spelled "Xichén."

This transformation of the name of an iconic archaeological site to conform to the company's brand is consistent with the larger homogenization of regional cultural attractions that some local bloggers have referred to as "Xcaretification." This process has proved culturally insensitive and offensive to academics and many Yukatek Maya speakers. But it also speaks to a larger reconfiguration of the regional tourism industry that has inflicted a catastrophic degree of negative infrastructure on many members of local communities. Xcaret's business model emphasizes the transportation of clients to different sites joined by common branding and tightly controlled logistics. Embraced in the 2000s by a state government that took the development of "cultural infrastructure" as one of its chief mandates, this genre of tourism places as much emphasis on the development of routes of transportation and communication used by tourists as on the actual destinations on an itinerary.

Xcaret's clients are dropped off at a given site, where they are led by guides employed by the parent company. These tours take place according to a fixed schedule, rain or shine, to ensure that tourists will be ready to leave for their next destination at the appointed hour. During occasional rain showers or particularly sunny days, clients are issued large pink umbrellas emblazoned with the Xcaret logo, allowing them to keep their schedule while serving as walking billboards for other visitors at the site.

These captive tours have dealt a significant blow to independent tourism operators in Pisté and other communities on the Highway 180 corridor. In many ways, Xcaret's model of tourism is an extreme example of the logistical "bubbles" (Carrier and Macleod 2005) that distance captive travelers from the larger social and economic contexts through which they move. The company's logistical teams determine when and if tourists will stop for lunch between attractions, largely mooting any attempts by local restaurant owners to independently lure in large tourist groups. Today, smaller restaurants are limited to flagging down individual families of Mexican tourists who still arrive in their own cars. Xcaret's practice of entering archaeological zones with their own guides has also disrupted the work of local licensed tour conductors, who traditionally "hooked" their fares from entries at the door of the attached tourism complex (Castañeda 1996). Adding insult to injury, Xcaret's guides often discourage their "captive" tourists from purchasing handicrafts from the locals who have set up stalls inside the archaeological zone.

The highly mobile, brand-focused style of tourism promoted by Xcaret embodies economic, political, and technical transformations that make twenty-first-century capital a different creature from its twentieth-century precursor. As John Urry and Mimi Scheller (2004) observe, contemporary mass tourism feeds into global economic processes that simultaneously reduce distances between human populations and tend to destabilize older forms of place-making. Xcaret's fleet of black buses promote a style of tourism that is not tied to any given location but has the freedom to move customers between various interchangeable "eXperiences" as time and other contingencies permit. This emphasis on transport logistics over site-specific consumption opens new avenues of profitability for capitalists and the governments with which they partner. Taking a broader perspective, the Marxist media scholar McKenzie Wark has noted that twenty-first-century capitalism has been transformed—if not replaced—by a new "vectorial" means of production. Outright control of material resources is no longer the primary means of profit and exploitation. As Wark (2019, 55) observes, "If the capitalist class owns the means of production, the vectorialist class own the vectors of information. They own extensive vectors of communications, which traverse space. They own intensive vectors of computation, which accelerate time. They own copyrights, the patents, and the trademarks that capture attention or assign ownership to novel techniques. They own the logistical systems that manage and monitor the disposition and movement of any resource."

As an enterprise, Xcaret Group is dwarfed by Walmart, Google, Amazon, and the other primary examples of the vectorial class in Wark's writing. But outside of these questions of scale, there is something distinctly "vectorial" in Xcaret's dominance of the regional tourist trade. Writing in the mid-1990s, Castañeda (1996, 1997) characterized Chichén Itzá as an "apparatus" that controlled the movement of the tourist body through a purpose-constructed space of entertainment, education and consumption. Xcaret controls an analogous apparatus, but one that spans from global advertising to sites scattered across the Yucatán Peninsula. Whereas the guides that Castañeda studied in the 1990s "hooked" tourists when they arrived at the entrance of Chichén Itzá, Xcaret's vectorial management of advertising, branding and transportation essentially "hooks" tourists from their arrival in Cancún, if not before (see also Córdoba Azcárate 2020, 84). Once reeled in, they engage in a series of "eXperiences" that are guided by the company for more or less the duration of their stay in Mexico.

Insofar as it can be considered a "vectorial" enterprise, Xcaret is an organization that translates older alliances between national business leaders and the state into a model of expansion and exploitation that is uniquely suited to the realities of twenty-first-century capitalism. Tourism depends on global market conditions and is as vulnerable to economic downturns and pandemics as it is to the hurricanes that devastate coastal infrastructure in the peninsula with increasing frequency (Córdoba Azcárate 2010, 32). And, as rural Mayan speakers have learned over the decades, a well-timed blockade of a road or site entrance can be used to apply pressure on local governments or business magnates. But the decentralized nature of Xcaret's tourism model allows it to adapt quickly to economic, ecological, and political contingencies that can limit the flow to specific sites by swapping one "eXperience" for another. Even at its lowest ebbs, it is a solidly profitable enterprise with no need for the constant infusions of cash that were required by older homegrown industries like henequen or sugar.

As I will discuss below, the synergy between the vectorial power embodied by Xcaret and the twenty-first-century iteration of the Mexican state is evident in some important changes in the basic structure of state-sponsored heritage management. The increased importance of "cultural infrastructure" as a general term for state interventions in tourism and cultural heritage is at the heart of this synergy. These transformations emerge against the backdrop of a new electoral landscape in which control of both state and federal government could shift between political parties. To understand this process, it is important to place it in the post-2000 political context.

CULTURAL INFRASTRUCTURE AND
THE "RESURGENT" PRI

In 2000, Patricio Patrón Laviada became the first Panista to hold the governorship of the state of Yucatán, marking the end of the fifteen-year Cerverato. In doing so, he inherited control of a series of state-level institutions that had been founded by Cervera to manage the tourism infrastructure of archaeological sites like Chichén (see Breglia 2006). Patrón Laviada also inherited an alliance with the Xcaret Group, whose leadership had made overtures toward the Partido Acción Nacional (National Action Party, or PAN) in the waning days of Cervera's tenure. By 2000, with little undeveloped real estate left on the Caribbean coast, the tourism conglomerate was expanding its empire inland. A group of investors associated with Patrón Laviada's family had purchased former ejidal land from communities in the municipality of Chan Kom, which were rumored to be part of a larger project to create inland ecopark attractions in collaboration with the Xcaret Group (Armstrong-Fumero 2013, 149). The purchases in Chan Kom municipality were not developed on any significant scale, as the Partido Revolucionario

Institucional (Institutional Revolutionary Party, or PRI) reclaimed the governorship in 2006, shifting the center of political power once again. The new governor, Ivonne Ortega Pacheco, would make ambitious projects to bolster the state's tourism a signature of her tenure.

The personal debts and clientelistic connections that marked Ortega Pacheco's political rise are a matter of conjecture among Mexican and Yucatecan pundits. Most commentators are quick to observe that she is a niece of Víctor Cervera Pacheco. In her autobiography, Ortega Pacheco (2015, 73–75) downplays the familial bond, noting again and again how "Don Víctor" kept her at arm's length for fear of being accused of nepotism. This denial is generally contested in the press, which tends to list her among other prominent Yucatecan Priístas of the early 2000s who were formed within the family and patronage networks of cerverismo (Revista Yucatán 2010). Whatever the depth of her actual nepotistic connection, Ivonne's penchant for both folksy populism and close partnership with national corporate interests strongly echoes the 1980s and early 1990s. She herself refers to the old cacique as "a model to be copied in politics. . . . Nobody can deny his passionate love for his ideals and his sacrifice of so many things in the name of the people" (Ortega Pacheco 2015, 93).

If cerverismo tied Ivonne to a PRI dynasty with deep roots in Yucatán, journalists also refer to other political ties linking her to the quasi-mythical Grupo Atlacomulco in the state of Mexico (Villamil 2012b). Referred to as camarillas or simply as grupos in the political science literature, multigenerational associations like the reputed Grupo Atlacomulco are based on biological kinship, compadrazgo, patronage, and shared economic interests (Ai Camp 1985; Wells and Joseph 1996). For decades, political journalists have insinuated that an especially powerful camarilla traces its roots to Carlos Hank González, a billionaire who held a number of prominent political positions beginning in the 1950s and 1960s. Still powerful after its founder's death in 2007, this political network is considered to have been instrumental in the 2012 rise to the presidency of Priísta Enrique Peña Nieto (Cruz Jiménez and Montiel 2009; Martínez 1999). Speculation about Ivonne Ortega Pacheco's (2015) connections to this group focuses on her early collaboration with future president Peña Nieto, and on her reliance on corporations owned or controlled by Hank González's sons in various projects that were sponsored by the State of Yucatán during her tenure as governor.

Through these connections, Ortega Pacheco is an important figure in the "resurgent" PRI that was able to recover from its humiliating losses in 2000 and retake the presidency of Mexico in 2012. Beginning her own period as governor under Panista president Felipe Calderón Hinojosa, Ortega Pacheco's tenure was marked by a number of innovative means of sidelining federal institutions that were controlled by the political opposition. As I noted earlier, one of the hallmarks of her gubernatorial sexenio was an unprecedented assertion of state-level agencies' power over the management of the region's tourism. Historically, this has been a sensitive jurisdictional terrain, as the Instituto Nacional de Antropología e Historia (National Institute of Anthropology and History, or INAH) exercises direct control over the management and protection of archaeological and historical sites in all of the Mexican Republic. In many cases, Ortega Pacheco's strategy involved control of the infrastructure linking archaeological sites and peripheral services that did not technically impinge on the physical antiquities that are controlled by INAH.

The key institution in Ortega Pacheco's assertion of state-level control over archaeological tourism was an agency called CULTUR. CULTUR was founded in 1987 by Cervera Pacheco as a means of establishing the state's management over services to tourists at archaeological sites that were traditionally administered by the federal INAH (see Castañeda 1996; and Breglia 2006). In return for maintaining bathrooms, renting out concession stands, and running light and sound shows at sites like Chichén Itzá and Uxmal, CULTUR collects ticket revenues that often exceed the share pocketed by INAH. CULTUR is closely tied to the office of each sitting governor, who is the formal head of the agency and appoints its principal administrators.

Ortega Pacheco was able to expand CULTUR's original mandate in a number of important ways. The most notable was the state government's purchase of the lands on which the archaeological site of Chichén Itzá is located. Since the 1930s, these had belonged to the Barbachano family, relatives of the tourism magnate who was humiliated by President Echeverría in Uxmal in 1974. While the family maintained legal title to the land, and profited from a series of luxury hotels that they owned on the periphery of the site, formal stewardship of all archaeological remains was in the hands of INAH (see Breglia 2006). The Ortega Pacheco administration's purchase of the majority of the Barbachanos' landholdings resulted in a unique arrangement in which the state of Yucatán owned the surface of the land surrounding the ruins, while INAH retained its federal mandate over the ruins themselves. Sitting gubernatorial administrations had already had a stake in tourism receipts through the on-site visitor facilities operated by CULTUR. Now, the State of Yucatán was the site's landowner, cementing the governor's control over the regional cash cow.

If the change in ownership might be invisible to most visitors to the Chichén Itzá, Ortega Pacheco also funded a high-tech revamping of the light and sound show that had been run nightly in the archaeological zone for decades. Today, this is an expensive add-on to a visit to Chichén Itzá. In the first few weeks of its operation, the new light and sound show was open to community members from Pisté. I was invited to tag along with some friends to one of the first showings. The new show, consisting of crystal-clear sound and digital video projected on the surface of the iconic Castillo pyramid, was a stunning improvement on the bare-bones spectacle that had existed since the time of Loret de Mola. My friends were also very impressed but expressed their annoyance as we walked back into town. At one point, the digital projection "dresses" the pyramid structure of the Castillo in an *ipil*, the traditional female garment of Yucatán. The specific color pattern and embroidery on the borders of the projected ipil were copied from the signature garment that Ortega Pacheco wore to many public events. For the foreseeable future, the most iconic structure of Chichén Itzá will be transformed nightly into a stony simulacrum of the former governor.

Ortega Pacheco left an equally durable stamp on archaeological tourism in the capital city of Mérida through the creation of the Gran Museo del Mundo Maya (Great Museum of the Maya World). Boasting state-of-the-art installation techniques and replete with expensively produced immersive video and audio elements, the museum aims to provide a more visitor-friendly experience than many of the older and more curatorially conservative museums in the peninsula. But, located near a new convention center in the extreme northwest of the city, it is not accessible to the foot traffic of downtown Mérida. The admission fee of 100 pesos for adults and 50 for children is relatively high by the standards of similar institutions in Mexico, and prohibitive for many local families.

More controversial than the museum's price and location was the confluence of state-level planning and private finance that contributed to its construction. The museum's foundation involved agreements between CULTUR, the Fundación Cultural Yaxché (an organization closely tied to Governor Ortega Pacheco), and Grupo Hermes. This last organization is a Mexican infrastructure conglomerate that would manage and collect revenues from the museum. Through Grupo Hermes, this project was associated with Carlos Hank Rhon, a Mexico City– and Tijuana-based industrialist who is the son of Carlos Hank González and closely tied to the Atlacomulco Group. Rumored connections between the Hank clan and narco trafficking, which have circulated in the Mexican and international press for decades, cast a shadow on some coverage of the museum (*Proceso* 2011). There was also considerable concern over the transfer of a very large part of the collection that had been displayed in the INAH-operated Palacio Cantón museum. Objects that had been accessible to the public in a relatively inexpensive and centrally located public institution for generations were suddenly placed in a space where access to them would be regulated by Grupo Hermes, which possessed a twenty-one-year contract to collect entrance fees. As a number of outraged journalists observed, this and other elements of the contract between Grupo Hermes and Ortega Pacheco would indebt the state of Yucatán to the Hank clan for decades to come (Montero 2020).

It is telling that Ortega Pacheco's private sector partner in the development of the museum was Grupo Hermes, whose primary business is infrastructure construction. Infrastructure is both a literal and metaphorical component of the state's relationship to Maya culture in twenty-first-century Yucatán. As I noted earlier, the term "cultural infrastructure" became more prominent in the discourse of CULTUR and related institutions in the 2000s. The exact meaning of cultural infrastructure in CULTUR's interventions varies across several contexts. However, two consistent elements of the polyvalent term are worth highlighting. First, there is the transformation of cultural policy from a question of top-down communication to bottom-up accessibility. Second, there is a broadening of the terrain of culture to include spaces that fall outside of the strict jurisdiction of federal institutions.

From a longer historical perspective, the question of bottom-up accessibility represents a reversal of an older Revolutionary vision that characterized culture as something that was "brought" to the rural masses by urban educators. The rural teachers who "brought" Western culture to isolated Maya peasants in the 1930s often described arduous journeys down narrow bush trails. In contrast, CULTUR's mandate in the early 2000s focused on staging sites that would be visited by highly mobile travelers on modern highways, be they local consumers of culture or international tourists. A 2012 reform to CULTUR's charter emphasized the importance of creating a physical infrastructure that allowed access to the "cultural, archaeological, colonial, and natural" sites within the state (Gobierno del Estado de Yucatán 2012). In this context, the role of government is not to "bring" culture to deprived citizens but to provide the infrastructure that makes cultural sites available to Mexicans and foreigners who expend their own time and money to seek them.

CULTUR's semantic distinction of "cultural" sites from "archaeological, colonial, and natural" ones is also telling. This gesture distinguishes the state of Yucatán's cultural infrastructure from the specific heritage and conservation sites where INAH and other federal agencies have clear jurisdiction. Mentions of elements of "infraestructura de carácter cultural o turística" (infrastructure of cultural or touristic character) in the law refer specifically to spaces that can be directly purchased, built, and managed by the state-level agency. In effect, the institutional definition of "culture" used by Ortega Pacheco and her collaborators posited a terrain in which the state government could exercise independent authority from federal institutions. Thus, from an agency that maintained bathrooms and managed vendors at a few sites, CULTUR evolved into the planner and coordinator of works of road infrastructure that had the potential to alter the region's geography.

A MAYA DISNEYLAND

One of the alterations of the state's cultural infrastructure that was planned during Ortega Pacheco's sexenio involved the Palacio de la Cultura Maya (Palace of Maya Culture), a project playfully dubbed a "Maya Disneyland" by the governor herself. Designed as a multipurpose campus built around a cenote in the rural municipality of Yaxcabá, the palace would allow visitors to experience the interplay between Maya culture and the natural environment of the Yucatán Peninsula. Given this emphasis on the "ecological" dimensions of the attraction, it's no surprise that Ortega Pacheco's private partners were the Xcaret Group. The new complex matched the tourism conglomerate's strategy of expanding inland with the construction of new attractions around Yucatecan "Xenotes."

This "palace" was a frequent topic of conversation during my research visits after its construction was announced in 2009. The first indication that people in Pisté had of this project was the state's purchase of a rustic ranch known as Dzonot Abán, located near the village of Popolá on the road to Yaxcabá (see map 6.1). I recalled Dzonot Abán from fieldwork trips between 1999 and around 2001, when I was conducting oral history research and teaching an informal English class in Popolá. At the time, the road to Yaxcabá was a narrow, rocky "white road" of layered rocks, gravel, and fine limestone powder that I traveled several times a week by bicycle. I always gave Dzonot Abán a wide berth, because the ranch was patrolled by a family of irritable dogs that threatened to jump the fence and chase me every time I pedaled by.

For generations, Dzonot Abán and the rest of the municipality of Yaxcabá have existed on the southern fringes of the tourist economy that developed around the Highway 180 corridor. Change there always seemed to come more slowly than in Pisté and other centrally located communities. It wasn't until

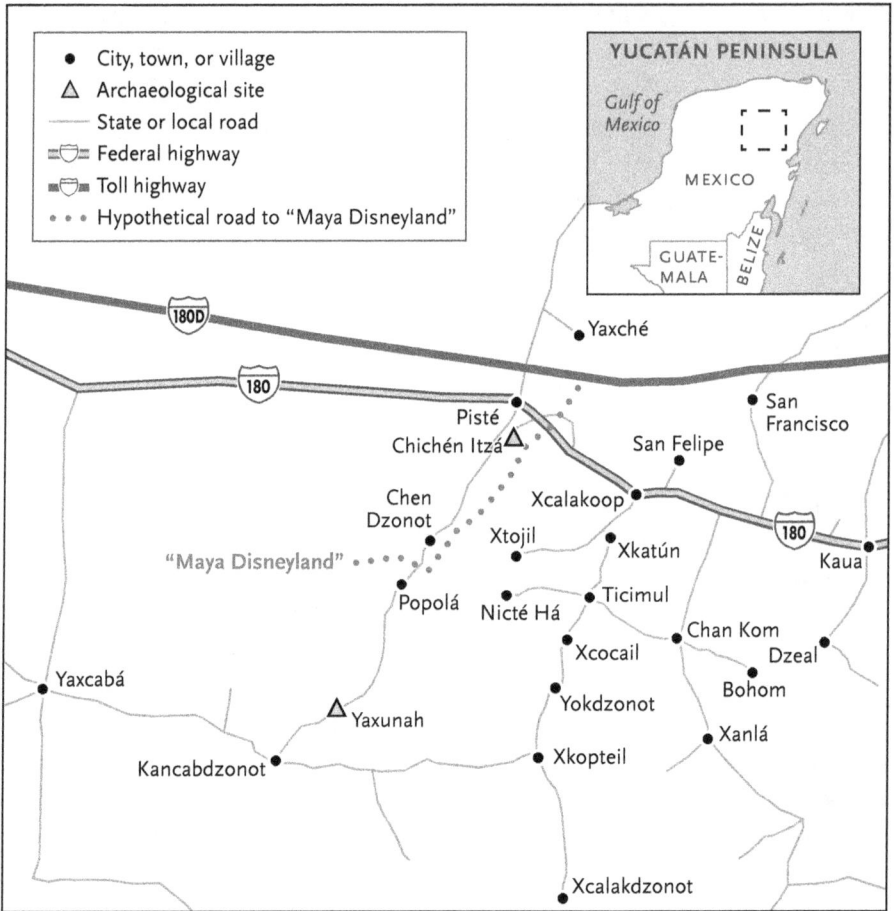

Map 6.1. The road to Yaxunah and Federal Highway 180. The dotted line
represents the hypothetical route of a road connecting the "Maya Disneyland"
directly to Chichén Itzá and the toll road (Federal Highway 180D).
*Map created by Nicolás Reyes, Heather Rosenfeld, and Kala'i Ellis
at the Spatial Analysis Lab, Smith College, Northampton, MA.*

2005, after decades of petitioning by local residents, that the stretch of road
linking these communities to Highway 180 had been releveled and finished
with a modern asphalt pavement. This expansion was meant to make the
rarely visited archaeological site of Yaxunah more accessible, along with a
cenote and cultural center in the nearby village of the same name. Ending
in the town of Yaxcabá, with its impressive eighteenth-century church, the
finished road also presented a new link between the Highway 180 touristic

Chapter 6

corridor and the "Route of the Convents" that took travelers through pictur-esque colonial towns in the south of the state.

On paper, the plan to build the Maya Disneyland at the site of Dzonot Abán seemed very sound. The complex would generate employment in a his-torically underserved municipality and create a geographical bridge between two established tourism corridors. But within a few years of its announce-ment to the press, this project had become one of the most visible failures of Ortega Pacheco's intervention into the state's touristic and cultural landscape. One of the causes was a conflict between the governor and a Panista political faction dominant in Pisté, which held ejidal title to much of the bushland that would have been needed for the completion of the project. Beyond party politics, Ortega Pacheco's expansive vision of "cultural infrastructure" collided with a longer history of intercommunity conflicts and competition that was tied to the creation of roads linking towns and municipalities in this part of Yucatán. Understanding this process will require a series of historical digressions in the next section.

THE ROADS ALREADY TAKEN

CULTUR's twenty-first-century iteration of "cultural infrastructure" may have changed the dynamics of tourism development in Yucatán, but the idea of purpose-built roads linking existing thoroughfares to archaeological sites was hardly new. The first such project was imagined, though apparently never realized, by a private entrepreneur named Emilio Ontiveros Machado.[1] In August 1913, Ontiveros solicited a concession from the state government to build and operate a series of Decauville rails connecting the ruins of Uxmal and Chichén Itzá to the nearest railway hubs (Muna and Dzitas, respectively).

Ontiveros's Decauville project never seems to have functioned, but the proposed connection between Chichén Itzá and the train station at Dzitas would be the first specially built tourism artery to a Maya archaeological site. The original dedication of this route in 1922 by the legendary Socialist governor Felipe Carrillo Puerto has a prominent place in the oral history of Pisté (Armstrong-Fumero 2013, 54). Today, if you visit the town's small tourist district, you can see a monolith dated to 1935, which commemorates improvements to the original road sponsored by Governor César Alayola Barrera (see fig. 6.1). The Dzitas-Pisté road would be the primary means of accessing Chichén Itzá until the completion of the Highway 180 corridor in the late 1950s.

Figure 6.1. Monolith for the dedication of 1935 improvements to the road from Dzitas to Pisté. In the mid-2010s, it was moved to a more prominent position in the town plaza near a hieroglyphic stela created by local artists. *Photos by Fernando Armstrong-Fumero.*

Dzonot Abán and the rest of the municipality of Yaxcabá remained on the periphery of these early developments. A side road linking Yaxcabá to Highway 180 was first proposed, unsuccessfully, at some point in the 1960s. In 1974, the municipal president of Yaxcabá, Eusebio Po'ot Mena, appealed directly to Governor Carlos Loret de Mola in a letter to the *Diario de Yucatán.* As reported in the "Municipios" section on 7 October, he proposed a twenty-kilometer road that would connect the largely unexcavated archaeological site of Yaxunah—the origin of the famous archaeological road to Cobá—to Chichén Itzá. The timing of this request was fortuitous. Expanding the state's network of rural roads, and generating temporary jobs in the process, was a point of pride for Loret de Mola. The governor approved the plan, but the proposed roadway would evolve slowly, and in fits and starts, over the course of three decades.

The road that was proposed by Po'ot Mena passed through the ejido landholdings of two communities in the municipality of Tinum and two communities in the municipality of Yaxcabá. Because of this, men from both sides of the municipal border found work in the project. This collaboration represented a rare détente in a low-level feud that had simmered between the municipalities for half a century. In the early 1920s, while Tinum was a stronghold of the revolutionary Partido Socialista de Yucatán (Socialist Party of Yucatán), Yaxcabá came under the control of the elite-backed Partido Liberal Yucateco (Yucatecan Liberal Party). Enabled by sympathetic federal police in the local garrison, Partido Liberal Yucateco militants from Yaxcabá conducted a campaign of armed terror against Partido Socialista de Yucatán–controlled communities to their north. In the summer of 1921, Socialists from communities in the Tinum municipality formed a coalition with allied towns to the east (Domínguez 1979). The resulting raid was still remembered by some of my elderly informants in the early 2000s as "the burning of Yaxcabá." Memories of this conflict were still fresh twenty years after the fact and played a role in the negotiations between the founders of the border village of Popolá, local municipal authorities, and federal agrarian agencies (Armstrong-Fumero 2013, 168–70). In the 1970s, the people who collaborated on the road linking Yaxunah to Highway 180 were children and grandchildren of those who had lived through the original cycle of violence.

When I met him in 2000, Javier Maas of Pisté was in his late sixties and a local authority on tourism infrastructure. Besides having planned several public works during his tenure as comisario municipal in the 1970s, he had spent decades working with restoration projects at Chichén Itzá. He mentioned the construction of the road to Yaxunah as a secondary development to the consolidation of the Highway 180 corridor. Don Javier recalled that while the heavy work on the span between Valladolid and Puerto Juárez "arrancó en 1950" (took off in 1950), work on the branch leading to Yaxunah didn't begin "until the 1960s." Later, he referred to it as being completed under the Manos de Obra program begun by the Echeverría presidential administration, which would place the event somewhere between 1970 and 1976 (see Mitchell 2001, 60). This seems to confirm that the 1974 letter to the editor of the *Diario* by Eusebio Po'ot Mena was the immediate catalyst for its construction.

Though the road construction project represented a rare moment of collaboration between the normally hostile municipalities, Javier Maas made a point of stating that it still involved a clear boundary between different jurisdictions. He referred to Vías Terrestres, the parastatal company that coordinated the work, as transferring the *mando* (command) of the project to the correct municipal authorities on either side of the border. That is, the municipal authorities of Yaxcabá would oversee recruiting and compensating workers from local communities as work progressed northward to the ejido of Popolá, which bordered the municipal jurisdiction of Tinum. At that point, the municipal authorities of Tinum would take over, filling positions with residents of their own communities. The recruitment of labor through community-level organizations was common throughout Mexico (Bess 2017; Waters 1999). But in this case, the practice may have been especially important for keeping the peace. Although Yaxcabá and Tinum were working toward a common goal, men from opposite sides of the border would rarely if ever have worked on the same crews.

Though Javier Maas himself did not work on the road, I interviewed a municipal politician from Yaxcabá municipality who had. Carlos Cocom of Popolá had worked on several sections of the span linking his community to the neighboring village of Chen Dzonot. He shared more ambivalent recollections of the process of soliciting state funds and conducting the work of construction in collaboration with the normally hostile residents of Tinum municipality. He noted that, by the time that workers from Pisté joined in from the Tinum side of the project, communities in the municipality of Yaxcabá had spent years unsuccessfully soliciting funds and permissions. Whatever benefit the people of Pisté derived from roadwork came at the expense of political groundwork laid by their poorer southern neighbors.

Geography itself seemed to favor the people of Pisté. Cocom recalled that workers were paid for piecework, with 300 pesos as the going rate for work on a twenty-meter stretch of four-meter-wide road. The catch was that the terrain between Popolá and the border of Tinum municipality included a hilly stretch of solid karst limestone. If a crew were lucky, they would be offered work on a fairly flat stretch that they could complete in two or three weeks, for the respectable sum of twenty to fifteen pesos a day. If they were unlucky, they would earn the same 300 pesos over a month or more of backbreaking work. Complaints about these conditions were enough that the state government offered workers a daily ration of food as a further enticement.

What struck me as most remarkable about Carlos Cocom's account was that the vast majority of this work took place without the use of heavy machinery and explosives. As Cocom put it, crews from his home village attacked the limestone bedrock with "picks, shovels, wheelbarrows, and sledgehammers." It wasn't until work stalled at an impassible mass of limestone on the border of the two municipalities that the workers hired in Popolá refused to continue. I remember this stretch of terrain well from the late 1990s. Even two decades after it had been "leveled," it was hilly enough that I dreaded bicycling down its steep and rocky surface on my way to Popolá. As Cocom recalled, it was at this treacherously hilly stretch that the government realized it had already "thrown away a lot of budget" making the road. Within a few weeks, heavy pneumatic drills arrived to help place explosives, and heavy earthmoving equipment cleared and flattened the surface in a fraction of the time that it would have taken a local road crew.

Carlos Cocom told me this story in 2001, with almost thirty years of hindsight on the usefulness of the road. Although the request communicated to Governor Loret de Mola in 1974 characterized the road as a means of bringing tourists "in" to the relatively untouched ruins in the municipality of Yaxcabá, Cocom's account treats the road as a means of allowing locals to get "out." He noted that the road saved the lives of many people who would have died without visiting doctors, and that it made it possible for him and his neighbors to participate in the handicraft trade in Pisté. Cocom's cousin, Doña Marta Cahum, had first informed me about this commerce when I interviewed her in 2000. She, her sons, and in-laws were all heavily involved in the lively commerce in small wood carvings. The rocky road made possible the twice-weekly visit of a three-ton truck that picked up unfinished wood carvings to be bought wholesale by artisanry merchants in Pisté. Thrifty wood carvers like Doña Marta's sons could make their own trips on bicycles and sell directly to their favorite middleman. It was a tiring trip but manageable if one left before dawn, conducted business, and returned south in the late afternoon.

The fact that the road linking Yaxunah to Pisté was better at getting handicrafts "out" than it was at bringing tourists "in" remained a persistent point of contention for people in the impoverished municipality to the south. When I interviewed him in 2001, Carlos Cocom said that he and other local residents had spent close to a decade seeking funds to widen and properly pave the road, a process that was still several years in the future. It was their dream to see cars and vans full of tourists drive by their communities on the way to the ruins of Yaxunah and the various cenotes in the area, stopping to buy handicrafts and snacks along the way. As things currently were, a woodcarver in Popolá was likely to sell a small figure to a middleman in Pisté for five to ten pesos. The merchant would then sand, paint, and polish the figure and sell it for anywhere from twenty-five to even fifty pesos. As Carlos Cocom put it, "[The merchants] draw more benefit than the person who did the work."

This suspicion, even resentment, toward the comparatively wealthy residents of the town of Pisté extends beyond simple economics to very real differences in political patronage. I didn't delve too deeply into presidential politics with Carlos Cocom, but I got a sense that he was less optimistic about his village's future in 2001 than he would have been a few years earlier. Mexico's historic 2000 election, which brought the Panista Vicente Fox to the presidency, held a foreboding tone for many in the staunchly Priísta municipality of Yaxcabá. During our interview, Cocom had heaped praise on former president Carlos Salinas de Gortari, who had been vilified in the national press for the financial crash that took place at the end of his sexenio and for corruption scandals that were made public in the 1990s. He acknowledged many criticisms of the former president but noted that he was much loved in the municipality of Yaxcabá for a project that had electrified most of the smaller communities. The state-level PRI had also delivered a number of benefits to the same rural hamlets. As I noted in chapter 3, most of the homes that I visited in Popolá had cement floors stamped with a commemorative inscription that referenced a home improvement project implemented by Víctor Cervera Pacheco. Regarding ongoing attempts to pave the road linking their communities to Highway 180, Carlos Cocom laconically stated, "We'll see how it goes with this new government. With this Fox."

By the time that Ivonne Ortega Pacheco took office in 2007, political fractures between the municipalities had only deepened. There are still many staunch Priístas in Pisté and other communities in the municipality of Tinum. But, since the 1990s, the homegrown Panistas had exerted more and more dominance in the town of Pisté. Given that that town had at least twice the population of the municipal seat of Tinum, it shifted the political balance of the entire municipality. If they are able to run up a significant vote tally in the municipality's outlying comisarías, Pisté's Panistas can reliably overwhelm PRI opposition to elect their own candidates to the municipal presidency.

A decade after I interviewed Carlos Cocom and Javier Maas about their respective memories of the road linking Pisté and Popolá, the political differences between these municipalities would come to a head. Priístas from Yaxcabá found a sympathetic governor in Ivonne Ortega Pacheco, who promised political opportunities that had been rare during the previous Panista administration. In contrast, a very popular PAN administration in the municipal presidency of Tinum faced an increasingly hostile governor, which they mitigated by making direct appeals to different federal institutions. This was the environment in which Ivonne Ortega Pacheco sought to construct her Maya Disneyland.

DEATH OF THE MAYA DISNEYLAND: AN UNSTOPPABLE FORCE MEETS AN IMMOVABLE OBJECT

I remember that the first reports of the construction work at Dzonot Abán, in 2009, were received with cautious optimism by some people in Pisté. Several Priísta friends of mine in town had a very high opinion of Governor Ortega Pacheco. They observed that, like the road and hotel construction of previous decades, the project at Abán would likely create temporary construction jobs for dozens, or even hundreds of local workers. Even if the primary beneficiaries of the Palacio de la Cultura Maya would be residents of villages in the neighboring municipality, there was reason for people from Pisté to be optimistic about the project. Had traffic to the Maya Disneyland passed through the existing road network, travelers leaving Chichén Itzá would have to pass through downtown Pisté. For enough of a commission, the guides might be induced to take advantage of a number of local charter lunch restaurants, and maybe even revitalize some handicraft shops whose business had slumped since the early 2000s.

Such optimism was short-lived, however. Skepticism began in 2011 with the ejidatarios, the users and managers of Pisté's collectively titled agricultural land. They had been contacted by representatives of Governor Ortega Pacheco who wished to purchase part of their holdings. The purchase would allow the state government to develop a larger "master plan" for the tourist zone around Chichén Itzá (*Excélsior* 2010). As the ejidatarios understood it, the governor intended to build a new road linking Chichén Itzá directly to the Maya Disneyland, bypassing downtown Pisté entirely (see map 6.1). This would essentially translate the model of "captive" tourism employed by the Xcaret Group into a physical road that would exercise a significant amount of negative infrastructure on Pisté and its immediate vicinity. Over the years, Xcaret's guides had become quite adept at convincing the tourists they brought to "Xichen" that the food and crafts offered by independent vendors from Pisté were less safe, less authentic, and more expensive than those provided within their package deal. Now, if the rumors were true, a purpose-built road would do that work for them. Adding insult to injury, the state government hoped to build this road through Pisté's own collective landholdings.

The Ortega Pacheco administration was confident enough in the completion of this project that it proceeded with major work at Dzonot Abán before purchasing all of the lands needed for the completion of the planned complex. In the summer of 2011, when I drove down the road from Yaxcabá on the way back to Pisté, I noticed the very large parking lot in the stretch of bush that had once been a rustic ranch. Freshly paved and painted, with fully modern light fixtures, it reminded me of the parking lot at the Cancún airport. There was a narrow unpaved path leading far into the bush behind the asphalt, and piles of cinderblock hinted at further construction that the tree cover made invisible from the road.

A decade later, the parking lot is as much of the Palacio de la Cultura Maya that is visible to tourists and other passersby. Several Mexican newspapers and websites have published eerie photos of the unfinished frames of buildings that, by 2015, were quickly turning into a modern ruin (see fig. 6.2). In 2020, a study by Mexico's federal auditing institution determined that the project failed due to a combination of poor planning, an inability to secure federal funds, and an inability to purchase some of the lands required for its completion. The audit also documented the apparent theft of millions of pesos from the project (Casares Cámara 2020). Some of the very literal roadblocks to integrating the Maya Disneyland into a larger development plan came from the people of Pisté. At the heart of this was a strengthening of municipal-level political opposition to Governor Ortega Pacheco under the aegis of a charismatic local leader.

That leader was Evelio Mis Tun. Mis had risen from humble origins to become one of the wealthiest handicraft vendors working in the periphery of Chichén Itzá. The distinctly Mayan diction of his Spanish and his tendency to use pointed language against political rivals have made him a frequent target of racist attacks on social media and in the regional press. This has also made more elitist elements in the state-level PAN reluctant to embrace his candidacy in some election cycles. But Mis's charismatic influence among

Figure 6.2. A parking lot to nowhere, ca. 2015.
Photo by Fernando Armstrong-Fumero.

the local Panistas is strong enough that he has been able to rally large-scale defections to third parties when members of his political network have been refused formal PAN endorsement. Thus, while a significant portion of voters who support Evelio Mis identify as lifelong Panistas, the unpredictable twists and turns that marked the politics of the later 2000s and 2010s sometimes make the term "*evelista*" seem more appropriate.

One of the hallmarks of Evelio Mis's period of political dominance was an unprecedented level of investment in local infrastructure, which included the renovations of municipal buildings and the town square, the construction of a new municipal marketplace, and the paving of many roads. In this regard, Mis benefited from tensions between the PRI-controlled statehouse of Yucatán and the Panista presidential administration of Felipe Calderón. Given their recent history of conflicts with Yucatán's governors, Pisté's municipal authorities had ample cause to appeal directly to federal institutions for funds, and were very successful in soliciting them.

Less visible to the casual visitor, but perhaps more important in defining the town's relationship to state and federal governments, was an increasing assertiveness over access to Chichén Itzá. Mis and his collaborators began to articulate stronger demands that the community of Pisté be able to derive income from tourism at the archaeological zone. Given that several spans of roadway leading into and out of the archaeological zone pass through Pisté's ejido, members of the local agrarian committee claimed the right to charge tolls to passing tour buses. At other times, the ejidatarios have demanded that CULTUR guarantee that a percentage of their entrance fees be earmarked for the municipal coffers.

As the state government rebuffed most of his demands, Evelio Mis's ability to mobilize the local agrarian committee contributed to the collapse of the Maya Disneyland project. With no feasible plan for construction that didn't pass through Pisté's ejido, the state government was dependent on the ejidatarios for permission to build. Despite months of lobbying, the committee would not budge. Though Mérida-based journalists have pointed to misappropriation of funds as a primary cause for the demise of the Maya Disneyland, a number of ejidatarios to whom I've spoken give their committee credit for ultimately "stopping" future construction.

Whatever the ultimate cause of the Maya Disneyland's demise, the direct confrontation between an increasingly assertive municipal government and the state's dominant PRI faction would have lasting consequences. Given the centrality of "vectorial" tourism in their vision for Yucatán's prosperity, Ivonne Ortega Pacheco and her Priísta successor Rolando Zapata were highly motivated to dislodge the popular faction whose control of ejidal lands could thwart projects like the Maya Disneyland. During the period between 2010 and 2018, the municipality of Tinum experienced a series of particularly violent election cycles. Intimidation, brawling, and extrajudicial detentions are fairly common features of municipal elections in rural Yucatán (Armstrong-Fumero 2018). But the years of restored PRI dominance of the Yucatecan governorship led to a relatively new phenomenon in which multiple units of state police—ultimately commanded by the governor in Mérida—became a permanent presence in the streets of Pisté. This created potentially dangerous situations, like a 2015 incident in which state and federal police took part in an hour-long standoff to prevent PAN-affiliated municipal police from harassing a local PRI candidate (*Proceso* 2015). Other incidents would involve PAN candidates and activists being threatened by PRI-affiliated police forces, and will be discussed below.

Despite the growing threat of violence, Evelio Mis initially governed over what Panistas in Pisté consider to be a golden age for local infrastructural development. Due in part to his initial successes, the 2012 election in Tinum municipality was relatively peaceful. This is somewhat ironic, given that that same year brought the PRI back into the presidency through Enrique Peña Nieto, and secured Ivonne Ortega Pacheco's legacy in Yucatán's statehouse through the election of Rolando Zapata. But with the PRI of Tinum municipality still in disarray after a disastrous local election cycle in 2009, their candidate was easily defeated by Evelio Mis's young daughter Natalia. Though many of the Priístas stated the obvious and complained that Evelio would remain the real power behind the municipality, this seemed to trouble few voters.

With federal funds remaining from the previous round of requests, the rapid pace of construction of downtown infrastructure continued. By 2015, Pisté boasted a new medical center, a cultural center, and major additions to the municipal hall. My friend Rubén Dzul played a number of roles in the administration, and loved to take me on long drives through town to show off miles of new pavement that had been a network of rocky and muddy roads just months before. He would take deep breaths of fresh asphalt and say, "Ki' u book, maas[im]a?" (Mayan: It smells lovely, doesn't it?).

Conflict, however, was just on the horizon. After the election of Priísta Enrique Peña Nieto to the Mexican presidency in 2012, Evelio Mis and his supporters had lost much of their leverage with federal institutions. Politically isolated, they turned to time-tested forms of direct action. In 2015, on the eve of a new municipal election in which Mis was a candidate, members of Pisté's ejido committee demanded a payment from the state government for the passage of tourist vehicles through the town's collectively held lands. This could have included allotting as much as 15 percent of CULTUR's tourism receipts to the town's municipal coffers. This gambit proved less successful than the earlier refusal to permit road construction for the Maya Disneyland project. The laws giving the agrarian committee jurisdiction over new construction through their lands were clear, but the basis for making similar demands for passage through those lands on the existing Highway 180 was more tenuous. So, just as Rubén Dzul and his classmates had blocked the federal road to Quintana Roo in the 1970s, several groups of community members blocked access to Chichén Itzá several times for multiple days in early 2015 (*Tribuna* 2015).

While the *evelistas* sought media attention for their demands, supporters of the state PRI mounted their own press campaign. In 2014, charges had appeared that Mis and his family derived much of their income from importing and reselling dubiously sourced silver jewelry at his handicraft stores, and that they were evading federal taxes on the sale of precious metals (*Novedades Yucatán* 2014c). Though no formal charges ever seem to have been filed, state police confiscated several million pesos' worth of silver destined for one of Mis's stores. Close to a year later, at the height of the 2015 election season, state police attempted to detain Evelio Mis himself as he left town for an election event in one of the outlying villages of the municipality. Again, no formal arrests were made or specific charges filed. The questionable detention, which many Panistas in Pisté referred to as the attempted kidnapping of a political candidate, was filmed on smartphone cameras. Widely distributed on Facebook and uploaded to YouTube, it became a rallying cry during the election (*Periódico PorEso* 2015).

In the end, popular outrage about targeted armed harassment of a municipal candidate was not enough for the Panistas to overcome the united resistance of the federal government, the state's governor, and their own local rivals. The election was decided in San Felipe, Tohopkú, and Xcalakoop, three smaller communities in Tinum municipality. According to some locals, these comisarías had seen relatively little improvement during the six years in which Mis was the formal and de facto leader of the county. Some municipal buildings had received new veneers and a number of streets were paved each year. Mis personally purchased an expensive set of portable bleachers that could be set up for bullfights and rodeos at community fairs. But the kind of infrastructural investment that had transformed Pisté was far less evident in Xcalakoop, Tohopkú, San Felipe, and Yaxché. People in these communities, who travel frequently to Pisté to work, shop, visit a doctor, and attend secondary school could not ignore the contrast. For many voters, the Mis dynasty seemed no different from other municipal politicians insofar as it "abandoned" the outlying villages.[2]

Three years later, the faction associated with Evelio Mis was once again in power in Tinum under the administration of Evelio's daughter, Natalia Mis Mex. The Priísta municipal president who handed them a defeat in 2015 proved to be highly unpopular and seems to have failed at fortifying his base of support in the outlying villages. The 2018 election, during which municipal officials shared the ballot with candidates for the governorship and national presidency, proved to be even more violent than 2015. In early July 2018, Evelio Mis's campaign caravan was stopped in the village of San Francisco by PRI party militants from Pisté, who were supported by state police. The scuffle that resulted led to another attempted extrajudicial detention, this time with reports of shots being fired. Several Mis supporters were severely beaten, detained for hours in the back of a police vehicle, and threatened with shotguns and automatic rifles (*Diario de Yucatán* 2018a, 2018d). But when the votes were tallied, the violence that had occurred throughout the election cycle seemed to have galvanized the Panistas, and Natalia Mis was seated for her second term as municipal president.

The 2018 election also ended twelve years of PRI control of the Yucatecan statehouse, with the election of Panista Mauricio Vila Dosa. By then, the Maya Disneyland that had been planned for Dzonot Abán, and that contributed to the early phases of conflict between the Panistas of Pisté and two successive gubernatorial administrations, was largely forgotten. A new conflict developed around the Tren Maya megaproject that incoming president Andrés Manuel López Obrador intended to round the entire peninsula. This project, which I will discuss more in the conclusion of this book, seemed to be generating a growing opposition from the *evelista* camp. But then, of course, COVID-19 came and changed everything.

NEW VECTORS AND OLD FORMS OF RESISTANCE

In the opening pages of this book, I discussed the importance of approaching neoliberalism from comparative, national, and vernacular commonsense perspectives. The story of the Maya Disneyland offers some important examples of the intersection of all three. Closely tied to the branding and logistical support provided by the Xcaret Group, the original project embodied the "vectorial" iteration of tourism that became dominant in the region at the end of the millennium. This was itself representative of broader global transformations in the nature of capital, which place greater emphasis on intellectual property, intangibles like "eXperience," and the logistics of scheduling and transport.

When members of Mexico's political elite engage with this "vectorial" capitalism, they tend to adapt novel economic schemes to existing factional and partisan realpolitik. Ivonne Ortega Pacheco's interventions in "cultural infrastructure" served a dual purpose. Ostensibly, they helped to create synergies between the state and its "vectorialized" corporate partners. But just as important, Ortega Pacheco carved out an institutional space in which the state government could operate with relative autonomy from a federal government that was controlled by an opposition party. Through the proposed Maya Disneyland, this terrain of cultural infrastructure could benefit both the governor's corporate partners and more traditional rural clients in the municipality of Yaxcabá.

Both of the "vectorial" and clientelistic dimensions of this project ultimately ran aground on a series of institutions and historical memories with deep roots in the municipalities of Tinum and Yaxcabá. Whether or not members of the Ortega Pacheco administration were aware of the history of violence between the two municipalities, rivalry simmered in the collective memory of local residents. It likely compounded the outrage that many Pisteños felt over the negative infrastructure that the project would inflict on their local businesses. Vestiges of the early twentieth century also provided them with a powerful tool for resisting the governor's plan. Insofar as Panistas in Pisté can take credit for derailing the Maya Disneyland, it was through their use of formal agrarian institutions enshrined in the 1917 Constitution.

What about the common sense dimension of local communities' engagement with this instance of "vectorialized" neoliberal capital? In chapters 4 and 5, I discussed the mixture of agrarian heritage, ethnic identity, and neoliberal political theology with which many people in Pisté characterize the expansion of their political horizons since the 1970s. This heterodox perspective allows them to contest the state's claim to promote projects in the name of Maya culture, and to do so in the very language of capitalist development that has been a source of legitimacy for national and regional elites. These narratives help to legitimate the idea of local autonomy—both in terms of traditional agrarian territories and of entrepreneurial access to Chichén Itzá—that was at the heart of Evelio Mis's political successes.

This postpeasant identity, which incorporates traditional customs, the heritage of the Mexican Revolution, and more recent conceptions of entrepreneurialism, figured in some surprising forms of political expression in the conflicts of the 2000 and 2010s. As I mentioned earlier, social media took on an expanded role in municipal campaigns, enabling residents of Pisté and neighboring communities to publicize information and opinions that are not well-represented in the legacy press. However, the content and form of these communications, like the historical process that made them accessible to rural Yucatecans, follow patterns of mainstream media consumption that are very distinct from better-known examples of digital activism by Indigenous communities. This contestatory use of "mainstream" media, and its relationship to a longer history of rural communities' engagement with communications infrastructure, will be the focus of the next chapter.

7

FACEBOOK IN PISTÉ, OR DIGITAL POLITICS GOES MAINSTREAM

As I discussed in chapter 6, online social media played a role in publicizing different incidents in the conflict between the *evelista* municipal faction of Pisté and two successive Partido Revolucionario Institucional (Institutional Revolutionary Party, or PRI) governors. Still, most uses of social media in political campaigns in Pisté bear little resemblance to the communication strategies of internationally known Indigenous movements like the Ejército Zapatista de Liberación Nacional (Zapatista National Liberation Army, or EZLN), or to hashtag campaigns that gained prominence in Mexico in the 2010s. In fact, election-season content creation in the community remains consistent with patterns of online behavior that many of Mexico's public intellectuals associate with "mainstream" acquiescence to the country's state-friendly media environment. In this chapter, I will offer an alternative reading of this online political culture that situates it within a longer collective experience of expanding media infrastructure on the Yucatán Peninsula. Viewed within this context, "mainstream" patterns of media consumption become an integral part of the vernacular neoliberalism that shapes local politics on the periphery of Chichén Itzá.

Since the late 1990s, most discussions of Indigenous Mexicans' uses of the internet have begun with the EZLN movement of Chiapas. The EZLN's early successes in reaching global publics through emailed communiqués hinted at new means of circumventing the military might and media controls of authoritarian states (see Gómez Menjívar and Chacón 2018). During the waning years of the PRI's national hegemony, many academics interpreted this innovative media strategy as the creation of alternative spaces for solidarity and mobilization, and as a model for a new kind of social movement that was uniquely suited for the changing realities of a neoliberal world (Cleaver 1998; Nash 1997; Rob 2005, 132–38). The EZLN's use of media to generate alternative oppositional publics remains an inspiration to some more recent forms of urban hashtag activism.

Recent research has been more ambivalent about the politics of online media, noting more complicated intersections between Indigenous activism, corporate controlled media platforms, and disinformation in the age of Twitter, Facebook, and Instagram (see Lupien 2020). Roberto González's 2020 ethnography of the highland Zapotec community of Telea highlights some of these complexities. González documents how alliances between local leaders, global activists, and an NGO led to the creation of an autonomous community wireless network in 2013. This brought cellular connections to an area that major telecom companies considered too isolated to service. But despite its initial successes, this homespun network was ultimately replaced by service from a transnational conglomerate, just as the popularization of social media platforms exposed the community to patterns of digital consumption that threatened to undermine more traditional forms of sociality.

This more ambivalent portrait of digital media in Indigenous communities resonates with my own observations of municipal politics in the 2010s. As I will show in this chapter, social media users in Pisté seem to have relatively little interest in establishing the kinds of translocal solidarities that gave the EZLN global visibility. Many of the memes, denunciations, and event announcements that circulate online would not be intelligible beyond the geographical boundaries of the municipality of Tinum. Also, given that the town is located in a region that received early and extensive network coverage, there are no local parallels to the grassroots mobilization that "connected" Telea and other isolated communities in Oaxaca. Patterns for the adoption and use of cell phones in the communities on the periphery of

Chichén Itzá resemble those of more urbanized populations as much as they do those of isolated Indigenous communities in other parts of the republic.

Two factors of the "mainstream" politics of social media in Pisté and its neighboring communities will figure prominently in this chapter. First, most political posts seem to be directed at a local audience that is committed to the electoral processes whose history I have traced throughout this book. These tend to be individuals who identify with existing mainstream political parties, and whose networks of online debate and mobilization tend to be circumscribed by the traditional boundaries of municipal elections. Second, the most prolific political posters in Pisté and neighboring communities use Facebook almost exclusively, and tend to draw on themes and images from popular broadcast media. In so doing, they employ a platform and manipulate content that many Mexican critics associate with consumerism and with the ideological apparatus of the old authoritarian PRI. Thus, just as the geographical scale of most Pisteños' online political networks mirrors that of municipal partisanship, the form and content of their posts reflect their experience as local consumers of the most widely accessible commercial media.

While Pisté's Facebook users rarely seem to promote a radical departure from politics as usual, they do use national and global symbolic languages to politicize their daily reality. As I've discussed throughout this book, many local people associate the prosperity that came from their privileged place on the Highway 180 corridor with a political awakening that led them to question traditional forms of rural clientelism. Mainstream or not, contemporary patterns of social media use figure prominently in the performance of post-peasant identities that many Pisteños consider to be politically empowering.

In later sections of this chapter, I will provide brief sketches of the history of telephone and broadcast industries in Yucatán. Like the roads that connected towns and villages to Cancún, media infrastructure was an important symbol of modernity for rural Yucatecans. But unlike those scarce public goods, communications and entertainment media became readily accessible in rural communities when quasi-monopolistic private firms sought to expand their markets into the Mexican countryside. This privatized exception to the interplay of negative and positive infrastructure makes cell phone connectivity distinct from other experiences of development, and contributes to the particular role that it plays in the expression of local political identities. Before delving into the process that consolidated Mexico's quasi-monopolistic communications ecosystem, I will provide an ethnographic sketch of how I observed the expansion of these media in Pisté and neighboring communities over the course of twenty years.

When I began conducting fieldwork in 1997, the 1994 manifestos that catapulted the EZLN of Chiapas onto the global stage were as fresh in my mind as they were in those of millions of college students around the world. Like many of my peers from other US universities, I arrived in Mexico primed to look for emergent forms of digital activism in an increasingly "connected" countryside. But soon after I first arrived, the "Zapatista effect" (Cleaver 1998) began to seem like an exception to the vast digital divide that limited online access for rural Mexicans through the 1990s and early 2000s.[1]

In spite of its relative prosperity and prime location in the state's transport and communications infrastructure, the Pisté of the late 1990s was not a promising haven for anti-neoliberal cyberguerrillas. Cell phones were still a rare sight in the community, and only a few of the wealthier families in town had landlines. In emergencies, people could make calls from a public landline in the city hall or use card-operated payphones in the street. The latter were my primary means of making a weekly call home.

The lack of telephone options in a community of 5,000 reflected the broader situation in Mexico, where decades of notoriously inefficient monopoly by the state-owned Teléfonos de México (Telmex) were just coming to an end. Before 1996, Telmex users waited from three to six months for the installation of a connection after completing the initial applications process and fee payments (Santos Corral 2008, 59–60). The wait tended to be longer in rural communities, where basic phone cable installations were limited to downtown areas and were often more poorly maintained than their urban counterparts. Beyond the generally poor service, Telmex fee structures remained among the highest of any country from the earliest available records into the 2000s (Ordóñez and Bouchain 2011, 129). Fines to restore service that had been disconnected for lack of payment were also high, and clients often waited months to receive attention from technicians. Thus, most families that I knew in rural Yucatán avoided installing telephone service altogether during the landline era.

This lack of telephone use was particularly striking to me given the prevalence of other technologies in most homes. Even the poorer households that I visited had at least one television—often connected to cable—and a radio with cassette or compact disc player. Families owned stacks of bootleg VHS tapes and later DVDs, and the machines to play them on. But phone usage seemed to be a relatively uncommon experience for most people who weren't involved in hotel work, education, or local government. I remember one middle-class family laughing as they told me about a debate they had had before phoning birthday wishes to a brother who was living in Playa del Carmen in 1994 or 1995. One older lady in the family didn't speak much Spanish and was sure that her message would not be transmitted. She reasoned that the cables had been designed to transmit the sounds of the "national" language, and that the distinct phonology of Mayan would be garbled beyond comprehension in the process. Her children tried to convince her that this was not how telephones work, but she insisted on delivering her greetings in halting Spanish, just in case.

Email was even less familiar to most Pisteños at the end of the 1990s. I knew a few local teenagers and twenty-somethings who had opened email accounts as students in secondary and postsecondary schools in the city. But since there were no real options for checking their mail in their hometown, they almost never used them. That changed somewhat after 2000, when two cybercafés had opened in town. Besides traffic from tourists, these businesses catered to local teenagers who edited and printed homework assignments, downloaded music, played video games or visited friends from other towns in chatrooms. As late as 2000, I only knew a handful of well-off families who had internet connections in their home. But the *ciber* was well established as a place where teenagers would spend a few pesos for an hour's entertainment, just as their younger siblings would visit the arcade consoles outside of the larger grocery stores in town.

By 2002 or 2003, cell phones had become common in the community, and essentially made landlines obsolete. Telcel, a subsidiary of the vast holding company that purchased Telmex after its privatization in 1994, found a market niche in the later 1990s by offering pay-as-you-go services for a large and relatively low-income public (Ordóñez and Bouchain 2011, 196–201). Like most Mexicans, people in rural Yucatán paid some of the highest premiums for air time of anyone in the world in the 1990s and early 2000s (Ordóñez and Bouchain 2011, 150). But the relative ease of establishing a new cell phone line, and of reestablishing a connection after a lapse in payment, was a vast improvement over the local experience of landlines. For thousands of rural Yucatecan families that had never possessed a landline, the household phone became a blocky but remarkably durable dark blue Nokia device that was promoted by Telcel through the affordable pay-as-you-go Amigo plan.[2] By 2005 and 2006, I saw many people in the community using more expensive and fashionable flip phones, though these were always activated with the same plan as the blocky Nokia devices.

Home internet access was still rare in Pisté in the early 2000s, as it was in most of the rest of Mexico. I knew some young people who had designed personal web pages as part of their coursework in Valladolid, but who didn't invest much time in updating and maintaining them. Though members of local artisanry organizations and dance troupes might use email when communicating with clients, there seemed to be little motivation to establish an online presence through personal websites. A friend from Pisté who worked in the artisanry trade made this clear to me in 2004 when I suggested that he create a website to expand the customer base for his wholesale business. He dismissed the idea by observing that most business with buyers in the peninsula relied on one-to-one contacts and networking, and that the cost and inconvenience of shipping made retailing artisanry online too much of a hassle.

This lack of a viable conduit and economic rationale for creating online content changed with the local proliferation of smartphones around 2012. One of the most popular features of the new technology involved the ability to work around the high price of standard cell phone data by using wireless internet. Locals could easily log on to wireless hotspots in restaurants and hotels that catered to tourists, and free Wi-Fi was installed in the town hall and schools. Apps like WhatsApp and Facetime allowed smartphone users to make "calls" with wireless internet, thus saving precious minutes of prepaid cellular service.

Besides the well-established use of text messaging, Facebook was by far the most prominent dimension of Pisté's smartphone revolution. I remember months between 2013 and 2014 as a time when I got a flurry of "friend" requests from people that I knew in the community, and then from their friends in towns and villages throughout the state. By 2016, as twenty-four-year-old Marcelino Huchim from Tizimín told me, "Even the eighty-year-olds have Facebook." As an example of this, he cited a friend's elderly mother, who spent hours every day uploading images of her grandchildren and monitoring their online activities.

I interviewed several of my Facebook friends from Pisté, and some of their friends from other communities in the eastern part of the state, to get a better sense of what the transition to the new social media looked like from their perspective. Selena Cahuich and Ángela Dzul were in their late twenties when I interviewed them in 2016 and had been close friends since their teens. Both created their first online account in 2004 when they were secondary school students in Valladolid. Neither had a home computer or internet connection, so for the next decade they accessed these accounts at various cybercafés in Valladolid or their hometown of Pisté. Besides finishing school assignments, they mostly used the messenger function to chat with friends from school. After a brief experiment with several other short-lived platforms, Selena, Ángela, and most of their friends migrated to Facebook around 2009. They were impressed by their new ability to "meet" people outside of predetermined networks, and by the range of video and audio content that it was possible to share on the newer platform. Their activity was still limited to cybercafés in town until they bought their first smartphones, around 2013 or 2014.

Selena's husband Xavier May had a somewhat different trajectory to Facebook. He had been a late adopter of the internet, creating his first email account as a student at one of the private universities in Valladolid. Some of Xavier's friends at the university started a Facebook group around 2009, which was his first exposure to social media. Unlike most people I know in Pisté, Xavier had also experimented with Twitter. But, he said, he got bored with it and closed his account. "I'm the type of person who likes to observe [other people's posts], comment on them, 'like' them, that sort of thing. I'm not much into posting myself. And that's what Twitter is all about."

Of the group of friends, Ángela's husband José Juan Mo was the only one who first encountered social media outside of school. He confessed to having absolutely no interest in computers in his teens. When his peers were spending time in the *ciber*, he was busy building the handicraft business that he still runs today, and learning how to paint graffiti murals. He recalls being bemused when his friends asked him if he was on Facebook, recalling how funny the unfamiliar word was to him. "Feibook? Feisbook? What *is* that?" What pulled him in was the realization that many friends he had made at graffiti art events kept pages, which they used to set up events or to organize local clubs. Inside of a year, José Juan found that "se me pegó el vicio" (I became addicted) to the network, which he used to organize his own events in town.

José Juan Mo's characterization of his Facebook habit as an "addiction" is not surprising. In fact, a number of media outlets in Yucatán have reported on a moral panic related to "nomophobia," a psychological disorder that emerges from "addiction" to cell phones. A portmanteau of "NO MObile PHOone phoBIA," this term was coined in the United Kingdom in 2008 and has since gained some traction in the international clinical community (Bhattacharya et al. 2019). As reported in the Yucatecan press, symptoms include a compulsive dependence on screen time, a withdrawal from face-to-face activities, poor performance in work or school, and an excessive emotional attachment to the physical object of the cell phone (Díaz Navero 2014). Like the fear of bullying that I discussed in chapter 5, overidentification with a medium and technology forms part of a constellation of novel psychopathologies that are feared by many parents in Pisté and other rural communities.

The same week that I interviewed Selena, Javier, José, and Ángela, I realized that I had been visiting Pisté for nearly twenty years. I reflected back on my first field seasons, when I looked excitedly for the kind of digital activism that generated global solidarity for the EZLN. I was amused by the degree to which my expectations of Pisté had been shaped by a media narrative of "connectedness" that didn't reflect the technological and commercial realities of millions of rural Mexicans. This is not to say that there was not something inherently political behind many local uses of cell phones and social media. The sociality and conspicuous consumption that figured in my friends' Facebook use embodied a lifestyle that they and many of their neighbors consider to have liberated them from dependency on older forms of political clientelism. But this seemed like a distinctly neoliberal liberation, and one that had little need for transnational solidarity with students and activists from the Global North.

The dominant forms of social media use in Pisté also distanced community members from the cutting edge of online activism in 2010s Mexico. For many urban and university-educated Mexicans, including some prominent public intellectuals, Facebook was a far less prestigious platform than the former international "gold standard" of Twitter. Jenaro Villamil, a political journalist and longtime collaborator of the late Carlos Monsiváis, was one such prominent Twitter user. Since the mid-2000s, much of his writing has focused on the search for media alternatives to Televisa, the near-monopolistic television conglomerate with historical ties to the PRI.[3] For Villamil (2017, 107), as for many other Mexican authors, the 2012 Twitter movement known as #YoSoy132 was a pivotal moment that turned social media into a vessel with the potential to disrupt the PRI's stranglehold over mainstream broadcasting (see also Villamil 2017; Corona 2016; Rivera Hernández 2016; Rodríguez Cano 2015, 84–90).[4] Twitter, he argued, became "the ideal medium for sharing information, disseminating causes, generating debate, seeking justice, giving free play to humor and sarcasm, and shining a light on the errors of those in power" (Villamil 2017, 162). In contrast, Villamil (2017, 171–73) characterizes Facebook as a platform popular among consumerist youth, with an emphasis on promoting existing commercial brands and the personal "brands" of users.

It's not surprising that Villamil himself had been a very active Twitter user, with more than half a million followers. His attitude toward Facebook is common among the Mexican intelligentsia (see Rodríguez Cano 2015), including a Yucatecan colleague and close friend of mine who deleted his Facebook account a decade ago but remained active on Twitter until the Elon Musk takeover. When I mentioned my observations about social media use in communities like Pisté, he attributed the local preference for Facebook to a question of cultural capital. Like Villamil, he suggested that Facebook was the preferred platform of the consumerist masses, while more educated users preferred Twitter.[5]

Statements such as this equate the intellectual prestige that was once ascribed to certain corners of the Twitterverse to "authentic" political engagement. Based on my own experience, it *is* fair to say that Pisté is not hotbed of the kinds of hashtag activism associated with #YoSoy132 and other national-level mobilizations. But this may reflect the fact that the community's vibrant politics are intensely local, limiting the appeal of these larger online movements. Furthermore, the "consumerism" that is at the heart of Villamil's dismissal of Facebook is an aspect of postpeasant identities and vernacular neoliberalism that gives it a distinct local relevance. Facebook encourages users to put their choices in food, fashion, and lifestyle on display, a kind of conspicuous consumption that allows Pisteños to showcase the prosperity that resulted from their community's privileged place in the touristic infrastructure that developed since the 1970s. These celebrations of consumption may lack the pithy debate that Villamil and many other intellectuals once ascribed to Twitter, but they play a central role in many Pisteños' sense of having transcended rural poverty and the need to participate in the "old" style of clientelistic politics.

There is a common thread to Villamil's love of Twitter and my own early search for 1990s digital activism. Both are based on an expectation of rupture. Just as I had hoped to find a rupture from the traditionally local politics of rural Mexico, Villamil saw Twitter as a seismic rupture from Mexico's state-friendly media environment. Neither of these expectations is a good fit for the online experience of people in communities like Pisté, just as neither accurately reflects the political common sense that generations of local people have used to push against the undesirable impacts of economic development. In the next two sections, I will place the contemporary media culture of Pisté in a longer historical perspective, and highlight some of the shared experiences and cultural factors that make platforms like Facebook the site of a distinctive blend of consumerism and political engagement. At the heart of this is a relationship to media technology and content in which the expansion of quasi-monopolistic firms has delivered connectivity and entertainment in ways state investment and small-scale enterprise never could.

As I mentioned earlier, most families in Pisté were excluded, or chose to abstain, from telephone ownership until the 2000s. This lack of local connectivity reflected the limited development of telephony in the region during its first decades as a private industry, and its slow expansion after the later consolidation and parastatalization of Telmex. The "explosion" of cell phone and later smartphone usage resulted from the confluence of digital technology and a reprivatization of the industry in the neoliberal era.

As far as I have been able to determine, the very first telephone line to pass through Pisté was laid in 1910. That year, Edward Thompson, the Anglo-American adventurer and amateur archaeologist who had purchased the hacienda Chichén Itzá, wrote to the state legislature of Yucatán seeking permission to establish a telephone line on his property.[6] At the time, commercial telephones had existed in Mexico for twenty years.[7] However, phone ownership remained a luxury even in urban areas. By 1931, the Compañía Telefónica y Telegráfica Yucateca had added fewer than 700 lines to its service in the city of Mérida, which by then had over 96,000 inhabitants. The company's published directory only listed a few additional subscribers in the nearby port city of Progreso and the satellite town of Umán.[8]

A limited expansion of telephone access in rural Yucatán took place in tandem with the larger process of parastatal development that I discussed in chapter 2. Telmex was first consolidated as a private company in 1947 and received significant subsidies before coming under majority government ownership in the 1970s.[9] Whether in private or public hands, however, Telmex was a notoriously overpriced and inefficient company whose services remained out of reach for most rural consumers. By 1974, the state of Yucatán had just under 30,000 telephones, or just a little over three for every hundred inhabitants.[10]

As unpopular as Telmex was with much of the Mexican public, the 1989 privatization of the parastatal is often cited as one of the most controversial moments of the country's neoliberal transition.[11] Telmex was acquired by a holding company controlled by the Mexican industrialist and PRI stalwart

Carlos Slim Helú, who would be ranked as the richest person on Earth at several points between 2010 and 2014. In 2000, Slim's holding company founded América Móvil, the parent company of Telcel, Mexico's largest cell phone service provider.

Notwithstanding public criticisms of the privatization process, Mexico became a far more "connected" country in the Telcel era. Over the course of the 2000s and 2010s, Telcel consolidated an overwhelming market share, which allowed it to greatly reduce its own prices, much to the detriment of its smaller competitors.[12] Census data show that the number of cell phone lines in Yucatán grew 900 percent between 2002 and 2012, from roughly 8.6 to 80 lines for every hundred residents. Later surveys provided more fine-grained data, such as a 2018 study that tracked cell phone lines per number of citizens in each state in Mexico. Again, Mérida had the highest proportion of lines per capita in the state, with 110 lines for every hundred adult residents. However, the gap in telephone usage separating rural communities from the capital had reduced considerably, with 97 lines for every 100 residents when these were tallied for the state as a whole (*Novedades de Yucatán* 2014a).

The aggressive tactics that consolidated Telcel's overwhelming share of the national market helped transform Yukatek Maya speakers like the people of Pisté into the most "connected" Indigenous ethnic group in all of Mexico. Demand for cell service in the tourist sector, along with the explosion of cell phone use by workers who spent part of each week in their home communities, prompted the expansion of cellular infrastructure far beyond the major road corridors of the state. A major national survey found that the Mayan-speaking people of Yucatán were the Indigenous ethnic group with the greatest degree of access to 2G, 3G, or 4G cell phone connectivity, with at least 96 percent of the population having coverage.[13]

This level of connectivity presents a rare exception to the struggles over infrastructure that have been at the center of this book. Rather than being the result of negotiations between communities and state agencies that create public infrastructure, rural cellular access reflects the expansion of private capital beyond saturated urban markets to a new consumer base. Seen within the longer arc of Yucatecans' relationship with telephone technology, this phenomenon seems to—at least partially—vindicate privatization. Like the vast majority of Mexicans, rural Mayan speakers were excluded from telephone ownership during the first decades of the national industry. Telephone use did not grow that significantly during the eras of Stabilizing Development or parastatalization, even as the burgeoning tourism industry began to change local lifestyles. Telephones became a means of conspicuous consumption, and then an indispensable part of everyday life, when that newfound prosperity collided with the privatization of the notoriously inefficient company.

Here, contrasts with Nikhil Anand's discussion of water resources reflect important differences in both resource type and contexts of neoliberalization. Like the parastatal iteration of Telmex, Mumbai's formal institutions for water infrastructure are technically inefficient and difficult for the city's poorer residents to navigate. Faced with exclusion from legal access to a basic necessity, marginal urban dwellers employed a range of social networks and informal arrangements to exploit "leaks" in the system. For many of them, the established public infrastructure is viewed as preferable to emergent private providers, which entailed a tighter policing of now-commodified water resources (Anand 2017, 36). But unlike water, telephone and internet connections are a resource that people in communities like Pisté could choose to live without in the age of parastatal inefficiency. Like millions of other rural Mexicans, they were drawn into digital communications infrastructure when quasi-monopolistic firms lowered their rates to suppress competition and expand beyond saturated urban markets. However much local consumers complain about fees for airtime or the ill-gotten billions of Carlos Slim, the historical process of how they became so "connected" hinges on the privatization of Telmex. Thus, for many local consumers, the very experience of acquiring cell phone technology was consistent with the critique of inefficient parastatal industry that is at the heart of vernacular neoliberalism.

TELEVISION: MONOPOLIES OF
TECHNOLOGY AND CONTENT

In many ways, the history of the communications industry that made cell phones ubiquitous in Pisté mirrors that of the entertainment industry that influences the content that many local users post online. Like the telephone infrastructure that preceded Mexico's current digital network, national broadcast media developed in an environment that has favored state-friendly quasi-monopolies (see Castro 2016; and Hayes 2000). In this case, the national proliferation of radio and later television technology allowed the northern business magnate Emilio Azcárraga Vidarrueta to build a family empire that exists to this day. Since the 1930s, three successive generations of Azcárragas have filled the airwaves with content friendly to the Mexican state (see Castro 2016, 118–20, 203–5; and Hayes 2000, 70).

One significant way the history of broadcasting in Yucatán differs from that of telephones is in the early development of an independent regional tradition.[14] In the 1930s, the official radio station XEY, "La voz del Mayab," beamed political news and cultural programing from the headquarters of the Partido Socialista del Sureste (Socialist Party of the Southeast) in the city of Mérida (Echeverría 1999). Yucatecan authors tend to cite these first decades of radio in the state as playing an integral role in defining lo yucateco through the transmission of live performances of regional theater and the music of the state's most prominent trova performers (see Ocampo Escamilla 2000; see also Eiss 2017). This period of broadcasting was also notable for the early presence of Mayan-language content. In the late 1930s, the Academia de la Lengua Maya (Academy of the Mayan Language) coordinated with regional artists, educators, and anthropologists to broadcast La hora del campesino maya, which included traditional and modern songs, poetry, prose narrative, and lectures on utilitarian topics in the Yukatek language.[15] These early media helped translate older canons of regional culture into themes and aesthetics that are still evident in popular genres of music, theater, and standup comedy.

This independent era was short-lived. The first radio transmitters in Yucatán were locally built and had both a limited range and a limited ability to operate in adverse weather conditions. This changed in 1947, when the Yucatecan radio entrepreneur Perfecto Villamil Cicero entered into a partnership with the magnate Emilio Azcárraga Vidarrueta to import the RCA Victor equipment that would form the basis for Radio XEQW.[16] Regional music, humor, and news were still common on the airwaves. But by the 1950s, the most popular and widely accessible programing in the state also bore the commercial and ideological stamp of the Azcárraga dynasty.

By 1947, Mexico's industrialists and political leaders were also paying close attention to the development of television.[17] David Arceo (1948), the founder of the first major electronics store in Mérida, made his own exploratory trip to various broadcasting outlets in the United States, which he described in an article submitted to the Diario de Yucatán. As Arceo might have predicted, more than a decade passed before the technology proliferated on the peninsula. The first television station concessions in Mexico were granted by the federal government at the beginning of the 1950s, and Emilio Azcárraga Vidarrueta successfully outmaneuvered his rivals to consolidate Telesistema Mexicano, the precursor of Televisa (see Corral Corral 2006, 60; Hayes 2000, 116–20; and Pérez Espino 1979). This national company cofounded and operated the first commercial television broadcaster in the state of Yucatán, albeit with a significant input of capital from Mérida-based entrepreneurs.[18]

As many Mexican critics have observed, this corporate consolidation of media infrastructure went hand-in-hand with ideological consolidation of media content. The merger that created the modern Televisa conglomerate took place in the 1970s, just as President Luis Echeverría began asserting greater censorship pressure on national media (González de Bustamante 2012, 177–90; see also Smith 2018, 67–70). The Azcárraga family responded to these pressures with a series of policy changes that consolidated executive control over news content, guaranteeing favorable coverage for the PRI for decades to come (Fernández and Paxman 2013, 201–3). The privatization of Mexico's remaining state-owned television stations in the early 1990s created an opening for the rise of a new conglomerate named TV Azteca. But, as Villamil (2017) notes, the new conglomerate was quickly drawn into a similar political symbiosis, establishing a comfortable duopoly of ideologically consistent mainstream media. By the turn of the millennium, Televisa and TV Azteca controlled 97 percent of television transmissions in Mexico.

This media duopoly still commands a large portion of the attention of rural people in states like Yucatán. A 2022 national survey showed that television sets were the most common electronic appliance in Yucatecan homes, with 92.6 percent of households owning at least one. This is slightly above the national average of 91.6 percent (¡Por Esto! 2022). Mainstream nationally produced content seems to dominate the viewing habits of much of this population. A 2018 survey found that a solid majority of Yucatecans reported that they preferred to view the "free" national chains of Televisa/TV Azteca affiliates, with only around 17 percent getting most of their visual entertainment or educational content from phones or computer devices. The roughly 30 percent of the population who prefer foreign or alternative television programming enjoy this through paid services, implying that consumption of Televisa/TV Azteca content tilts even more heavily toward the rural and urban poor (Diario de Yucatán 2018e).

When public intellectuals like Genaro Villamil decry the viewing habits of most Mexicans, it is with an eye to the presumably low-quality and politically enervating content that the duopoly delivers to this large population. The steady stream of musical variety shows, professional sports, and mass-produced soap operas is a target of critics ranging from some of the country's most influential public intellectuals to the rap-metal group Molotov (Mejía Madrid 2013; Monsiváis 1997). In a 1993 interview, Televisa president Emilio

Azcárraga Milmo seemed to recognize and dismiss these critiques when he famously stated, "Mexico's working class is fucked, and will always be fucked. The obligation of television is to give those people entertainment that takes them out of their sad reality and difficult future" (quoted in Fernández and Paxman 2013, 478).

Given this blunt admission, it is little surprise that so many critical intellectuals bear a strong suspicion of forms of popular expression that draw from the nation's mainstream media. However, given the collective memory of rural poverty that is relatively fresh for many families in Pisté, indulging in forms of entertainment associated with the urban working class has a more complicated symbolic resonance. Furthermore, these same escapist entertainments are often rearticulated in surprising ways in local humor and political discourse. This is particularly evident in the jokes, memes, and insults that permeate Pisté's Facebook during political elections, which will be the focus of the next section.

RURAL MEME CULTURE AND POLITICAL COMMENTARY

Part of the political impact of Facebook in Pisté stems from its blending of the escapist traditions of Mexican entertainment media with explicitly partisan content during the tense months around electoral campaigns. As most of the people I interviewed acknowledged, stories, memes, and other content posted and shared online are not usually serious business. The most common phrases used to describe them was that they "dan risa" (provoke laughter) and were a common means of pranking friends. Marcelino Huchim, whom I interviewed in 2016, described one of the most popular memes of that year. "I have a cousin named Juan [who is on Facebook]. Then I find an image of an unattractive person online, and I add the text, 'Does anyone here know Juan? I'm looking for Juan.' Then I post it on his page and watch everyone 'Like' and comment on it."[19]

Other popular jokes poke fun at local lifestyles and reference shared experiences behind the town's culture of consumerism. Given the local popularity of Televisa and TV Azteca, it is no surprise some of the most popular macro memes include well-known characters from mainstream programming. One that I saw repeatedly between around 2015 and 2020 involves the actress Delia "Macaria" de la Cruz in her role from the popular comedy *Vecinos*, in which she plays a working-class woman with humorously deluded class pretensions. The meme superimposes text over an image of the actress in character, and refers to some object with her catchphrase "carísima, por cierto" (very expensive, of course!). With that meme, inexpensive foods like Dondé breakfast crackers, household implements like hand-crank mills, or low-end clothing brands that are familiar to residents of rural communities are ironically referred to as "carísimos, por cierto" (*La Prensa Gráfica* 2018).

Other popular memes that circulated in the 2010s bore sentimental echoes of the regional musical, theatrical, and humoristic traditions that have been a mainstay of regional Televisa affiliates since the 1940s. A popular set of memes focused on an evocative image of a "traditional" Yucatecan activity—from sleeping face down in a hammock to playing with a hand-carved wooden top—with the caption "If you don't know what this is, you didn't have a childhood." Other "local color" memes give a Yucatecan spin on globally known macro images. For example, the popular "Bad Luck Brian" image macro is often captioned with references to stereotypically Yucatecan activities that cause suffering to the blonde teenager. In one example, Bad Luck Brian eats *guaya* fruit with lime and chili powder, only to suffer from *chotnak'*, a Mayan word for diarrhea with painful stomach cramps.

This Mayan-language punchline at the expense of a very gringo-looking Bad Luck Brian touches upon a tradition of vernacular humor that is a mainstay of regionally themed shows in mainstream broadcast media. In many popular standup routines and skits, characters with thick Yucatecan accents, often dressed in stereotypical Indigenous clothes, misunderstand urban customs or modern technology. In most cases, the nature of the rural person's "misunderstanding" sets up a joke that will be made at the expense of a non-Maya character (see Armstrong-Fumero 2009a, 2009b). Bad Luck Brian's chotnak' evokes a common gag in such routines, in which a city person or foreigner has no choice but to eat local foods that are unfamiliar to them, and suffers the inevitable digestive consequences.

Another macro meme that draws from this popular tradition involved an image of two older women in typical Maya clothing chatting in a municipal market while staring into a smartphone. These women are often referred to as "las tías" (the aunties) by people in Pisté. In one iteration of the meme, the text had one auntie asking the other what the acronym WTF meant. Apparently reading the context of the cryptic acronym, the other auntie replied that it meant "Way! 'Ta feo!" a colloquial Spanish-Mayan phrase meaning "Yikes! That's ugly!"[20] The aunties' resignification of the digital anglicism embodies the playful appropriation and rearticulation of global culture that is at the heart of local engagements with social media (see Milner 2016).

In interviews that I conducted and in informal conversations, it's clear that most people enjoy memes like these as a light form of entertainment.

The fact that they draw on characters and themes that are familiar from the most widely consumed types of television media makes them relatable to a broad audience. By extension, these familiar characters and themes helped rapidly transform the macro meme into a genre of humor that is broadly intelligible and enjoyable in the community.

Light entertainment is not necessarily apolitical. Explicitly partisan versions of these memes already seemed common by the time I began adding people from Pisté as Facebook "friends." People I've asked suggest that this trend began around the 2012 election. That would place the origins of this practice very early in the explosion of local smartphone use. It also situates the origin of Pisteños' political memes in the same historical moment as the nationally famous #YoSoy132 campaign. While Twitter and #YoSoy132 don't seem to have gained much traction on the peripheries of Chichén Itzá, local Facebook users were marshalling familiar images from mainstream media to comment on their own political realities.

Like Bad Luck Brian's case of chotnak', some popular election-year memes use internationally recognizable themes and characters. One popular image macro is a version of the Kermit the Frog "But it's none of my business" meme that first appeared in English in 2014. In the anglophone original, an image of Kermit sipping tea is accompanied with some critical political observation followed by the sarcastic phrase "But it's none of my business" (see Shifman 2013). The Spanish-language versions that I have seen from Yucatán have a somewhat different structure, with the text usually reading, "A veces pienso en X, pero entonces recuerdo Y, y se me pasa" (Sometimes I think about doing X, but then I remember Y and I get over it). Some iterations that I have seen during election seasons include comments like "Sometimes I think about voting for the PRI, but then I remember the 200 pesos I now get monthly, and I get over it."[21] This is a reference to different forms of public assistance that are often "politicized" in rural communities, giving families affiliated with the party currently in power early or preferential access. Other examples take the form of humorous ad hominem attacks against candidates or party activists. One example from the highly contested four-party race of 2018 had Kermit saying that "Sometimes I think of going to a PRD [Partido de la Revolución Democrática, or Party of the Democratic Revolution] party meeting, but then I remember how badly Don Chucho Tamay [a local party leader] plays the keyboard at the rallies, and I get over it."[22]

Besides the use of internationally popular image macros, producers of political memes often use images or video stills of actual local events. In 2015, for example, several public Facebook groups posted memes based on photos of local operatives who were allegedly caught in flagrante delicto illegally distributing gifts to potential voters.[23] That same year, following the attempt to detain the candidate Evelio Mis, a number of memes circulated using image stills of two of the state police who were filmed during the incident.[24] The humorous captions tended to echo the phrasing, or even repeat jokes, taken from popular television comedians.

While these memes employ much of the same broad humor that is popular in nonpolitical posts, the fact that many include images and names of local political figures does bring an additional layer of risk in a close-knit community. In 2015, backlash against the attempted arrest of Evelio Mis resulted in several roadblocks and other confrontations between local Panistas, Priístas, and the state police. Given this volatile political environment, some of the most active creators of political memes rely on the anonymity offered by Facebook to post material through accounts with cryptic names like "Anonymous Pisté" and "The Circus of Evelio." The detailed local knowledge displayed in their content—from the names of political figures and businesses to references to local events that happened hours before a particular meme first appeared—makes it clear that the users are residents of Pisté or nearby communities. But many dress their online personae with familiar images from international hacker and troll culture, such as the Guy Fawkes mask of the Anonymous movement and Heath Ledger's Joker character from 2008's *The Dark Knight*.

Many of the behaviors in which these incognito posters engage, from posting abusive text to stating contrarian opinions for the sheer joy of offending more "mainstream" users, are consistent with what English speakers would refer to as trolling. None of the people I interviewed were familiar with the term "trolling" or any Spanish- or Mayan-language equivalent; instead they simply referred to these behaviors as "rudeness" (*grosería* in Spanish; *poch* in Mayan). As Ángela Dzul commented when I interviewed her, the whole point of creating digital alter egos was to be able to post outrageous things while minimizing the risk of social repercussions. She found this aspect of online behavior to be somewhat cowardly but admitted that the content of the anonymous accounts was some of the most entertaining for casual political observers like herself.

The role of these anonymous accounts in Pisté's digital ecosystem embodies a distinctive intersection of the local and cosmopolitan. The use of digital platforms, like the appropriation of symbols from international troll and hacker culture, references the global nature of the digital media of which Pisteños have become avid consumers. However, the specific characters and events referenced by these messages tend to be so local that they would be unintelligible to audiences from other regions of Mexico, let alone other countries. Unlike the Zapatista-esque communications that I had hoped to find in the 1990s, these subversive posters use a cosmopolitan "cultural style" (see Ferguson 1999) to produce content for a decidedly local audience.

In some cases, these desires to inhabit the role of a troll or hacker collide with the realities of local politics. This was the case with a poster who went by the handle of El Vato Donald ("Donald Dude," a play on Pato Donald or Donald Duck).[25] El Vato Donald was a supporter of Evelio Mis, and a passionate critic of the Priísta municipal administration that ousted him in 2015. His exposé of several embarrassing incidents that had occurred in the municipal offices suggested that he was somehow connected to the local leadership. For most of that year, my friends debated which of their neighbors was behind the account. The mystery was solved one evening, when a young man was detained by local police on a minor charge. His cell phone, which was confiscated, had been left open with no password protection. As the local police curiously skimmed his Facebook feed, they quickly realized that the man in their cell was none other than the troll that had been heaping insults on the municipal president, his allies, and the state police units. El Vato Donald suddenly found himself surrounded by a hostile crowd that bullied and threatened him to the point that he deleted his account and promised to stay off of social media before being sent on his way. Over the next several days, a few of the other PAN-sympathizing (Partido Acción Nacional, or National Action Party) anonymous accounts posted tributes to their "fallen" comrade. However much they might adopt the aesthetics of global online cultures, the political realities in which they try to intervene are too local for true anonymity.

THE ONLINE REVOLUTION THAT DIDN'T HAPPEN

Considered in contrast to the early EZLN communiqués or #YoSoy132, the Facebook culture of Pisté and neighboring communities does not seem particularly subversive, let alone transformative. In many ways, its prominence in local politics reflects the larger capitalist forces that have transformed the region since the construction of Cancún, and that accelerated after Mexico's national neoliberal turn. The cellular infrastructure that provides online access to rural Yucatecans emerged through an expansion of privatized cell phone markets into rural areas. Much of the visual and narrative content of local Facebook is drawn from sentimentalized aspects of regional culture and other elements of Mexico's most mainstream media. Both of these industries, the cellular infrastructure and media content consumed by local users, were shaped by quasi-monopolies that were historically friendly to the authoritarian PRI.

But as with other aspects of consumerism, Pisté's Facebook obsession is a component of the lifestyles that many local people associate with their "liberation" from older forms of political clientelism. In some respects, the meme as a cultural form is an apt metaphor for the relationship of vernacular neoliberalism to the larger historical processes through which rural Yucatecan communities negotiate their relationship to the modernizing state and national business elites. The communication scholar Ryan Milner (2016, 2) has characterized memes and mimetic communication as a form of "participation by reappropriation" through which communities of users produce a "vast cultural tapestry" of ever-mutable meaning (see also Dynel 2016; Shifman 2013). Many people in Pisté have reappropriated the political theology of neoliberalism to articulate locally meaningful claims on economic opportunity and political autonomy. During elections, even "mainstream" social media can become a site for challenging the economic and political actors who seek to exclude Pisteños from the sources of local prosperity.

"Participation by reappropriation" is also an apt metaphor for an adaptation to neoliberalism that differentiates Pisté and many other Maya communities in Yucatán from those in regions that have seen more grassroots Indigenous activism (see Mattiace 2013). One of the most prominent academic interpretations of the origin of the EZLN involves the neoliberal unravelling of the Revolutionary pact between the state and Indigenous communities. The loss of state protections of peasant agriculture created the pressures that eventually led thousands of Indigenous people to armed revolt in the state of Chiapas (see Collier and Quaratiello 1999). But by 1994, a generation of Mayan-speaking Yucatecans had already witnessed the rise of the tourist economy amid the concurrent decline of state-sponsored agriculture. These communities still face pervasive racial and socioeconomic exclusion. But their experience of a regional precursor of Mexico's neoliberal transition gave rural Yucatecans space to appropriate aspects of these new regimes of labor and consumption, and to adapt traditional means of political agency to new realities. In the conclusion, I will turn to events in the 2020s that once again tested these local traditions.

Conclusion

POLITICS AS USUAL
AND THE FOURTH
TRANSFORMATION

In 2018, I arrived in Mexico City in time to hear the celebrations that accompanied the election of President Andrés Manuel López Obrador (AMLO), whose Tren Maya megaproject set the stage for the incidents with which I opened this book. For well over a decade, AMLO had been a persistent figure in the national political scene as a left-leaning critic of Mexico's endemic corruption and the neoliberal consensus of *prianismo*. His popularity among youth and self-identified progressives had led to numerous comparisons to the popularity of Bernie Sanders in the United States. But this superficial similarity hides a more complex, and more distinctly Mexican, political trajectory.

AMLO was among a generation of left-leaning Partido Revolucionario Institucional (Institutional Revolutionary Party, or PRI) politicians who defected to form the Partido de la Revolución Democrática (Party of the Democratic Revolution, or PRD) in the late 1980s. He failed to win the Mexican presidency as the candidate of the PRD in 2006 and 2012. In each case, he refused to accept the legitimacy of election results and staged high-profile

179

protests against a system that seemed to guarantee the continued dominance of *prianismo*. By the 2018 election, he had abandoned the PRD and transformed his civic organization, the Movimiento de Regeneración Nacional (Movement for National Regeneration, or MORENA), into an electoral party. This resulted in a series of defections from mainline parties that led to a larger reconfiguration of the national electoral landscape. The PRD, facing a rapid descent into irrelevance, took the unprecedented step of joining an electoral coalition with the right-of-center Partido Acción Nacional (National Action Party, or PAN). This coalition was generally referred to as the Frente Ciudadano por México (Citizens Front for Mexico).[1] In another surprising move, groups closely associated with the Ejército Zapatista de Liberación Nacional (Zapatista National Liberation Army, EZLN) of Chiapas shifted from their historical position of rejecting Mexico's formal electoral system to field an independent candidate for the presidency. Though the traditional doctor and activist María de Jesús "Marichuy" Patricio did not gather enough signatures to appear on the ballot, her brief campaign embodied a confluence of Indigenous rights, feminism, and environmentalism that would continue to generate criticism from AMLO's left (Corona 2018).

In spite of this reconfiguration of legacy parties and the activist Left, AMLO and MORENA won a decisive victory in 2018, capturing not only the presidency but a strong majority in the federal Congress. For millions of his supporters, this initiated what the president had christened as the "Fourth Transformation." Often shortened to "4T," this project is framed as a peaceful transformation that would bring changes no less radical than those won during the independence struggle of 1810–21, the Reform Wars of the mid-nineteenth century, and the Revolution of 1910. The implication was that the end of single-party rule in 2000 had failed to fundamentally transform a flawed political system that had been consolidated over seven decades of authoritarianism. This, along with reasserting an interventionist role for the public sector, is precisely what AMLO and MORENA proposed to do (see Meyer 2021).

In 2018, the partisan realignment of the 4T seemed somewhat less transformative in Pisté and other rural Yucatecan communities. The two-party hegemony that AMLO hopes to ultimately displace proved very persistent in the state. Yucatán emerged from the 2018 election cycle with a Panista governor, a Priísta majority in the state legislature, and only 3 out of 106 municipal presidents representing MORENA. Unsurprisingly, given these trends, the municipal government of Tinum remained in the hands of the PAN, whose principal local opponent consisted of a demoralized but still active PRI.

When I visited Pisté in 2023, however, things had changed significantly. I found the downtown hotels, which had been moribund for decades, packed with long-term renters. But in this case, the renters were hundreds of engineers and laborers attached to the Tren Maya megaproject that was quickly taking shape in the bushland between downtown and the toll highway to the north. These changes in the physical landscape were mirrored in a restructuring of local politics. The charismatic leader Evelio Mis had once again distanced himself from the PAN, and it was rumored that he was hoping to launch a new campaign for the municipal presidency under the aegis of MORENA. The party of AMLO, all but invisible locally in 2018, now boasted a large following in the municipality.

In the section that follows, I will provide a sketch both of how the Tren Maya has impacted the local economy of the communities on the periphery of Chichén Itzá and of how this has shaped the growing partisan realignment and other strategies of local political engagement. Organized by Evelio Mis and other local political figures, people in Pisté employed many of the same tools for deriving economic and political benefit from infrastructural projects that I have discussed in previous chapters. These strategies met with mixed success, but the results seem to have underscored the necessity of direct involvement with AMLO's political party, MORENA. The need to engage with MORENA also reflects the perception that the Tren Maya and related 4T projects are being completed more quickly, and impacting local life sooner, than similar projects that had been proposed and canceled in the previous decades.

At present, it's impossible to gauge the full economic and political impact of AMLO's sexenio, let alone that of his successor, Claudia Sheinbaum Pardo. But based on the patterns of political engagement that I have described throughout this book, it is possible to offer some conjectures. I will close this book with a discussion of how some of the more likely outcomes would impact the economic and political life of rural communities in the peninsula, and how this relates to the broader themes of infrastructural development and political engagement that I have discussed throughout this text.

THE FOURTH TRANSFORMATION MEETS
THE GHOSTS OF PROJECTS PAST

In September 2018, the López Obrador administration unveiled the Tren Maya as a project that would "detonate" tourism in the southeast of Mexico. The proposed route would link the archaeological site of Palenque in the state of Chiapas to several towns in the neighboring state of Tabasco before veering north through Campeche to the city of Mérida. From there, it would take a route roughly parallel to the Highway 180 corridor to Cancún, from where it will continue south along the Riviera Maya, parallel to the Caribbean coast. Perhaps most surprising, the final portion of the circuit will run west from Chetumal to Escárcega in southern Campeche, running roughly parallel to the little-traveled Highway 186 to complete a circuit around the peninsula.

Even more surprising than the scale of the project was the claim that it was meant to be completed in 2023, well ahead of the end of AMLO's sexenio. Any rural Yucatecan who was alive during the completion of the three original transpeninsular roads would be justified in viewing this prediction with skepticism. The routes that were decreed by Cárdenas in the mid-1930s were not even nominally completed until the 1950s and 1960s. Since then, the generations of rural people who have requested better roads linking their communities to larger arteries have become accustomed to the public mantra that resources for infrastructure are very limited in Mexico. Many, like the residents of Popolá and other villages in the municipality of Yaxcabá, would resort to pleading with the governor in the press, and even then they had to invest years of their own time and labor for rudimentary roads. Several friends of mine who had voted for AMLO confessed to me that the overly ambitious reveal of the Tren Maya was the moment when they began to question whether the new candidate was really so different from his *prianista* opponents.

More recent history justified some of these doubts. The idea of a new transpeninsular train route linking Yucatán to Quintana Roo had first been presented to the public during Ivonne Ortega Pacheco's (2007–12) tenure as governor (see Schettino 2022, 109–11). I remember discussion of the project, popularly referred to as a "bullet train," by skeptical friends in Pisté in 2010. They compared it to the toll highway connecting Cancún to Mérida that had been constructed parallel to the original Highway 180 in the 1980s. Though it is used today by tourists and some bus companies, the toll highway failed to generate the income promised to the investors who helped finance it, and became an *elefante blanco* (white elephant). That is, the toll road is an expensive, overbuilt project whose final results fell far from those promised by the officials who first proposed it. As critics in the press have noted, the construction of the new road *did* prove profitable to construction and heavy transport companies closely tied to Víctor Cervera Pacheco and his allies. In 2010, locals reasoned that the "bullet train" would face a similar fate, particularly as it would compete with both the toll road and the original High-way 180 for travelers. But however limited its impact on day-to-day transport and commerce, the construction of this new white elephant was likely to line the pockets of relict Cerveristas in the resurgent PRI.

Despite popular skepticism, the 2010 bullet train project continued to figure prominently in Ortega Pacheco's press releases and public speeches. It even became a campaign promise of future president Enrique Peña Nieto during his electoral tour of Yucatán. Ultimately, however, the funding nec-essary for the project never materialized. Former members of the governor's administration observed that Ivonne Ortega Pacheco had been aware for years of studies that proved that the project was financially unfeasible. Not even a white elephant, the questionable train project never existed outside of political speeches and the skeptical public imagination (*Novedades Yucatán* 2015).

Like many of my friends in Pisté, I processed AMLO's 2018 promise through the memory of this earlier, "unfeasible" bullet train. But several years passed, and my own skepticism receded with each story I read in the newspaper. By April 2020, work had begun on modernizing and upgrading several existing train stations that would service the new route. In May, the private firms that had won bids to construct different spans of the route were announced. By June, construction began on two major spans of the project. The first, linking Palenque to the town of Escárcega in southern Campeche, would be developed in cooperation with the Consorcio Mota Engil, a Mexican subsidiary of a transnational infrastructure conglomerate based in Portugal (*Expansión* 2020). This linked to a second span that had been awarded to Grupo Carso, the holding company that had allowed Carlos Slim to purchase majority shares in Telmex and build the quasi-monopoly that turned him into one of the wealthiest people on the planet (*Forbes México* 2020).

AMLO's early critics, particularly those associated with the Frente Ciudadano por México (Citizens Front for Mexico) coalition of 2018, characterized the train as an ill-conceived pharaonic project that was sure to generate vast debt with minimal social benefits. The economist and politi-cal analyst Macario Schettino observed that ambiguities about the purpose of the project—variously characterized as serving the needs of the tourism industry or regional manufacturing—cast doubt on the planning behind the enterprise. Even in the likely scenario that its use would focus on the tourism industry, the Tren Maya would require an average of 16,000 to 25,000 daily passengers to be cost-effective. The availability of several alternative—and likely less expensive—transport options cast doubt on the sustainability of this level of use (Schettino 2022, 110–12).

Equally strident criticisms emerged from the Mexican left. Mirroring earlier protests over the construction of roads in Chiapas (Otto 2018), the EZLN stated that it would oppose a project that would ride roughshod over Indigenous territories and cause untold ecological damage (Lichtinger and Aridjis 2018; *Proceso* 2021). Environmentalists were critical of the impacts on fragile coastal and inland forest landscapes, and archaeologists of the inevitable damage to pre-Hispanic sites. Still, by the beginning of 2020, the federal agencies charged with planning the Tren Maya had manufactured a degree of consent among local stakeholders. Or, at least, they had created a simulacrum of consent. A series of public consultations held in late 2019 in communities that would be impacted by the construction showed overwhelming support for the project. This, however, was panned in the media after the Mexican offices of the UN Commission for Human Rights criticized the consultation process. Chief among the problems highlighted were the quality of translation of questionnaires into Indigenous languages and a lack of explicit mention of potential harms caused by the train and its construction. The commission also observed the overall low turnout of respondents, and particularly of Indigenous women (*El Universal* 2019). Despite this criticism, the AMLO administration remained bullish about the supposedly overwhelming support that the project enjoyed among affected communities.

One group that AMLO and his administration actively lobbied were the ejidatarios of Pisté and the formidable local political figure Evelio Mis. In doing so, MORENA representatives waded into older conflicts over local land use and access to tourist sites. In the winter of 2020, members of Pisté's ejido were in the process of constructing a stand for the sale of souvenirs near the archaeological zone. In late February, they were issued a federal cease-and-desist order over damages to the local forest ecosystem. In response, Evelio Mis and the ejidal committee expressed their opposition to the use of their town's communal lands for the Tren Maya, a public protest that the 23 February edition of the *Diario de Yucatán* (2020b) declared to be a "break" with the project. If the people of Pisté could not build on land that they considered to be their own, neither could AMLO.

By turning to their control of the ejido, Mis and his collaborators employed the same political gambit they had used to confront the "Maya Disneyland," which had set the stage for escalating violence during the local elections of the late 2010s. However, in 2020, the state and federal governments were more open to negotiation with local political leaders and their constituents.

Along with promises to respect the rights of ejidatarios to use of lands on the periphery of the train project, MORENA representatives reiterated earlier offers to create a small public university in the town of Pisté. By the late fall of 2020, Pisté's Universidad del Bienestar Benito Juárez had its first director, who was actively negotiating with the municipality and ejido for a plot of land on which to build the facilities.

In the end, the COVID-19 epidemic may have done as much to improve Pisté's acceptance of the Tren Maya as direct negotiations with MORENA. By mid-March, the archaeological site of Chichén Itzá closed to visitors, devastating the local economy. On 29 September, ¡Por Esto!, the Priísta organ that is typically hostile to Evelio Mis and his collaborators, interviewed locals in Pisté regarding their "divided" opinions on the train project. Mis himself expressed a cautious optimism about the Tren Maya. Though he harbored lingering concerns about the degree to which local workers would benefit directly from the new station, any increase in tourist traffic would be welcome as the community recovered from the closure of Chichén Itzá. Other local residents interviewed for the piece were more or less hopeful, but they also tempered their optimism with the assumption that the primary beneficiaries of the train project would be the large tourism chains, like Xcaret.

Work on the train continued at a surprisingly brisk space, pandemic notwithstanding. On 4 June 2020, the *Diario de Yucatán* (2020a) announced the completion of AMLO's tour of work sites for the initial span, which passed through the states of Chiapas and Tabasco en route to the southwest of Campeche. It was declared that work on the train would generate 80,000 jobs in 2020 alone, with close to half a million being generated over the three years of labor on the project. For those old enough to remember the construction of Cancún, these promises bore an echo of the promises of job creation and economic multipliers that had accompanied that megaproject a half century earlier. But instead of appealing to the hopes of the federally dependent agrarian region of the 1960s, the Tren Maya was being marketed to struggling voters in a once-thriving tourism economy where the effects of Xcaret's near monopoly had dovetailed with the closures of COVID-19. AMLO actually spent the night in the town of Pisté in late October 2020 before making an official visit to a work site adjacent to the Mérida-Cancún highway. In an interview published in the *Diario* on 12 October, he declared that, notwithstanding the delays caused by the pandemic, construction would be completed before the end of his sexenio.

Pisteños were slowly, and painfully, recovering from the initial pandemic closure of major tourist sites when a new blow landed. As the *Diario de*

Yucatán reported in October 2022, a plan had emerged to build a station for the Tren Maya beyond the eastern extreme of the town's commercial district, leading tourists bound for Chichén Itzá to bypass locally owned businesses entirely. Though the town's Panista municipal president stated her displeasure with this new development, she suggested that higher-ups in the state's party hierarchy had instructed her not to interfere (*Diario de Yucatán* 2022). Although her official statement to the newspaper leaves the rationale for this noninterference vague, it is likely that state-level negotiations for the development of the train offered some concession to PAN-affiliated interests from outside of the municipality.

So, at the start of 2023, the residents of Pisté were cut off from the promise of direct commercial benefits from the Tren Maya. The participation of wealthy tourism operators in the planning of the new station was a worrying sign of other forms of negative infrastructure that could be inflicted by subsequent developments of this new transit route. Worse still, the Panista municipal president's refusal to intervene damaged the reputation of what had become the town's dominant political party.

Some of the contours of the next round of state-level elections, set for June 2024, were already taking shape when I visited Pisté in 2023. Over the 2022 holiday season, accusations emerged that high-ranking Instituto Nacional de Antropología e Historia (National Institute of Anthropology and History) officials at Chichén Itzá were charging tourists thousands of pesos a head for exclusive nighttime or early morning access to iconic structures. These tours were in clear violation of the laws that govern the archaeological site from which most of the local population derives its income. Worse still, the violators in this case appeared to be the same federal officials who enforce rules and regulations on local vendors within the archaeological zone. By the second week of January 2023, a coalition of tour guides, ejido members, and artisanry vendors blockaded the federal road into the archaeological site, demanding the firing of those officials. Some of their spokespersons included representatives of the small but growing MORENA organization in Tinum County. They also included the charismatic local leader Evelio Mis, who was sidelined by the state-level PAN in 2021 (*Diario de Yucatán* 2023a; 2023b). This protest touched on grievances beyond the corruption of Instituto Nacional de Antropología e Historia officials, and seemed like a broader preelectoral flexing of political muscle. By early 2023, there was open speculation that Evelio Mis was seeking a new source of formal political endorsement as a representative of the 4T.

I watched the June 2024 election returns from Massachusetts and missed the celebrations that marked the election of Mexico's first female president, the *morenista* Claudia Sheinbaum. Mirroring the dramatic Panista sweep of 2000, Joachín "Huacho" Díaz Mena also won the governorship of the Yucatán for MORENA. Switching between the major newspapers and my Facebook feed, I also learned that Evelio Mis won his municipal election in 2024 as a candidate for the Partido Verde Ecologista de México (Green Environmentalist Party of Mexico), which was part of MORENA's national electoral coalition. Cementing the family's hold on local politics, his daughter Natalia Mis was elected to the state congress on the same ticket.

The Mis dynasty's return to power under new party affiliation reflects a statewide realignment that took place over the course of AMLO's sexenio, and that was evident in my 2023 visit to Pisté. Besides AMLO's popularity as a reformer of national bureaucracies and tax codes, the party and its affiliates were bolstered by high-profile defections from legacy parties. These included the now-governor-elect Joaquín "Huacho" Díaz Mena, a seventeen-year veteran of the PAN who had held several congressional posts at the state and federal level. For years, I had heard him mentioned as an important party elder who was highly respected by old-guard Panistas in Pisté. Frustrated by the lack of party support for his planned senatorial campaign, he defected to MORENA in 2018 and became a prominent booster of the Tren Maya project (*Animal Político* 2023).

Díaz Mena's defection may have been motivated by the frustration of his own political ambitions, but his public declarations that the PAN had lost its way resonated with many voters who were baffled by the partisan realignments of the 2020s. Reeling from national losses in 2018, the PRI took the unprecedented step of forming a national coalition with the PAN and PRD in hopes of pushing back the surging tide of MORENA. In the state of Yucatán, this was represented by a coalition of the PRI, PAN, and a minor regional party called Nueva Alianza Yucatán. Through the early months of 2024, the Facebook feeds of many of my friends in Pisté featured pictures of local rallies in which "red-boned" Priístas and Panistas stood shoulder to shoulder with the banners of their respective parties. Some comments were derisive, but many locals simply expressed wonder that local politicos who had despised each other for decades found a common cause against MORENA's coalition. Even many "red-boned" Panistas like Rubén Dzul agreed with Díaz Mena. In aligning with their old enemies, the PRI, the party *had* lost its way.

Still, while the 2024 elections in Yucatán were far better for MORENA's coalition than those of 2018, they were not an entirely *clean* sweep. The MORENA coalition made gains in local elections, though the PRI/PAN coalition managed victories in 61 of the state's 106 municipalities (*Diario de Yucatán* 2024). Evelio Mis's own victory over his Panista opponent by just over five percentage points suggests that the legacy parties are still a significant force in the municipality of Tinum (Santana 2024). Other positive signs for the legacy parties came from the all-important mayorality of the state capital of Mérida, which was handily won by Panista Cecilia Patrón Laviada, sister of former governor Patricio.

If nothing else, the 2024 elections proved that MORENA would remain a force in national and state-level politics *after* AMLO's sexenio, suggesting that the raft of policies promoted through the 4T will continue to have electoral consequences for the foreseeable future. This raises a series of more specific questions about the ideology and political behavior of the communities whose history I have traced in this book. Were the people who elected Evelio and Natalia Mis in 2024 newly convinced *morenistas*, or were they *evelistas* voting for a familiar local dynasty?

The Tren Maya remains a divisive topic in Pisté, but many people to whom I have spoken honestly believe that AMLO delivered on many of his "revolutionary" promises. Specifically, many members of communities like Pisté are set to benefit significantly from the 4T's restructuring of federal benefit payments. The AMLO administration replaced the direct cash transfer programs derived from Oportunidades and Progresa with a series of new scholarship, healthcare, and basic welfare schemes. Boosters of the 4T note that this new social safety net guarantees citizens' rights to basic benchmarks of well-being, rather than distributing conditional payments that could be manipulated by corrupt or partisan intermediaries (Salmón Perrilliat 2021). Critics have observed that AMLO's signature educational programs seem to offer fewer benefits to fewer citizens than the old Oportunidades and Progresa model (Rodríguez Gómez 2020f). The 4T's dramatic expansion of universal pensions for senior citizens, seemingly at the expense of earlier education and healthcare programs, has also been viewed by some as a thinly disguised strategy to court older voters (Martínez 2022).

It is too early to gauge the impacts of these policy changes on the local politics of communities like Pisté. Out of respect for tensions that these political reconfigurations have produced in the family and social circles of many of my friends in town, I have decided not to conduct formal interviews on people's evaluations of the 4T for at least a few years. But it's possible to speculate about a few key factors. Based on how they have been characterized by political analysts, scholarships provided for primary and secondary education through various 4T programs *will* cover fewer children per family than would have been covered by the older Oportunidades and Progresa schemes. However, students at the Universidad del Bienestar Benito Juárez that was founded in Pisté are eligible for a new higher education scholarship. This combination of a federal scholarship with local access to higher education provides options for local families that would have struggled to cover the cost of travel to universities in Valladolid. Perhaps more important, the scholarships provide an in-cash safety net for childless young adults who would not have benefited from earlier direct-transfer programs. This is also, coincidentally, the demographic most directly impacted by the disjuncture between an expansion of secondary or higher education opportunities and the lack of nontouristic professional employment in the region.

Unprecedented federal benefits being paid to senior citizens are likely to be even more impactful. Elderly people in Pisté who receive pensions after long-term formal employment are a minority in the community. Enrollment for a guaranteed bimonthly payment under the 4T is transformative for many elderly people who were heavily reliant on assistance from their children and grandchildren. Bolstered by a constitutional reform that mandated basic economic safety nets for disadvantaged groups (Ramos 2020), these pensions grew steadily over the course of AMLO's sexenio. By late 2023, Pisté residents over sixty-five years of age joined 11 million Mexicans receiving a bimonthly payment of 4,800 pesos, with expectations that that sum would rise to 6,000 in the 2024 fiscal year (*¡Por Esto!* 2023).

Even local voters who are not immediate beneficiaries of these programs may be acting on the sense that political winds were blowing against the legacy parties. AMLO's project for uprooting the system that enabled two decades of *prianismo* seems to hinge on concentrating power within a new "institutional" party. In late 2022, the president extended his overhaul of the political system through several attempts to replace long-serving appointees on Mexico's National Electoral Institute with a new slate of elected officials (*Latin American Advisor* 2022). This has only deepened the debate over whether the 4T is truly uprooting vestiges of corruption and elite dominance, or whether it is an attempt to concentrate political power under the aegis of a surging MORENA.[2]

From the perspective of voters and political leaders in communities like Pisté, these developments have strategic consequences that may trump more philosophical reflections about the future of Mexico's democracy. The original Panistas of Pisté had little in common socially or ideologically with the conservative urban middle class that was the traditional constituency of that "party of notables." But over decades, the PAN has served as a vital means for promoting alternative candidates and for articulating grievances that focus on the traditional paternalism of the PRI. It is possible that that alliance between local political actors and the established opposition party has worn too thin over two decades of competitive elections, during which the PAN leadership has remained inconsistent in its embrace of popular leaders like Evelio Mis. Just as the PAN embodied opposition to PRI clientelism in the 1980s, MORENA seems to embody opposition to the *prianista* stalemate of the 2000s.

FINAL REFLECTIONS

The story of this book has been one of material prosperity and political identities that are intimately tied to a multigenerational engagement with development. The historical precursors of AMLO's Tren Maya are at the heart of the story. Even without the ability to foresee things like the emergence of the tourism economy, Lázaro Cárdenas and his immediate successors set some of the most significant economic and geopolitical parameters for subsequent economic developments in the Yucatán Peninsula. Each of the three transpeninsular roadways brought a range of economic and political benefits to the communities through which it passed. Each also inflicted varying degrees of negative infrastructure on communities like Kantunilkín, which were excluded from the main arteries of modernization. These effects had lasting consequences. The relatively speedy completion of what would become Highway 180 was due in large part to the military exigencies of World War II. A quarter century later, this road determined the location of Cancún, and the spatial contours of the tourism economy that would radiate from it.

Material prosperity brought more intangible changes to local perspectives. Rural Yucatecans who were transitioning from agricultural labor to touristic entrepreneurship between the 1950s and 1980s might not have been familiar with the monetary subtleties that informed the planning of Cancún. But they developed a distinctly local knowledge of the risks and promises of this new economy through quotidian engagement with the dollars that arrived in the pockets of tourists, and by observing how those dollars changed the local dynamics of labor and consumption. As early negotiations over the routing of the Tren Maya showed, older agrarian institutions like the ejido are still an important means of exercising formal control over valuable land resources. But as many of my friends and informants have pointed out, local people have outgrown the paternalism associated with state-supported agriculture and aspire to forms of political engagement that reflect their active participation in the markets that have turned Maya identity into such a valuable commodity. The discourses of vernacular neoliberalism that shape this political subjectivity can be seen as a long-term consequence of the uneven regional development that spans back to the rapid completion of the Highway 180 corridor a generation earlier.

Will the Tren Maya represent a similar foundational moment for a new geography of prosperity? As I noted earlier, some political commentators have expressed skepticism regarding the 4T's qualitative departure from earlier political and economic traditions of Mexico. The Tren Maya seems to embody this ambiguity. As some suggest, its ultimate fate could be the same as older "white elephants" like Víctor Cervera Pacheco's toll road from Mérida to Cancún, or Ivonne Ortega Pacheco's abortive bullet train project. Once the hundreds of construction workers and engineers who crowd Pisté's hotels return home, the train will have to compete with existing road infrastructure to justify the cost of its construction. If it doesn't do so, AMLO and MORENA would have trod upon the same ground of the "failures" of development that filled the opinion pages of the *Diario de Yucatán* in the 1970s, and that so often provide the foil for the values that many rural Yucatecans find in market-driven prosperity.

What if the Tren Maya succeeds in its stated goal of "detonating" tourism and significantly transforms the spatial distribution of economic resources in the Mexican Southeast? The most likely beneficiaries of new forms of positive infrastructure would be the communities along the southern transit between Chetumal and Escárcega. The massive ruins of Calakmul and a dozen smaller archaeological sites in the region could see an unprecedented flood of tourism, albeit to the detriment of the delicate ecosystems of protected areas on the peripheries of Highway 186. By extension, older and more established tourist circuits would experience some degree of negative infrastructure. Though it's hard to imagine Calakmul displacing Chichén Itzá on the tourist market, even small reductions in the number of visitors can have lasting effects on local communities.

From the perspective of many rural Yucatecans, either of these outcomes for the Tren Maya would be consistent with earlier generations' experiences of state-sponsored infrastructural development. Failed projects make rural residents suffer for poor decision-making by political elites. Even successful projects can inflict harm on communities through negative infrastructure.

In either case, the most likely courses of action for local political leaders are established patterns of electioneering and direct action. Participating in electoral tours and sending well-timed critiques to the *Diario de Yucatán* served Don Javier Maas well in the 1970s, as he sought Governor Loret de Mola's aid in improving the downtown infrastructure of Pisté. During those same years, Rubén Dzul experimented with roadblocks and other tactics of direct action that could produce results when normal political channels failed. At least so far, both strategies seem to apply to working with the 4T. Local residents were initially able to use formal ejido institutions and public engagement with MORENA representatives to leverage a number of concessions from a federal administration eager to expand its support in the countryside. The blockade of Chichén Itzá in January 2023 shows that the most classic forms of protest are also still relevant when other options have been exhausted.

For those of us who comment from the academic sidelines, these histories of infrastructural development and local adaptation offer an important lesson on neoliberalism, Indigeneity, and development. As I learned during my first summers of undergraduate research, political movers in Pisté have little interest in the kinds of transnational solidarity networks made famous by the EZLN. If this revelation surprised me, it was because my expectations had been shaped by narratives about Indigeneity that have a real impact on the political lives of rural Yucatecans. As reporting in the regional press shows, Pisteños' entrepreneurial views of Maya identity are less intelligible to many urban Mexicans than the conflation of Indigeneity and anti-neoliberalism that defines contemporary Zapatismo. In this regard, the expectation of some global publics mirrors the assumptions of development regimes that view "authentic" Indigenous lifeways as incompatible with participation in modern market economies. In places like Yucatán, such romantic expectations of precapitalist "otherness" contribute to larger forces of ethnic and class-based exclusion.

As I've stressed throughout this book, people in communities like Pisté don't *need* to appeal to transnational solidarity, because they possess a number of well-worn local tools for political leverage. The ability to apply pressure on regional leaders through competitive municipal elections has been a mainstay of local political life since the 1980s. Even before that, during the height of the so-called *pax priísta*, petitions and well-timed complaints in the regional press could sway politicians who needed to secure rural votes. Mexican politics *is* tilted in favor of the powerful federal executive branch and the interests of well-connected business magnates. In many cases, this elite dominance forces rural people to resort to a range of informal mechanisms or outright direct action. But the structure of municipal governance assures that people like the residents of Pisté never entirely lacked leverage in electoral politics or through formal institutions like the ejido. Again, the aspirations and lived realities of people in these communities contradict academic narratives that tend to treat Indigenous people and other subaltern groups as being fundamentally alienated from the formal institutions of modern nation-states.

One final set of insights stems from the deep continuities in the political life of rural Yucatecan communities. In spite of a multigenerational critique of the classic anthropological dichotomy of "tradition" and "modernity," many of us enter the field seeking similar kinds of historical rupture. In particular, many social scientists are primed to establish a clear empirical distinction between life under neoliberalism and its immediate historical precursors. Again, this is an awkward fit for the experience of people in communities like Pisté. Though many of my friends and informants frame their vernacular neoliberalism as a political "awakening," this is a perspective that still operates within the mainstream of Mexico's national politics. Just as the rise of Cancún blurs the common distinction between the eras of Stabilizing Development and neoliberalism, the persistence of time-tested political strategies bridges the experience of the agrarian past with that of the entrepreneurial present. These subtle continuities and ambiguous changes might frustrate scholars and activists with an eye for radical historical transformations. But they embody a vernacular common sense that has guided generations of Yucatecans struggling to shape their own roads to prosperity.

NOTES

INTRODUCTION

1. Strictly speaking, "Stabilizing Development" refers to a combination of development and monetary strategies that were consolidated in the mid-1950s. Some forms of state-sponsored development and industry subsidies that I will discuss took place a decade earlier. But given the centrality of the 1960s and 1970s to the narrative of this book, I will use "Stabilizing Development" as a more general shorthand for state-sponsored industrial and agrarian development that was dependent on high tariff barriers and a relatively high valuation of the Mexican peso. See Gracida 2004.

The *pax priísta* was a period of institutional continuity and relative economic prosperity that began with the consolidation of single-party rule at the end of the 1920s. The PRI party-state faced a mounting crisis of legitimacy in the 1970s and ended definitively with the electoral victory of an opposition party in 2000. Particularly in the United States, historians and social scientists who were trained in the 1990s and early 2000s tended to view the first decades after the Revolution of 1910 as a period of "state formation" that produced a remarkably stable system that could rely on the strategic complicity of a diverse range of social groups (Joseph and Nugent 1994). A shift in the literature on the twentieth century is evident by the 2010s. For example, some authors turned to important mutations of the Mexican state that took place after the initial period of "consolidation," like the diplomatic compromises that challenged Revolutionary nationalism during the country's participation in the Second World War (Jones 2014; Rankin 2009). Others explored key topics like the formation of new kinds of political networks by leaders who were born and raised in the decades after the Revolution (Alexander 2016; Gillingham 2021; Hernández Rodríguez 2015), or the fluctuating relations between state, society, and the press (Smith

2018). Some of the most important new directions in scholarship were prompted by the opening of previously restricted archival sources based on the work of Mexico's national security forces at the end of the 1990s. New studies of rural and urban insurgencies since the mid-twentieth century suggested that the "Dirty War" was not so much a reaction to a late crisis in the single-party system as the expression of a more pervasive repressive apparatus (Aviña 2014; Illades 2018; Keller 2015; McCormick 2016; Mendiola García 2017).

2. The current name of the PRI dates to 1946. Previous iterations of the post-Revolutionary party-state were referred to as the Partido Nacional Revolucionario (National Revolutionary Party, 1929–38) and Partido de la Revolución Mexicana (Party of the Mexican Revolution, 1938–46). Although the naming reflected internal restructuring of the party, the historical literature considers all three to be iterations of the same single-party state.

3. Since the election of Adolfo López Mateos in 1958 (Hernández Rodríguez 2015), the handpicked successor has been referred to as the *tapado* (covered one), who is only "uncovered" to public scrutiny when the sitting president considers it unlikely that the selection can be effectively contested by disgruntled party factions. Once the candidate is "uncovered," the public anticipates a flood of spending, as the candidate promotes mass distribution of goods and political favors, just as the sitting president announces or approves projects that will boost the reputation of the party.

4. Cancún was first planned in 1968, with the major phases of construction beginning between 1971 and 1973. These straddled the presidential *sexenios* of Gustavo Díaz Ordaz (1964–70) and Luis Echeverría Álvarez (1970–76). The political repression and growing social inequality that marked the final years of the Díaz Ordaz sexenio tarnished the image of the both the PRI and the political foundations of Stabilizing Development. When he assumed the presidency in 1970, Luis Echeverría sought to restore the damaged reputation of the PRI party-state through a glut of public spending. But he also faced the very real exhaustion of Stabilizing Development as a strategy that had promoted noninflationary growth for the previous decade. So, despite his public critiques of the previous sexenio's economic policy, Echeverría soon embraced Cancún as a highly visible component of his own development agenda, and one of the rare successes of the mid-1970s (Martí 1985).

5. Given the underreporting of informal sales of handicrafts, food, and services by locals, the sum could be significantly higher. Numbers quoted here are derived from statistical data for 2008 available from the Instituto Nacional de Estadísticas y Geografía's public México en cifras app. Comparative numbers were drawn from neighboring municipalities of Yaxcabá, Dzitas, Uayma, Chan Kom, and Kaua. Note that data tables are inconsistently reported between municipalities, and few data are available at the town or village level.

CHAPTER 1

1. All documents pertinent to the 1939 commission to Puerto Juárez are archived in a single folder in the Archivo General de la Nación. Some texts will be referenced here by date. The main report is a single document dated 15 March 1939. Unless otherwise stated, the archival citation for all references to the commission is Fondo Lázaro Cárdenas, caja 634, exp. 515.1/582, Archivo General de la Nación, Mexico City.

2. Scientific names derived from Yucatán, Gobierno del Estado (n.d.).

3. The sparsely populated territory southeast of Kantunilkín through which García Mejía and his companions passed in 1939 had once been part of a vast private concession granted in 1889 to a Compañía Colonizadora de la Costa Oriental de Yucatán (Colonization Company of the East Coast of the Yucatán) headed by the Yucatecan businessman Faustino Martínez. This company struggled for decades to turn a profit from lumber and chicle extraction before yielding its assets to the Banco de Londres y México (Bank of London and Mexico) in 1902. The bank's title was nullified by the revolutionary Carranza administration in 1917, and title reverted to the federal government (Macías Zapata 2002, 112–17).

4. Letters dated between 6 and 9 June 1937, Fondo Lázaro Cárdenas, caja 629, exp. 515.1/156, Archivo General de la Nación, Mexico City.

5. SOP to Secretario Particular del Sr. Presidente, 27 July 1937, Fondo Lázaro Cárdenas, caja 629, exp. 515.1/156, Archivo General de la Nación, Mexico City.

6. The documents relevant to the charter date to March 1956 and are archived at the Historical Archive of the Banco de México, caja 64, exp. 4, Archivo Histórico, Banco de México, Mexico City.

7. This concession was part of a larger series of negotiations that also involved the exact placement of the long, straight border that separated Guatemala from present-day Campeche and Quintana Roo. Historically, the border had been set at 17° 49′ north latitude, a division inherited from the colonial-era border between the Audiencia of Guatemala and the Captaincy General of Yucatán. But, in the 1880s, Guatemalan negotiators insisted that a border at 18° north latitude was more appropriate, as it would include a number of settlements founded by Guatemalan citizens some decades earlier. To this, the Mexicans responded that those settlements were recent squatter camps occupied by "fugitives or criminals" and that they had since been reoccupied by Mexican troops and citizens from Campeche (Comisión Guatemalteca de Límites con México 1900, 154, 156). In the end, the Mexican negotiators were granted their version of Guatemala's northern border.

8. Early in his rule, Ubico had renewed Guatemala's historical claims to most of the territory within the British colony. Diplomatic communications between Mexico and the Allied powers suggested that, if the cessation of lands to Guatemala were to occur, Mexico would revive its own long-dormant claim to a portion of Belize that stretched considerably south of the 17° 49′ border with Guatemala's Petén. Kenneth Grieb reports that this claim dampened Ubico's ambition. The caudillo preferred Belizean territory to be the hands of a European power rather than in those of his troublesome northern neighbor (Grieb 1979, 139).

9. Maximino Ávila Camacho to Manuel Ávila Camacho, 26 May 1942, Fondo Manuel Ávila Camacho, exp. 151.1/311, Archivo General de la Nación, Mexico City.

10. Guevara to Maximino Ávila Camacho, 10 August 1943, Fondo Manuel Ávila Camacho, exp. 151.1/311, Archivo General de la Nación, Mexico City.

11. Guevara to Ávila Camacho, 14 August 1943, Fondo Manuel Ávila Camacho, exp. 151.1/311, Archivo General de la Nación, Mexico City.

12. Memo addressed to office of President Ávila Camacho, dated 28 April 1944, Fondo Manuel Ávila Camacho, exp. 151.1/311, Archivo General de la Nación, Mexico City.

13. Reports dated 28 December 1955, Fondo Adolfo Ruiz Cortines, exp. 151.1/595, Archivo General de la Nación, Mexico City.

14. Tourism development plan for 1960 fiscal year, dated 8 January 1958. Folder includes assorted telegrams and petition letters from local stakeholders. Fondo Adolfo López Mateos, caja 726, exp. 542/67, Archivo General de la Nación, Mexico City.

15. These numbers are derived from a collection of requests and an unpublished plan for road development in Quintana Roo compiled during the Adolfo Ruiz Cortines presidency. The documents date from 26 August 1954 to 5 January 1955. Fondo Adolfo Ruiz Cortines, exp. 151.1/412, Archivo General de la Nación, Mexico City.

16. Letters dated 11 November 1953 and 12 November 1953, Fondo Aldolfo Ruiz Cortines, exp. 515.1/56, Archivo General de la Nación, Mexico City.

17. Letters to President Díaz Ordaz dated between 20 June and 15 July 1966, Fondo Gustavo Díaz Ordaz, exp. "Yucatán" 726-4/4, Archivo General de la Nación, Mexico City.

18. Report dated 28 December 1955, Fondo Adolfo Ruiz Cortines, exp. 515.1/595, Archivo General de la Nación, Mexico City.

19. Development plan dated 16 June 1961, Fondo Adolfo López Mateo, caja, 726 exp. 547/67, Archivo General de la Nación, Mexico City.

CHAPTER 2

1. These institutions were consolidated as Banco Nacional de Crédito Rural in 1977, and even later reorganized as the Financiera Rural (Rural Financial). See Escalante 1988.

2. For more on the failure of projects in Santa Rosa and Maxcanú, see Loret de Mola 1978, 78–79.

3. In 1984, Cerveristas in the Confederación Nacional Campesina (National Peasant Confederation) orchestrated a string of mass protests that threatened the PRI's electoral prospects. Luna Kan's hapless successor, Graciliano Alpuche Pinzón, was forced from office (Ramírez Carrillo 2004, 59–62), and Cervera Pacheco finished his term as interim governor. Cervera Pacheco's immediate successor, Víctor Manzanilla Schaffer, embodied a last, and ultimately unsuccessful, attempt by non-Cerverista factions in the Yucatecan PRI to gain power. As Manzanilla Schaffer (1998a) narrates in his own memoirs, he was forced from office by President Carlos Salinas de Gortari for refusing to intervene illegally and prevent the election of Panistas in the state. His term in office was finished by the Cervera Pacheco ally Dulce María Sauri Riancho. By 1995, when Cervera Pacheco was elected to his second—and unconstitutional—term as governor, he had essentially cemented personal dominance over the Yucatecan PRI.

CHAPTER 4

1. This quote comes from a note in the 1976 issue of the internally circulated newsletter of the Fondo Nacional de Fomento al Turismo (National Fund for Tourism Development), titled "Turismo y balance de pagos." Original copies drawn from Fondo Enríquez Sauvignac, exp. C-177, Archivo Histórico, Universidad del Caribe, Cancún.

2. These figures are quoted from an internal Banco de México memo dated 1968 (no day or month) and titled "Bases para el desarrollo de un plan integral de infraestructura turística en México." This document is among the earliest formal articulations of the Cancún project, and is archived under the rubric "Infratur/Fonatur" files, vol. 1, Archivo Histórico, Banco de México, Mexico City. For a discussion of published versions of this memo, see Martí 1985.

3. The debate hinged on the exact location of a then-abandoned rural settlement known as Put, which had a significant population in the mid-nineteenth century. Since the 1850s, this place had been used as the starting point of a straight line of longitude that spanned south to the Guatemalan border and separated the state of Campeche from Yucatán. When Quintana Roo was declared as a federal territory in 1902, a diagonal line linking Put to a point east of one of the towers in the Church of Chemax became part of the new interstate border. Confusion was introduced in the twentieth century when some maps referenced the location of the then-abandoned settlement of Put (derived from the Mayan word for "papaya"), while others referred to a monument "at a point near Put" that had been erected by a cartographic expedition in 1922. This latter point was favored by the commission drafting a new state constitution for Quintana Roo in 1974. The more westerly location for Put would have absorbed hundreds of square kilometers of land that currently "belonged" to Yucatán, including the densely settled municipalities of Tihosuco and Tepich, into the new state (Loret de Mola 1974).

4. Disputes about the Yucatán / Quintana Roo border reemerged in 1990, and talk of "restoring" land to two Yucatecan municipalities was revived in 2019. When Quintana Roo was declared a federal territory in 1902, a diagonal line linking the settlement of Put to a point east of one of the towers in the Church of Chemax became part of the new interstate border. Disputes regarding the exact position of Put—which had been rebaptized from a Mayan toponym meaning "papaya" to the Spanish acronym for *punto de unidad territorial* (point of territorial juncture)—emerged in the 1990s (Cárdenas 2019). Most recently, the state legislature of Quintana Roo proposed a cartographic revision that would have "taken" lands from Campeche and the densely populated Yucatecan municipalities of Chemax and Peto (Barquet Loeza 2019; *Por Esto!* 2019b).

5. Though the Anglo-American traveler John Lloyd Stephens seems to have been aware of the site's existence in the early 1840s, the first recorded scholarly visit was in 1888, by the Yucatecan museum director Juan Peón Contreras. Thomas Gann is often credited with locating the *sacbe* linking it to Yaxunah in the 1920s. See also Graham 2004. Based on these reports, the Carnegie Institute of Washington project at Chichén Itzá mounted a small expedition directed by J. Eric Thompson (1963, 47), who considered himself to be "among the first dozen white men ever to ride [the sacbe to Yaxunah]." The site remained inaccessible, and was visited sporadically by foreign scholars who conducted basic test excavations, documented hieroglyphic inscriptions, and produced basic site plans.

6. The newsletter is attached to a letter directed to President Díaz Ordaz by Evelio Díaz Sierra, dated 6 April 1966, Fondo Gustavo Díaz Ordaz, exp. 726.4/4, Archivo General de la Nación, Mexico City.

7. The newsletter noted that the famed causeway to Yaxunah ran far to the west, near Chichén Itzá. Another, less well-explored sacbe tracked to the east, "probably to the village of Akumal," on the Caribbean coast.

8. For decades, the only road in or out of Cobá was a branch of the federal road linking the town of Nuevo Xcan in Quintana Roo to the town and archaeological site of Tulum, on the coast around eighty miles to the south of Cancún. This linked Cobá to an as-yet-undeveloped extreme of what was known as the "Cancún / Tulum corridor." This is the stretch of coast that came under the control of the Xcaret group and other politically connected entrepreneurs during the *cerverato*, and that would be officially rebaptized as the "Riviera Maya" in 1999.

CHAPTER 5

1. This expansion of secondary and tertiary education entailed a reconfiguration of the institutional landscape beyond the simple quantitative expansion of institutions. Historically, secondary and preparatory schools in Mexico were affiliated with universities to which they "fed" students, with the most prestigious institutions being clustered in Mexico City and the center of the republic (see Ai Camp 1985, 164–66). Until the 1980s, the Universidad Autónoma de Yucatán, founded in Mérida in 1922, was the only institution granting higher degrees in the Mexican Southeast (see Paoli Bolio 2004). Besides propaedeutic institutions associated with this flagship university, access to secondary and tertiary education hinged on geographical and financial access to private preparatory schools or public vocational schools that tended to cluster in major urban centers.

2. While the data that are available from the state Secretariat of Education of Yucatán list the locations and names of all secondary and preparatory schools in the state, many of the entries lack specific dates of foundation. However, the available information for Valladolid and the rural municipalities whose students tend to commute there for education makes some broad outlines clear. The specific set of data requested was for the municipalities of Valladolid, Chemax, Cuncunul, Chichimilá, Kaua, Chan Kom, Tinum, and Yaxcabá. I am grateful to Licenciado José González Ortega for assembling the data in spreadsheet form and making them accessible.

3. I have observed this phenomenon through particularly heartbreaking situations over the decades of my fieldwork. Bright and ambitious teenagers who finished the local secondary or preparatory school with "puro diez" ("all tens," equivalent to "straight As") are unable to score well enough in entrance exams to qualify for admission to the prestigious Universidad Autónoma de Yucatán. At that point, they contemplate the possibility of spending years saving up to enter a prohibitively expensive private institution, or for a less prestigious career path in a teacher's college.

4. Complaints that I have heard from parents in various communities follow a similar pattern. Usually, a young relative of a senior teacher in the local primary school completes coursework with a certification to teach a subject—let's say, mathematics—at the secondary school level. Seeing that their younger relative is eager to stay close to home and avoid an undesirable posting, the senior teacher uses connections in the teacher's union and the SEP bureaucracy to secure them a position in the local *secundaria*. In this case, the posting is complicated by the fact that there is already an established mathematics teacher at the secundaria. Calling in favors and maybe delivering a few well-placed payments, the senior teacher procures a certification in national history for his young relative, who begins to work in the secundaria. The result, parents have reported to me, are teachers who are teaching in subjects for which they are completely unqualified. In many cases, parents in rural communities lack the educational background or cultural capital to lodge successful complaints with the SEP against such abuses.

5. This is derived from data generously provided in spreadsheet form from the SEP of the State of Yucatán.

6. For example, the "Modelo" group of universities evolved from a prestigious private preparatory school founded in the state capital in 1910. The satellite institution in Valladolid was formally titled the Universidad de Valladolid Yucatán in 2006 was founded in 1990 as a preparatory school for teachers, adding a degree in physical education by 1994,

a law degree program by 1997, and a range of other degrees associated with tourism and the service sector by the 2000s. From the official Universidad de Valladolid Yucatán website (UVY, n.d.).

7. This information can be confirmed on the website of Mexico's SEP (n.d.), in the search option to confirm the "reconocimento de validez oficial de estudios" (recognition of official validity of studies) status of different institutions.

8. Until the mid-1980s, the majority of private universities in the country were well-funded elite institutions concentrated in Mexico City and in northern industrial centers like Monterrey. But the number and range of private universities exploded between 1990 and 2000, with over 167 percent sectorial growth. A further 60 percent growth in this sector between 2000 and 2010 reflects the persistent tendency to found new institutions to absorb the "excess demand" for higher education generated by the nationwide expansion of secondary education (see Cuevas-Cajiga 2015, 49).

9. At 8.8 years on average, it ranked below the national average of 9.2 and well below the 11 years or more that were typical in Mexico City. The neighboring states of Campeche and Quintana Roo fare better, with 9.1 and 9.6 years of education on average.

10. According to 2015 Instituto Nacional de Estadísticas y Geografía statistics, around a third of the population of the state of Yucatán are classed as *hablantes de lengua indígena* (Indigenous-language speakers, or HLI) who make extensive use of the Yukatek language in their everyday lives. Yukatek speakers account for 12 and 17 percent of the populations of Campeche and Quintana Roo, respectively. Other Mexican states with high populations of HLI people include Oaxaca and Chiapas, with 32 and 28 percent of HLI residents, respectively, and Guerrero, with around 15 percent. All of the latter states average fewer than eight grades of formal education per resident, significantly below the three peninsular states (INEGI, n.d.).

11. The language quoted here was from a section of Universidad Anáhuac Mayab's institutional website (UAM, n.d.). It has since been replaced by a new statement of academic vision adopted in 2025.

12. Students, and some academics at the more prestigious Universidad Autónoma de Yucatán, for years traced many of these educational and institutional irregularities to the fact that the Universidad del Oriente was chartered without the autonomy of older public institutions. Its directors are, in effect, political appointees of the sitting governor. Though some directors have been experienced academics, others have been bureaucrats and party apparatchiks with little or no background in higher education. This rule of an academic institution by nonacademics became the explicit focus of a new round of protests that began in 2018 and are described in the blog *Súbele al Volumen* (2011).

13. Some popular texts—including some of the more lurid tabloid publications that are around today—link this tendency to the pre-Hispanic deity Ix Tab, a supposed patron goddess of those who commit suicide by hanging (Reyes-Foster and Kangas 2016). Others associate the "tradition" with the days of debt peonage before the Mexican Revolution, when henequen workers ended their own lives to avoid further "enslavement" through debt (Canto-Valdés and Yanes-Pérez 2018).

14. This vernacularization of a once-uncommon anglicism reflects a discourse on violence in schools that became institutionalized in Mexico during the 2010s. An influential 2012 handbook on bullying written for Mexican public school teachers noted that the topic was not researched seriously in Mexico before 2006. It specifically referred to a tendency

in the national press to characterize the public debate on schoolyard violence as a "fad" or an "invented" crisis (Mendoza 2016, 17). Things had clearly changed by the 2010s, when government reforms and extensive press coverage made bullying a very real target for reforms. A number of nationwide surveys conducted between 2000 and 2010 first generated data on "school harassment" (*acoso escolar*), which informed the 2007 national Programa Escuela Segura (Program for Secure Schools). The Programa Escuela Segura included antibullying initiatives alongside traditional drug and gang enforcement, leading some critics to claim that "normal" forms of conflict between students were being criminalized alongside blatantly illegal gang activities (Saucedo Ramos and Guzmán Gómez 2018, 222–23, 234–36). Yucatán was among a handful of other Mexican states that took this program further, reforming the state's laws of education and public health in 2012 and implementing new best practices in schools a year later (see *Diario de Yucatán* 2018b; *Novedades Yucatán* 2014a).

CHAPTER 6

1. Ontivieros to Gobierno del Estado, 5 September 1913, Poder Legislativo, Archivo General del Estado de Yucatán, Mérida. Physical documents have deteriorated, and JPG files of them are stored on CD no. C89_8289_ab.

2. In some regards, the Panistas of Pisté also seem to have been caught off guard by just how different the political culture of their community had become from that of its neighbors. Most of my friends there commented on the increasing sophistication of electioneering in the larger town, which had expanded from the more traditional rallies and gifting to include social media strategies and even some polling. The "snapshots" of local opinion that one can derive from these means are difficult to reconcile with the patterns of voting still prevalent in villages like Tohopkú and San Francisco. In particular, these communities have a tradition of votes being "delivered" en masse by local political influencers who effectively determine the electoral choices of most of their relatives and neighbors. In some cases, these influencers are the traditional rural patriarchs referred to as *tatich* (Mayan: chieftain). In other cases, they are simply politically active members of prominent families who are personally courted by different political parties. These small-town influencers often play their cards close to the vest until the final days of an election. In 2015, they seemed prepared to "punish" Evelio Mis at the last moment for neglecting their roads and public buildings.

CHAPTER 7

1. Even in the 1990s, scholars observed that the romantic image of Subcomandante Marcos and the Indigenous leadership of the EZLN sending emails from the Selva Lacandona did not reflect the technological realities of the movement's Indigenous constituents. As in the village of Talea, direct internet connections were unavailable in most of rural Chiapas in 1994. The solidarity organizations most visible online were based in Mexico City or the United States. None of these groups claimed to represent an "official" line from

the EZLN (Rovira 2009, 77, 82–90), whose clandestine leadership lived a vastly different reality from that of their global allies.

2. Federal data on the state of Yucatán log an almost tenfold growth in the number of cell phone lines per citizen in the first decade of the millennium, from 8.6 lines per hundred residents in 2002 to 80 per hundred residents in 2012 (*Novedades Yucatán* 2014b).

3. Villamil has characterized the PRI "resurgence" under Peña Nieto as the "Televisa *sexenio*," stressing the role of televised political marketing in promoting the cameragenic candidate and suppressing the rise of leftist rival Andrés Manuel López Obrador (see Villamil 2012a; Villamil and Scherer Ibarra 2006). Villamil views the massive expansion of social media use in Mexico in the years immediately preceding and following the election of Peña Nieto as a revolution in mass information consumption that broke the generations-long monopoly of Televisa, notwithstanding the PRI's "resurgence." Tellingly, he draws inspiration from Manuel Castells (2009), the Spanish sociologist best known for his study *The Rise of the Network Society* and later discussions of movements associated with the Arab Spring and Occupy, who has been influential among Latin American authors.

4. On 11 May of that year, candidate Peña Nieto made an appearance at the private Universidad Iberoamericana for what was expected to be a tightly controlled campaign event. Protesters disrupted his speech, drawing attention to abuses against activists in the community of San Salvador Atenco during the candidate's term as governor of the state of Mexico. Following a well-established pattern, Televisa-affiliated media were quick to dismiss the protestors as *porros* (ringers) who had infiltrated the student body to disrupt the event. In response, a group of 131 student protestors from the Ibero posted an online video using their university IDs to demonstrate that they were, in fact, current students at the institution. In the weeks and months that follows, the hashtag #YoSoy132 (I am the 132nd) became a rallying cry for online and real-life protests against the policy proposals of Peña Nieto and the media machine that had transformed him into a seemingly inevitable candidate for the Mexican presidency.

5. For a general discussion of similar tendencies in other discussions of media, see Dean 2010, 28.

6. The formal approval and various undated notes regarding the approval of Thompson's telephone line are in a file dated 19 July 1919, Poder Legislativo, Archivo General del Estado de Yucatán, Mérida. Original files are damaged, but jpg images of original paper files are on CD no. C89_8289_ab. At the time, the nearest telephone connection was in the train depot in the town of Dzitas. The state legislature approved the project with the addendum that Thompson's telephone line be made accessible to any local political official who needed it to conduct government business. It's unclear how long even Thompson's telephone functioned at Chichén Itzá. As late as the 1930s, Robert Redfield (1941, 37) reported the telegraph as being the primary means of communication between the town of Dzitas and the city of Mérida. Even if it had remained in operation into the 1920s and 1930s, the telephone at the hacienda would have been an extreme rarity in rural communities of the eastern part of the state, where technologies even older than the telegraph remained in use. One very elderly man I interviewed in 2002 described a heliograph, a tall signaling tower that could be hired to send Morse code signals along a chain of relayed towers. Based on his recollections, this was still the main means of communicating between the municipality of Kaua and the telegraph lines in Dzitas during the 1920s (Armstrong-Fumero 2013).

7. The first private lines were established in the 1880s under the Compañía Telefónica Mexicana (Mexican Telephone Company, or Mextelco), a conglomerate of Mexican and foreign investors associated with the US-based Western Electric Telephone Company. By 1903, Mextelco faced competition from a national affiliate of the Swedish firm Ericsson Telephones (Telmex 1991, 47–54). Mextelco telephone service was available in Mérida from at least 1893 (Morales Blanco 2007), with Erricson introducing its own service some years later.

8. See Directorio de la Compañía Telefónica y Telegráfica Yucateca, S.A., 1931, archived at the Biblioteca Yucatanense, Mérida, Yucatán. The 96,000 population figure for Mérida was taken from Redfield 1941, and was itself derived from the 1930 census.

9. Telmex was consolidated after pressure on Ericsson by the Miguel Alemán administration allowed a group of Mexican investors to purchase a majority of shares, and later absorb Mextelco (Telmex 1991, 110–12).

10. State report prepared for the José López Portillo administration, "Apéndice estadístico," page 6, caja 2429, Archivo Histórico, Banco de México, Mexico City. The number of telephones per capita in Yucatán was slightly above the 1970 national average of about 2 lines per every 100 inhabitants, but well behind the 34 and 31 lines per 100 inhabitants in the United States and Canada, respectively (see Mariscal 2002, 69).

11. President Carlos Salinas de Gortari decreed that the state would withdraw its majority ownership of Telmex in 1989, privatizing the firm under the condition that it remain in majority Mexican ownership and meet certain benchmarks in expanding and modernizing service. Changes in fiber-optic technology and the emergence of cell phones allowed Mexican state regulatory agencies to adjust their policies, offering concessions to three additional national cell phone providers that operated alongside a Telmex subsidiary (de la Garza and Herrera et al. 1997).

12. Telcel's capture of at least 70 percent of the overall mobile telephone market allowed the corporation to lower rates. This was a boon for Mexican consumers, who had paid some of the highest premiums for cell service on Earth in the early 2000s. But it also helped secure Slim's near-monopoly control of the Mexican market. By 2019, leaders of his chief competitors argued that Telcel's slimmer profit margin made it difficult for other firms to compete and would retard the development of new technologies in Mexico (Celis 2019).

13. The first national survey of access to information technologies commissioned on the federal level in Mexico found that the Mayan-speaking people of Yucatán were the Indigenous ethnic group with the greatest degree of access to 2G, 3G, or 4G cell phone connectivity, with at least 96 percent of the Yukatek-speaking population having access to it (IFT 2018).

14. The first powerful radio transmitter was brought to the state shortly after 1915 by the revolutionary general Salvador Alvarado, and was used coordinate shipping off the north coast of the state and to establish reliable contact between Mérida and the distant outpost of Payo Obispo in the Bay of Chetumal (UADY, n.d.).

15. Two files on *La hora del campesino maya*, dated between 1937 and 1939, are archived under the rubrics XVII-1924-1938-052 and XVII-1924-1938-057, in the Centro de Apoyo para Investigación Histórica de Yucatán, Mérida.

16. Half of the capital of XEQW remained in Yucatecan hands, and distinctly "regional" content would remain central to its programming. But XEQW established two

key phenomena of broadcasting in twentieth-century Mexico: the dependence of imported technology to establish powerful transmitters, and a dependence on highly capitalized national companies (read, the Azcárragas) to purchase this technology. See Mérida de Yucatán 2018.

17. In a 1947 report commissioned by the presidential administration of Miguel Alemán, the prominent author Salvador Novo explored the contrasts between the British model (focused on a state-operated monopoly) and the US model (based on profit-driven private enterprise) (González de Bustamante 2012, 7; Pérez Espino 1979). Based on its reading of the Novo Report, the Alemán administration opted for the private model, albeit with a strong degree of intervention from the federal government. This was consistent with the rapprochement between the revolutionary state and national oligarchs for which the Alemán administration is famous (see Alexander 2016), and it set the tone for the relationship between the state and commercial television stations for generations to come. Looking back from the "revolt of audiences" in 2012, Villamil (2017, 52–58) characterized the "Mexican model" (*formula mexicana*) that emerged from the Alemán administration as an ironic hybrid in which a network of political favors, pressure, personal financial investment, and outright bribery blurred the lines between an ostensibly private television sector and the dominant PRI (see also González de Bustamente 2012, 83–87).

18. Founded in 1963, XHY-TV was co-owned and operated by Telesistema Mexicano and the newly created Grupo SIPSE, a media conglomerate founded by the Yucatecan businessman Andrés García Lavin. In the following decade, SIPSE would expand to found a number of print newspapers as well as radio and television stations throughout the states of Yucatán and Quintana Roo. Though much of this period, SIPSE remained closely affiliated to Telesistema Mexicano and its later iteration, Televisa (Vidal-Bonifaz 2019, 452).

19. Based on my own Facebook feed, the "I'm looking for X" meme was very popular in 2016. The joke petered out around 2018, though I still see the occasional example. I retrieved a relatively recent example, "Busco a Carlos," posted on 27 April 2018 as the profile photo of the Facebook account "Memes yucatecos," on 2 February 2022.

20. A version of this meme was tweeted publicly by user "RoGFIRE" on 25 June 2015. Retrieved by me on 2 February 2022.

21. "A veces quisiera ser del PRI . . ." Meme of unknown original author. Posted on a public Facebook page and retrieved by me on 20 September 2016.

22. "A veces quisiera ir al mitin . . ." Meme of unknown original author. Posted on a public Facebook page and retrieved by me on 20 September 2016.

23. "Es que nos dio chance." Meme of unknown original author. Posted on a public Facebook page and retrieved by me on 20 September 2016.

24. "Para que vea el Patroncito . . ." Meme of unknown original author. Posted on a public Facebook page and retrieved by me on 20 September 2016.

25. This is a pseudonym to the now-defunct account.

CONCLUSION

1. Just months before AMLO's 2006 electoral defeat, the historian Enrique Krauze, whose critique of Mexican personalism I touched upon in the introduction to this book, penned a mordant characterization of the candidate as a "tropical Messiah." AMLO, he

argued, possessed a fundamentally parochial vision of the world that he derived from the strongman politics of his home state of Tabasco. From this, the politician built his powerful following by undermining faith in Mexico's hard-won democratic institutions and framing his personal governance as the only viable route to true political change (Krauze 2018, 175–201; see also Grayson 2007). A little over a decade later, Krauze would express his support for the heterodox Frente Ciudadano. Faced with an entrenched PRI establishment and a surging AMLO, he saw the Frente as a means of fostering new forms of political debate that placed institutional democracy at the heart of Mexican politics (Krauze 2017).

2. Other critiques and countercritiques have focused on the president's style of governance. Three years into the *sexenio,* Frente collaborator Roger Bartra (2021) revisited his famous analysis of the intersections between revolutionary nationalism and PRI authoritarianism in the context of AMLO's rise to power. Mirroring aspects of Krauze's "tropical Messiah" narrative, he characterized the president as a populist who employs a combination of grievance and pseudo-religious nationalism to undermine the fragile electoral democracy that emerged in 2000. This, along with AMLO's stated admiration of figures associated with the Stabilizing Development of the 1960s and 1970s, seems to cast the new president in the same mold as the authoritarian populists of an earlier generation (Bartra 2021, 69–70). Some of AMLO's defenders respond by noting that a frontal assault on existing institutions is necessary to uproot the influence of business and political elites who maintained their privileges through two decades of competitive elections (see Rios 2021).

REFERENCES

Aguilar Camín, Héctor, and Lorenzo Meyer. 1993. *In the Shadow of the Mexican Revolution.* Austin: University of Texas Press.

Ai Camp, Roderic. 1985. *Intellectuals and the State in Twentieth-Century Mexico.* Austin: University of Texas Press.

Ai Camp, Roderic. 1995. *Mexican Political Biographies, 1935–1992.* Austin: University of Texas Press.

Ai Camp, Roderic. 2002. *Mexico's Mandarins: Crafting a Power Elite for the Twenty-First Century.* Berkeley: University of California Press.

Alexander, Ryan M. 2016. *Sons of the Mexican Revolution: Miguel Alemán and His Generation.* Albuquerque: University of New Mexico Press.

Aliskym, Marvin. 1980. "The Relations of the State of Yucatán and the Federal Government of Mexico, 1823–1978." In *Yucatán, a World Apart,* edited by Edward H. Moseley and Edward Terry, 235–75. Tuscaloosa: University of Alabama Press.

Anand, Nikhil. 2017. *The Hydraulic City: Water and the Infrastructures of Citizenship in Mumbai.* Durham, NC: Duke University Press.

Animal Político. 2023. "'Huacho' Díaz Mena: El forastero en Morena que busca quitarle la gubernatura de Yucatán al PAN." *Animalpolitico.com,* 18 December 2023.

Arceo, David R. 1948. "Cuando tendremos televisión en Yucatán?" *Diario de Yucatán,* 4 June 1948. Reproduced in the blog *Yucatán Ancestral,* 11 May 2018. https://Yucatánancestral .com/cuando-tendremos-television-Yucatán.

Armstrong-Fumero, Fernando. 2009a. "A Heritage of Ambiguity: The Historical Substrate of Vernacular Multiculturalism in Yucatán, Mexico." *American Ethnologist* 36 (2): 299–316.

Armstrong-Fumero, Fernando. 2009b. "Old Jokes and New Multiculturalisms: Continuity and Change in Vernacular Discourse on the Yucatec Maya Language." *American Anthropologist* 111 (3): 360–72.

Armstrong-Fumero, Fernando. 2013. *Elusive Unity: Factionalism and the Limits of Identity Politics in Yucatán, Mexico*. Boulder: University Press of Colorado.

Armstrong-Fumero, Fernando. 2014. "A Tale of Two Maya Babels: Vernacular Histories of the Maya and the Limits of Inclusion." *Ethnohistory* 61 (4): 761–84.

Armstrong-Fumero, Fernando. 2018. "Felipe Carrillo Puerto and the Maya Heroes That Weren't: Local Leadership and the Pathology of Politics in Yucatán." In *The Faces of Resistance: Maya Heroes, Power and Identity*, edited by Ashley Kistler, 121–35. Tuscaloosa: University of Alabama Press.

Armstrong-Fumero, Fernando. 2019. "Ouija Boards, Shape Shifters, and Dropouts Moral Panics and Neoliberal Precarity in Rural Yucatán." *Dialectical Anthropology* 43:333–46.

Arriaga Lemus, María de la Luz. 2015. "The Mexican Teachers' Movement: Thirty Years of Struggle for Union Democracy and the Defense of Public Education." *Social Justice* 42 (3–4): 104–17.

Ávila, José Luis. 2006. *Historia económica de México: La era neoliberal*. Mexico City: Océano.

Aviña, Alexander. 2014. *Specters of Revolution: Peasant Guerillas and the Cold War in the Mexican Countryside*. Oxford: Oxford University Press.

Babb, Florence. 2011. *The Tourism Encounter: Fashioning Latin American Nations and Histories*. Stanford, CA: Stanford University Press.

Babb, Sarah. 2001. *Managing Mexico: Economists from Nationalism to Neoliberalism*. Princeton, NJ: Princeton University Press.

Baklanoff, Eric N. 1980. "The Diversification Quest: A Monocrop Export Economy in Transition." In *Yucatán: A World Apart*, edited by Edward H. Moseley and Edward Terry, 202–42. Tuscaloosa: University of Alabama Press.

Banco de México. 1968. "Bases Para Desarrollar un Proyecto de Integral de Infraestructura Turística en México." Archivo Histórico del Banco de México, Mexico City.

Barquet Loeza, Daniel. 2019. "Quintana Roo quita territorio de Yucatán con reforma: Alistan controversia." *Milenio*, 12 June 2019.

Bartra, Roger. 1987. *La jaula de la melancolía*. Mexico City: Grijalbo.

Bartra, Roger. 2002. Prologue to *Anatomía del mexicano*, edited by Roger Bartra, 11–24. Barcelona: Plaza Janes.

Bartra, Roger. 2021. *Regreso a la jaula: El fracaso de López Obrador*. Mexico City: Debate.

Becker, Elizabeth. 2016. *Overbooked: The Exploding Business of Travel and Tourism*. New York: Simon and Schuster.

Benítez, Fernando. 1956. *Kí: El drama de un pueblo y una planta*. Mexico City: Fondo de Cultura Económica.

Benjamin, Thomas. 2000. *La Revolución: Mexico's Great Revolution as Memory, Myth, and History*. Austin: University of Texas Press.

Berger, Dina. 2006. *The Development of Mexico's Tourism Industry: Pyramids by Day, Martinis by Night*. New York: Palgrave.

Bess, Michael K. 2017. *Routes of Compromise: Building Roads and Shaping the Nation in Mexico, 1917–1952*. Lincoln: University of Nebraska Press.

Beteta, Ramón. 1951. *Tierra del chicle*. Mexico City: México Nuevo.

Bhattacharya, Sudip, Abu Bashar, Abhay Srivastava, and Amarjeet Singh. 2019. "NO-MOPHOBIA: NO MObile PHone PhoBIA." *Journal of Family Medicine and Primary Care* 8 (4): 1297–300.

Bleynat, Ingrid. 2021. *Vendor's Capitalism: A Political Economy of Public Markets in Mexico City*. Redwood City, CA: Stanford University Press.

Bonfil Gómez, Luis. 2004. "Murió el yucateco Víctor Cervera, figura del priismo de viejo cuño." *La Jornada*, 19 August 2004.

Breglia, Lisa. 2006. *Monumental Ambivalence*. Austin: University of Texas Press.

Brown, Denise Fay. 2007. "The Cah: Place and Identity of the Chemax Maya." In *Negotiating Identities in Modern Latin America*, edited by Hendrik Kraay, 215–34. Calgary: University Press of Calgary.

Brown, Michael. 2004. *Who Owns Native Culture?* Cambridge, MA: Harvard University Press.

Brown, Wendy. 2017. *Undoing the Demos: Neoliberalism's Stealth Revolution*. London: Zone.

Cámara Barbachano, Fernando. 1958. *Colonización interna de Yucatán*. Mexico City: INAH.

Canto Sáenz, Rodolfo. 2001. *Del henequén a las maquiladoras: La política industrial en Yucatán, 1984-2001*. Mérida: UADY.

Canto-Valdés, Luis Roberto, and Maritel Yanes-Pérez. 2018. "El suicidio y la melancolía en algunas haciendas porfirianas de Yucatán." *LiminaR: Estudios Sociales y Humanísticos* 16 (2). www.scielo.org.mx/scielo.php?script=sci_abstract&pid=S1665-80272018000200158&lng=t.

Cárdenas, Israel. 2019. "Revive Yucatán la polémica del Punto Put con Quintana Roo." *Novedades Quintana Roo*, 7 May 2019.

Carmona, Fernando. (1970) 1990. *El milagro mexicano*. Mexico City: Nuestros Tiempos.

Carrier, James, and Donald Macleod. 2005. "Bursting the Bubble: The Socio-cultural Context of Ecotourism." *Journal of the Royal Anthropological Institute* 11 (2): 315–34.

Carrier-Moisan, Marie-Eve. 2020. "The Dramatic Losses of Brazil: City-Staging, Spectacular Security, and the Problem of Sex Tourism during the 2014 World Cup in Natal." *City and Society* 23 (2): 530–55.

Casares Cámara, Hernán. 2020. "Comprueban desvío de fondos en el Palacio de la Civilización Maya." *Diario de Yucatán*, 6 February 2020. www.yucatan.com.mx/merida/2020/02/06/comprueban-desvios-de-fondos-en-el-palacio-de-la-civilizacion-maya.html.

Castañeda, Jorge. 2011. *Mañana o pasado: El misterio de los mexicanos*. New York: Vintage.

Castañeda, Quetzil. 1996. *In the Museum of Maya Culture*. Minneapolis: University of Minnesota Press.

Castañeda, Quetzil. 1997 "On the Correct Training of *Indios* in the Handicrafts Market at Chichén Itzá: Tactics and Tactility of Gender, Class, Race and State." *Journal of Latin American and Caribbean Anthropology* 2 (2): 106–43.

Castañeda, Quetzil. 2004. "'We Are Not Indigenous': An Introduction to the Maya Identity of Yucatán." *Journal of Latin American and Caribbean Anthropology* 9 (1): 36–61.

Castellanos, Bianet. 2010. *A Return to Servitude*. Minneapolis: University of Minnesota Press.

Castellanos, Bianet. 2020. *Indigenous Dispossessions: Housing and Mayan Indebtedness in Yucatán*. Redwood City, CA: Stanford University Press.

Castellanos, Bianet. 2023. "A Cartography of Tourist Imaginaries." In *The Transnational Construction of Mayanness*, edited by Fernando Armstrong-Fumero and Ben Fallaw, 179–97. Boulder: University Press of Colorado.

Castells, Manuel. 2009. *The Rise of the Network Society*. New York: Wiley-Blackwell.

Castillo Cocom, Juan. 2005. "'It Was Simply Their Word': Yucatec Maya PRInces in YucaPAN and the Politics of Respect." *Critique of Anthropology* 25 (2): 13–55.

Castillo Cocom, Juan, with Saul Rios Luviano. 2012. "Hot and Cold Politics of Indigenous Identity: Legal Indians, Cannibals, Words, More Words, More Food." *Anthropological Quarterly* 85 (1): 229–56.

Castro, Justin. 2016. *Radio in Revolution: Wireless Technology and State Power in Mexico, 1897–1938*. Lincoln: University of Nebraska Press.

Celis, Fernanda. 2019. "Monopolio en telecomunicaciones disminuye rentabilidad en México: Movistar." *Forbes México*, 8 May 2019. www.forbes.com.mx/monopolio -en-telecomunicaciones-disminuye-rentabilidad-en-mexico-movistar.

Chan, Joaquín. 2019. "Yucatán tercer lugar nacional con menor desempleo." *Diario de Yucatán*, 31 July 2019. www.Yucatán.com.mx/merida/Yucatán-tercer-lugar-nacional -con-menor-desempleo.

Checa-Artasu, Martín M. 2009. "Patrimonio, naturaleza recreada y gestión turística: El parque eco arqueológico de Xcaret." *Journal of Tourism Research* 2 (1): 45–58.

Chu, Julie. 2010. *Cosmologies of Credit*. Durham, NC: Duke University Press.

Chua, Jocelyn. 2014. *In Pursuit of the Good Life*. Berkeley: University of California Press.

Clancy, Michael. 2001. "Mexican Tourism, Export Growth and Structural Change since 1970." *Latin American Research Review* 36 (1): 128–50.

Cleaver, Harry M. 1998. "The Zapatista Effect: The Internet and the Rise of an Alternative Political Fabric." *Journal of International Affairs* 51 (2): 621–40.

Collier, George A., and Elizabeth Lowery Quaratiello. 1999. *Basta! Land and the Zapatista Rebellion of Chiapas*. San Francisco: Food First Books.

Comaroff, John, and Jean Comaroff. 2009. *Ethnicity, Inc.* Chicago: University of Chicago Press.

Comisión Guatemalteca de Límites con México. 1900. *Memoria sobre la cuestión de límites entre México y Guatemala*. Guatemala City: Tipografía Nacional.

Córdoba Azcárate, Matilde. 2020. *Stuck with Tourism: Space, Power, and Labor in Contemporary Yucatán*. Berkeley: University of California Press.

Corona, Ignacio. 2016. "Representación, espontaneismo, y la nueva esfera pública: El caso de #YoSoy132." In *Del Internet a las calles*, edited by Raúl Diego Rivera Hernández, 111–22. Raleigh, NC: A Contracorriente.

Corona, Jo. 2018 "Marichuy: Weaving Resistance Beyond the Mexican Elections." *Latin American News Dispatch*, 11 July 2018. https://latindispatch.com/2018/07/11/marichuy -weaving-resistances/?utm_source=Today+in+Latin+America&utm_campaign =35a10ec607-EMAIL_CAMPAIGN_2018_07_11_02_27&utm_medium=email&utm _term=0_73d76ad46b-35a10ec607-15292279.

Corral Corral, Manuel. 2006. *La ciencia de la comunicación en México*. Mexico City: Trillas.

Correa Rachó, Víctor. "Henequén." *Diario de Yucatán*, 5 June 1975.

Cruz, Francisco, and Marcos Durán. 2017. *Los depredadores: La historia oscura del presidencialismo en México*. Mexico City: Planeta.

Cruz Jiménez, Francisco, and Jorge Toribio Montiel. 2009. *Negocios de familia: Biografía no autorizada de Peña Nieto y el Grupo Atlacomulco*. Mexico City: Temas de Hoy.

Cuevas-Cajiga, Yazmín. 2015. "La educación superior privada en México: Representaciones sociales de estudiantes. Privilegio y prestigio." *Universia* 6 (16): 46–66.

Dawson, Alexander S. 2001. "'Wild Indians,' 'Mexican Gentlemen,' and the Lessons Learned in the Casa del Estudiante Indígena, 1926–1932." *The Americas* 57 (3): 329–61.

Dean, Jodi. 2010. *Blog Theory*. Cambridge, UK: Polity.

Dehart, Monica. 2010. *Ethnic Entreperneurs: Identity and Development Politics in Latin America*. Stanford, CA: Stanford University Press.

de la Garza, Enrique, and Fernando Herrera (with Germán Sánchez, Joel Oropeza, José Cruz Guzmán, and Alejandro Espinosa). 1997. *Telecommunications: Restructuring Work and Employment Relations Worldwide*. Ithaca, NY: Cornell University Press.

Diario de Yucatán. 1970. Front page. 3 March 1970.

Diario de Yucatán. 1974a. "El Plan Tabi." 21 July 1974.

Diario de Yucatán. 1974b. "Las nuevas instalaciones agropecuarias del Estado." 3 March 1974.

Diario de Yucatán. 1974c. "Pisté." 8 February 1974.

Diario de Yucatán. 1974d. "Pisté." 3 December 1974.

Diario de Yucatán. 1974e. "Tensa situación en Ticul." 10 January 1974.

Diario de Yucatán. 1975a. "Denuncia de los líderes cañeros." 18 March 1975.

Diario de Yucatán. 1975b. "La industria azucarera es una actividad que corresponde al sector privado." 29 February 1975.

Diario de Yucatán. 1975c. "La nacionalización de la industria azucarera es necesaria—López Portillo." 19 February 1975.

Diario de Yucatán. 1975d. "Los representantes de miles de caneros invaden el local del CNC." 19 March 1975.

Diario de Yucatán. 1975e. "Pisté." 2 April 1975.

Diario de Yucatán. 1975f. "Pisté." 10 July 1975.

Diario de Yucatán. 1975g. "Pisté." 1 December 1975.

Diario de Yucatán. 1975h. "Voces del público: Ingenio azucarero en el sur de Yucatán." 25 June 1975.

Diario de Yucatán. 2018a. "Aparece exalcalde de Tinúum." 4 July 2018. www.yucatan.com .mx/yucatan/2018/7/4/aparece-exalcalde-de-tinum-47012.html.

Diario de Yucatán. 2018b. "El bullying es algo común en escuelas." 3 November 2018. www .Yucatán.com.mx/Yucatán/bullying-algo-comun-escuelas.

Diario de Yucatán. 2018c. "Estudiantes de la Universidad del Oriente rechazan un nombramiento." 4 October 2018.

Diario de Yucatán. 2018d. "Salvaje detención y golpiza." 3 July 2018. www.Yucatán.com.mx /Yucatán/salvaje-detencion-y-golpiza.

Diario de Yucatán. 2018e. "Yucatecos prefieren la 'tele' abierta." 3 September 2018. www .yucatan.com.mx/merida/2018/9/3/yucatecos-prefieren-la-tele-abierta-61714.html.

Diario de Yucatán. 2019a. "Joven estudiante intenta suicidarse en Valladolid." 2 November 2019.

Diario de Yucatán. 2019b. "Por qué tanto suicidio en Yucatán?" 26 August 2019. www .Yucatán.com.mx/merida/por-que-tanto-suicidio-en-Yucatán.

Diario de Yucatán. 2019c. "Publica mensajes en Facebook y luego se suicida." 20 March 2019.

Diario de Yucatán. 2020a. "AMLO supervisa obras del Tren Maya en Yucatán" 4 June 2020.

Diario de Yucatán. 2020b. "Rompen con el Tren Maya" 23 February 2020.

Diario de Yucatán. 2022. "AMLO asegura en Yucatán que el Tren Maya estará listo en 2023." 12 October 2020.

Diario de Yucatán. 2023a. "Llevaran diálogos a siete comunidades Mayas del Oriente." 7 January 2023.

Diario de Yucatán. 2023b. "Sin solución un conflicto en Chichén Itzá." 6 January 2023.

Diario de Yucatán. 2024. "Más alcaldías opositoras en Yucatán." 12 June 2024.

Díaz Navero, Coral. 2014. "La dependencia al celular: Un nuevo vicio que sale de control." *Novedades Yucatán,* 7 September 2014. https://sipse.com/novedades-Yucatán/nomofobia-dependencia-al-celular-vicio-fuera-control-adiccion-111204.html.

Domínguez, José. 1979. "Luchas campesinas en Yaxcabá." Tesis de licenciatura, Universidad Autónoma de Yucatán.

Dorantes Carrión, Jeysira Jacqueline. 2019. "La educación secundaria y México, su historia, desarrollo y proceso de reforma: Memoria y olvido." *Revista de Humanidades* 2:69–94.

Dumond, Don E. 1997. *The Machete and the Cross.* Norman: University of Nebraska Press.

Dunphy, Robert. 1972. "Why the Computer Chose Cancún." *New York Times,* 5 March 1972.

Dynel, Marta. 2016. "I Has Seen Image Macros: Advice-Animal Memes and Visual-Verbal Jokes." *International Journal of Communications* 10: 660–88.

Echeverría, Pedro. 1999 "La Radio Yucateca (Esbozo Histórico)." *Revista Latina de Communicación Social,* no. 17. https://mdc.ulpgc.es/files/original/5124558c38fc8a55c41434b0c2ad6efcb22067cb.pdf.

Eiss, Paul. 2004. "Deconstructing Indians, Reconstructing *Patria*: Indigenous Education in Yucatán from the *Porfiriato* to the Mexican Revolution." *Journal of Latin American and Caribbean Anthropology* 9 (1): 119–50.

Eiss, Paul. 2010. *In the Name of the Pueblo.* Durham, NC: Duke University Press.

Eiss, Paul. 2017. "Playing Mestizo: Festivity, Language and Theater in Yucatan, Mexico." In *The Politics and Performance of Mestizaje in Latin America: Mestizo Acts,* edited by Paul Eiss and Joanne Rappaport, 30–53. New York: Routledge.

El Universal. 2019. "Rechaza ONU consulta sobre Tren Maya." 20 December 2019. www.eluniversal.com.mx/nacion/rechaza-onu-consulta-sobre-el-tren-maya.

Escalante, Roberto. 1988. *The State and Henequen Production in Yucatán, 1955–1980.* London: Institute of Latin American Studies, UCL.

Espinosa-Coria, Horacio. 2013. "El origen del proyecto turístico Cancún, México: Una valoración de sus objetivos iniciales a 42 años de su nacimiento." *LiminaR: Estudios Sociales y Humanísticos* 11 (1). www.scielo.org.mx/scielo.php?script=sci_arttext&pid=S1665-80272013000100011.

Excélsior. 2010. "Detonaran turismo con plan maestro Chichén Itzá." 6 December 2010. www.excelsior.com.mx/node/694332?utm_source=694332&utm_medium=contentrelated&utm_campaign=main.

Expansión. 2020. "El Tren Maya inicia su construcción en el tramo Palenque-Escárcega." 17 June 2020. https://expansion.mx/bespoke-ad/2020/06/17/tren-maya-inicia-su-construccion-en-palenque-escarcega.

Fabila, Alfonso. 1941. "Exploración económico-social del Estado de Yucatán." *Trimestre Económico* 8 (30): 205–52.

Fabinyi, Michael. 2010. "The Intensification of Fishing and the Rise of Tourism." *Human Ecology* 38 (3): 415–27.

Fallaw, Ben. 2001. *Cárdenas Compromised.* Durham, NC: Duke University Press.

Fallaw, Ben. 2004. "Rethinking Mayan Resistance: Changing Relations between Federal Teachers and Mayan Communities in Eastern Yucatán, 1929–1935." *Journal of Latin American and Caribbean Anthropology* 9 (1): 151–78.

Ferguson, James. 1999. *Expectations of Modernity.* Chicago: University of Chicago Press.

Fernández, Claudia, and Andrew Paxman. 2013. *El Tigre: Emilio Azcárraga y su imperio Televisa.* Mexico City: Grijalbo.

Forbes México. 2020. "AMLO pide a Grupo Carso acelerar la obra del Tren Maya." 19 December 2020. www.forbes.com.mx/politica-amlo-tren-maya-carso.

Ford, Annabelle, and Ronald Nigh. 2016. *Maya Forest Garden: Eight Millennia of Sustainable Cultivation of the Tropical Woodlands.* New York: Routledge.

Foster, George. 1987. *Tzintzuntzan.* New York: Waveland.

Fredericks, Rosalind. 2018. *Garbage Citizenship: Vital Infrastructures of Labor in Dakar, Senegal.* Durham, NC: Duke University Press.

Freeman, Brian. 2011. "'La Carrera de la Muerte': Death, Driving, and Rituals of Modernization in 1950s Mexico." *Studies in Latin American Popular Culture* 29 (1): 2–23.

Gabbert, Wolfgang. 2004. *Ethnicity and Social Inequality in Yucatán since 1500.* Tucson: University of Arizona Press.

Gálvez, Alyshia. 2018. *Eating NAFTA: Trade, Food Policies, and the Destruction of Mexico.* Berkeley: University of California Press.

Gama Tejada, Francisco Antonio. 2017. *Mercerización de la educación superior.* Mexico City: ANUIES.

Ganti, Tejaswini. 2014. "Neoliberalism." *Annual Review of Anthropology* 43: 89–104.

Gillingham, Paul. 2021. *Unrevolutionary Mexico: The Birth of a Strange Dictatorship.* New Haven, CT: Yale University Press.

Gobierno del Estado de Yucatán. 2012. *Poder Ejecutivo, Decreto Número 535.* www.yucatan.gob.mx/docs/regulaciones/muazzgsf.pdf.

Gómez Menjívar, Jennifer, and Gloria Elizabeth Chacón. 2018. "No Static: Re-indigenizing Technology." In *Indigenous Interfaces: Spaces, Technology and Social Networks in Mexico and Central America,* edited by Jennifer Gómez Menjívar and Gloria Elizabeth Chacón, 3–55. Tucson: University of Arizona Press.

Góngora Paz, Pedro. 1974. "El balance de Cordemex." *Diario de Yucatán,* 9 June 1974.

González, Roberto 2020. *Connected: How a Mexican Village Built its own Cell Network.* Berkeley: University of California Press.

González de Bustamante, Celeste. 2012. *Muy Buenas Noches: Mexico, Television, and the Cold War.* Omaha: University of Nebraska Press.

González Casanova, Pablo. 2001. *La universidad necesaria en el siglo XXI.* Mexico City: Era.

González Velarde, Fernando. 2018. "Tourism and Fishing Communities in Peru: Dominant Discourses and Social Exclusion." *ERLACS* 105:1–20.

Gracida, Elsa. 2004. *El desarrollismo (Historia económica de México).* Mexico City: Océano.

Graham, Ian. 2004. "Cobá." In *Corpus of Maya Hieroglyphic Inscriptions.* Cambridge, MA: Peabody Museum of Harvard. www.peabody.harvard.edu/cmhi/site.php?site=Coba.

Grayson, George W. 2007. *Mexican Messiah*. State College: Penn State University Press.

Grieb, Kenneth. 1979. *Guatemalan Caudillo: The Regime of Jorge Ubico, 1933–1944*. Columbus: University of Ohio Press.

Gruel Sández, Víctor Manuel. 2017. "The Opening of the Pan American Highway. Tourism and Stereotypes between Mexico and United States." *Estudios Fronterizos* 18 (36): 126–50.

Guevara Niebla, Gilberto. 1981. "Introducción: Los múltiples rostros de la crisis universitaria." In *La crisis de la educación superior en México*, edited by Gilberto Guevara Niebla, 11–22. Mexico City: Nueva Imagen.

Gutmann, Matthew. 2002. *The Romance of Democracy*. Berkeley: University of California Press.

Hale, Charles. 2005. "Neoliberal Multiculturalism: The Remaking of Cultural Rights and Racial Dominance in Central America." *Political and Legal Anthropology Review* 28 (1): 10–28.

Harvey, David. 2005. "Neoliberalism as Creative Destruction." *Geografiska Annaler* 2 (88): 145–58.

Harvey, David. 2007. *A Brief History of Neoliberalism*. Oxford: Oxford University Press.

Harvey, Penny, and Hannah Knox. 2015. *Roads: An Anthropology of Infrastructure and Expertise*. Ithaca, NY: Cornell University Press.

Hayes, Joy Elizabeth. 2000. *Radio Nation: Communication, Popular Culture, and Nationalism in Mexico, 1920–1950*. Tucson: University of Arizona Press.

Heath, Jonathan. 1999. *Mexico and the Sexenio Curse: Presidential Successions and Economic Crises in Modern Mexico*. Washington, DC: Center for Strategic and International Studies.

Hernández Rodríguez, Rogelio. 2008. *El centro dividido: La nueva autonomía de los gobernadores*. Mexico City: Colmex.

Hernández Rodríguez, Rogelio. 2015. *Presidencialismo y hombres fuertes en México: La sucesión presidencial de 1958*. Mexico City: Colmex.

Hervik, Peter. 2002. *Mayan People within and beyond Boundaries: Social Categories and Lived Identity in the Yucatán*. New York: Routledge.

Herzfeld, Michael. 2010. "Engagement, Gentrification and the Neoliberal Hijacking of History." *Current Anthropology* 51 (2): 259–67.

Hodge, G. Derrick, and Walter Little. 2014. "Introduction: Tourism Development and the Policing of Urban Space in Latin America and the Caribbean." *Journal of Latin American and Caribbean Anthropology* 19 (3): 389–95.

Hota, Pinky. 2019. "Money, Value, and Indigenous Citizenship: Notes from the Indian Development State." *Modern Asian Studies* 54 (1): 251–85.

Huchim, Eduardo. 1974. "Frutos sin fugas ni vicios." *Diario de Yucatán*, 18 June 1974.

IFT (Instituto Federal de Telecomunicaciones). 2018. "Presenta el IFT el primer Diagnóstico de Cobertura Garantizada del servicio móvil en pueblos indígenas." 9 August 2018. www.ift.org.mx/comunicacion-y-medios/comunicados-ift/es/presenta-el-ift-el-primer-diagnostico-de-cobertura-garantizada-del-servicio-movil-en-pueblos.

Illades, Carlos. 2018. *El marxismo en México: Una historia intelectual*. Mexico City: Taurus.

INEGI (Instituto Nacional de Estadísticas y Geografía). n.d. "Educación: Yucatán." Accessed 20 July 2021. www.cuentame.inegi.org.mx/monografias/informacion/yuc/poblacion/educacion.aspx?tema=me&e=31.

Jeffrey, Craig. 2010. "Timepass: Youth, Class and Time among Unemployed Young Men in India." *American Ethnologist* 37 (3): 465–81.

Jones, Halbert. 2014. *The War Has Brought Peace to Mexico*. Albuquerque: University of New Mexico Press.

Joseph, Gilbert, and David Nugent. 1994. "Popular Culture and State Formation in Revolutionary Mexico." In *Everyday Forms of State Formation*, edited by Gilbert Joseph and Daniel Nugent, 2–24. Durham, NC: Duke University Press.

Keller, Renata. 2015. *Mexico's Cold War: Cuba, the United States, and the Legacy of the Mexican Revolution*. Cambridge: Cambridge University Press.

Kennelly, Jacqueline. 2015. "'You're Making Our City Look Bad': Olympic Security, Neoliberal Urbanization and Homeless Youth." *Ethnography* 16 (1): 3–24.

Kim, Jessica. 2015. "Destiny of the West: The International Pacific Highway and the Pacific Borderlands, 1929–1957." *Western Historical Quarterly* 46 (3): 311–33.

Kotsko, Adam. 2018. *Neoliberalism's Demons: On the Political Theology of Late Capitalism*. Redwood City, CA: Stanford University Press.

Krauze, Enrique. 1987. *Biografía del poder*. 8 vol. Mexico City: Fondo de Cultura Económica.

Krauze, Enrique. 2013. *La presidencia imperial*. Rev. ed. Mexico City: Tusquets Editores.

Krauze, Enrique. 2017. "Justificación del Frente." 19 November 2017. https://enriquekrauze.com.mx/justificacion-del-frente.

Krauze, Enrique. 2018. *El pueblo soy yo*. Mexico City: Debate.

La Jornada. 2014. "México primer lugar en bullying a nivel mundial." 15 March 2014. www.jornada.com.mx/2014/03/15/sociedad/034n2soc.

La Jornada Maya. 2017. "Yucatecos de educación media superior, de los mejores del país." 8 October 2017. www.lajornadamaya.mx/2017-10-08/Yucatecos-de-educacion-media-superior--de-los-mejores-del-pais.

La Prensa Gráfica. 2018. "El meme que ha sido 'carísimo por cierto.'" 27 September 2018. www.laprensagrafica.com/tendencias/El-meme-que-ha-sido-carisimo-por-cierto-20180922-0053.html.

Lara Zavala, Hernán. 2007. *Charras*. Mérida: Diario de Yucatán.

La Revista Peninsular. 1998. "La tierra de caciques." 30 December 1998.

Larkin, Brian. 2013. "The Politics and Poetics of Infrastructure." *Annual Review of Anthropology* 42: 327–43.

Latin American Advisor. 2022. "What Would AMLO's Electoral Reforms Mean for Mexico?" *The Dialogue*, 30 November 2022. www.thedialogue.org/analysis/what-would-amlos-electoral-reforms-mean-for-mexico.

Levinson, Bradley. 2001. *We Are All Equal: Student Culture and Identity at a Mexican Secondary School, 1988–1998*. Durham, NC: Duke University Press.

Levy, Santiago. 2006. *Progress against Poverty: Sustaining Mexico's PROGRESA-OPORTUNIDADES Programs*. Washington, DC: Brookings Institution.

Lichtinger, Victor, and Homero Aridjis. 2018. "Opinion: The Mayan Trainwreck." *Washington Post*, 4 December 2018. www.washingtonpost.com/news/theworldpost/wp/2018/12/04/amlo.

Lomnitz, Claudio. 2001. *Deep Mexico, Silent Mexico: An Anthropology of Nationalism*. Minneapolis: University of Minnesota Press.

Loret de Mola, Carlos. 1974. "El caso de los límites con Quintana Roo." *Diario de Yucatán*, 19 September 1974.

Loret de Mola, Carlos. 1978. *Confesiones de un gobernador*. Mexico City: Grijalbo.

Lupien, Pascal. 2020. "Indigenous Movements, Collective Action, and Social Media: New Opportunities or New Threats?" *Social Media Society* 6 (2). https://journals.sagepub.com/doi/10.1177/2056305120926487.

Macías Zapata, Gabriel Aarón. 2002. *La península fracturada: Conformación marítima, social y forestal del territorio de Quintana Roo, 1884-1902*. Mexico City: Miguel Ángel Porrúa.

Mancera, Miguel. 1992. *Palabras del Lic. Miguel Mancera, con motivo del reconocimiento de la trascendencia turística otorgada al Banco de México por el Consejo de Promoción Turística de Cancún*. Mexico City: Banco de México.

Mantilla Gálvez, Diana Karina. 2018. "El impacto de la educación telesecundaria en México y su relación con la educación intercultural: El caso de la telesecundaria Tetsijtsilin en la Sierra Norte de Puebla." *Tla-Melaua: Revista de Ciencias Sociales* 12 (44): 164–80.

Manzanilla Schaffer, Víctor. 1998a. *Confesiones políticas*. Mexico City: Grijalbo.

Manzanilla Schaffer, Víctor. 1998b. *Neoliberalismo versus humanismo: La defensa de nuestro proyecto nacional*. Mexico City: Grijalbo.

Marginson, Simon. 2016. "The Worldwide Trend to High Participation Higher Education." *Higher Education* 72 (4): 413–34.

Mariscal, Judith. 2002. *Unfinished Business: Telecommunications Reform in Mexico*. New York: Praeger.

Martí, Fernando. 1985. *Cancún, fantasía de banqueros*. Mexico City: Fernando Martí.

Martínez, José. 1999. *Lecciones del maestro*. Mexico City: Océano.

Martínez, Marco Antonio. 2022. "4T aumenta recursos a adultos mayores y se los quita a los niños." *La Silla Rota.com*, 21 November 2022. https://lasillarota.com/nacion/2022/11/21/4t-aumenta-recursos-adultos-mayores-se-los-quita-los-ninos-ellos-no-votan-expertos-402687.html.

Martínez Valle, Adolfo. 2000. *El Partido Acción Nacional: Una historia política*. Mexico City: Porrúa.

Matthews, Michael. 2013. *The Civilizing Machine: A Cultural History of Mexican Railroads, 1876–1910*. Lincoln: University of Nebraska Press.

Mattiace, Shannan. 2013. "Multicultural Reforms for Mexico's 'Tranquil' Indians in Yucatán." In *Latin America's Multicultural Movements: The Struggle between Communitarianism, Autonomy, and Human Rights*, edited by Todd Einstadt, Michael S. Danielson, Moisés Jaime Ballón Corres, and Carlos Sorroza Polo, 217–44. New York: Oxford University Press.

Maurer, William. 2006. "The Anthropology of Money." *Annual Review of Anthropology* 35 (1): 15–36.

McCormick, Gladys I. 2016. *The Logic of Compromise in Mexico: How the Countryside Was Key to the Emergence of Authoritarianism*. Chapel Hill: University of North Carolina Press.

Medina, Arturo. 2014. "Sería Universo Maya de Pancho Córdova primer parque en Cancún." *Reportur.mx*, 11 April 2014. www.reportur.com/mexico/2014/04/11/seria-universo-maya-de-pancho-cordoba-1er-parque-tematico-en-cancun.

Mediz Bolio, Antonio. 1974. *La desintegración del Yucatán auténtico: Proceso histórico de la reducción del territorio yucateco a sus límites actuales*. Mérida: Zamná.

Mejía Madrid, Fabrizio. 2013. *Nación TV: La telenovela de Televisa*. Mexico City: Grijalbo.

Melly, Caroline. 2017. *Bottleneck: Moving, Building and Belonging in an African City*. Chicago: University of Chicago Press.

Mendiola García, Sandra C. 2017. *Street Democracy: Vendors, Violence and Public Space in Late Twentieth-Century Puebla*. Lincoln: University of Nebraska Press.

Mendoza, Brenda. 2016. *Bullying: Los múltiples rostros del acoso escolar*. Mexico City: Editorial Pax México.

Mérida de Yucatán. 2018. "Historia de la radio en Yucatán." 30 April 2018. www .meridadeyucatan.com/historia-de-la-radio-en-Yucatan.

Meyer, Lorenzo. 2021. "La 4T y Cambio de régimenes anteriores." In *4T: Claves para descifrar el rompecabezas*, edited by Blanca Heredia and Hernán Gómez Bruera, 37–53. Mexico City: Grijalbo.

Mijares Lara, Marcela. 2019. "'Por los caminos del Sur': La construcción de la carretera México-Acapulco, 1925-1940." *Alquimia* 65:76–80.

Milner, Ryan M. 2016. *The World Made Meme*. Cambridge, MA: MIT Press.

Mitchell, Lenneth Edward. 2001. *State-Society Relations in Mexico: Clientelism, Neoliberal Stare Reform and the Case of Conasupo*. New York: Ashgate.

Mitchell, Timothy. 2002. *Rule of Experts: Egypt, Modernity, Technopolitics*. Berkeley: University of California Press.

Mizrahi, Yemile. 2003. *From Martyrdom to Power: The Partido Acción Nacional in Mexico*. Notre Dame, IN: Notre Dame University Press.

Moncada Jiménez, Pedro. 2011. *Turismo, población y territorio en Quintana Roo*. Mexico City: Miguel Ángel Porrúa.

Monsiváis, Carlos. 1997. "Azcárraga Milmo y la 'filosofía de Televisa.'" *Revista Proceso*, 23 April 1997.

Montalvo Ortega, Enrique. 1996. *México en una transición conservadora: El caso Yucatán*. Mexico City: INAH.

Montero, Aarón. 2020. "Museo del Mundo Maya, gran negocio para Yvonne Ortega y Carlos Hank Rhon." *Diario de Yucatán*, 9 July 2020. www.yucatan.com.mx /merida/2020/07/09/museo-del-mundo-maya-gran-negocio-para-ivonne-ortega-y -carlos-hank-rhon.html.

Mora, Martín, and Rosana Santana. 2001. "Se resquebraja el PRI Yucateco." *Proceso*, 3 March 2001.

Morales Blanco, Leonardo. 2007. "La telefonía en México, 1878-1930." Lecture presented at the Universidad Autónoma de Queretaro in 1999. https://telmendez.com/?p=16.

Morales Ramírez, Rafael. 2006. "La imagen de los gobernantes de México: El cacicazgo de Víctor Cervera Pacheco en Yucatán." *Catoblepas* 47: 4.

Nash, June. 1997. "The Fiesta of the World: The Zapatista Uprising and Radical Democracy in Mexico." *American Ethnologist* 99 (2): 261–74.

Navarro Leal, Marco Aurelio, and Koryna Itze Contreras Ocegueda. 2014. "Gobernanza y evaluación." In *Educación superior: La discusión de temas emergentes*, edited by Marco Aurelio Navarro Leal, 113–53. Bloomington, IN: Palibrio.

Nicks, Trudy. 1999. "Indian Villages and Entertainments." In *Unpacking Culture: Art and Commodity in the Colonial and Post-colonial World*, edited by Ruth Phillips and Christopher Steiner, 301–14. Berkeley: University of California Press.

NotiRASA. 2014. "Movimiento de protesta estudiantil en Valladolid." 19 November 2014. https://notirasa.com/noticia/movimiento-de-protesta-estudiantil-en-valladolid/18999.

Novedades Yucatán. 2014a. "Aprietan tuercas' en lucha contra el bullying en Yucatán." 21 June 2014. https://sipse.com/novedades-Yucatán/emitiran-nueva-norma-de-convivencia -en-escuelas-de-Yucatán-97729.html.

Novedades Yucatán. 2014b. "Celulares cada vez más desechables." 24 June 2014.

Novedades Yucatán. 2014c. "Ex-presidente municipal trafica con plata." 3 May 2014. https:// sipse.com/novedades-Yucatán/ex-presidente-municipal-trafica-con-plata-88674.html.

Novedades Yucatán. 2015. "De Tren Bala a Tren Pluma que se esfumó." 30 January 2015. https://sipse.com/novedades-Yucatán/tren-transpeninsular-proyecto-fallido-desde -nacimiento-135196.html.

Núñez Tapía, Francisco Alberto, and Jesús Méndez Reyes. 2018. "El camino de Tijuana a Ensenada: De la precariedad al potencial turístico. Notas sobre empresas de transporte, movilidad y turismo estadounidense en Baja California, 1896-1940." In *Enfoques desde el Noroeste de México*, edited by Norma del Carmen Cruz González and Diana Lizbeth Méndez Medina, 95–129. Ensenada: UABC.

Ocampo Escamilla, Rubén Eloy. 2000. *Historia del radio en Yucatán*. Mérida: Instituto de Cultura Yucatán.

Offner, Amy. 2019. *Sorting Out the Mixed Economy*. Princeton, NJ: Princeton University Press.

Ordóñez, Sergio, and Rafael Bouchain. 2011. *Capitalismo del conocimiento*. Mexico City: UNAM-IIE.

Ornelas Delgado, Jaime. 2002. *Educación y neoliberalismo en México*. Puebla: BUAP.

Ortega Pacheco, Ivonne. 2015. *En el viejo sillón*. Mexico City: Planeta.

Ortiz Mena, Antonio. 1969. *Stabilizing Development: A Decade of Economic Strategy in Mexico*. Mexico City: International Monetary Fund.

Ortiz Yam, Inés. 2013. *De milperos a henequeneros en Yucatán, 1870-1937*. Mexico City: Colmex.

Osorio, Juan Antonio. 2022. "Tren Maya causa fatal destino a Pisté." *Diario de Yucatán*, 12 October 2022.

Otto, Jonathan. 2018. "State-Building and Roads in Post-Revolutionary Chiapas and at the Turn of the Twenty-First Century." In *The Oxford Research Encyclopedia of Latin American History*, edited by William Beezley. New York: Oxford University Press. https:// doi.org/10.1093/acrefore/9780199366439.013.585.

Pacheco Bailón, Fernando. 2007. *Las élites políticas yucatecas: Proceso electoral 2001*. Mérida: UADY.

Pacheco Ladrón de Guevara, Lourdes. 2010. "Los últimos guardianes: Jóvenes rurales e indígenas." In *Los Jóvenes en México*, edited by Rosana Reguillo, 217–41. Mexico City: Fondo de Cultura Económica.

Paerregaard, Karsten, Astrid Bredholt Stensrud, and Astrid Oberborbeck Andersen. 2016. "Water Citizenship: Negotiating Water Rights and Contesting Water Culture in the Peruvian Andes." *Latin American Research Review* 51 (1): 198–217.

Palco Quintanarroense. 2019. "Tasa del desempleo en Quintana Roo menor al promedio nacional." 26 August 2019.

Paoli Bolio, Francisco José. 2004. *Historia y cultura en Yucatán*. Mérida: Instituto Cultural de Yucatán.

Pérez Espino, Efraín. 1979. "El monopolio de la televisión comercial en México." *Revista Mexicana de Sociología* 41 (4): 1435–68.

Pérez Islas, José Antonio. 2010. "Las transformaciones en las edades sociales, escuela y mercados de trabajo." In *Los jóvenes en México*, edited by Rosana Reguillo, 52–81. Mexico City: Fondo de Cultura Económica.

Perfiles Educativos. 2002. "La educación superior privada en México: Una aproximación." 24 (97–98): 128–46.

Periódico PorEso. 2015. "MAS TV: Detiene policía estatal al candidato del PAN de Tinum Evelio Mis." 00:08:20. Posted 26 May 2015, YouTube, 8 min., 20 secs. www.youtube.com/watch?v=DUjCNsMY9bs.

Ponce Jiménez, Martha Patricia. 1990. *La montaña chiclera de Campeche: Vida cotidiana y trabajo (1900-1950)*. Mexico City: CIESAS.

¡Por Esto! 2019a. "Joven estudiante se suicida en el campus del CUV." 22 April 2019. www.poresto.net/2019/04/22/joven-estudiante-se-suicida-en-campus-del-cuv.

¡Por Esto! 2019b. "Otro problema de límites entre Yucatán y Quintana Roo." 7 May 2019.

¡Por Esto! 2022. "Apagón analógico en Yucatán." 27 January 2022. www.poresto.net/yucatan/2022/1/27/apagon-analogico-en-yucatan-16-de-los-hogares-conserva-su-vieja-tv-311987.html.

¡Por Esto! 2023. "Cambios en Pensión Bienestar: 'El regalo' de AMLO para los adultos mayores en 2024." 11 October 2023. www.poresto.net/republica/2023/10/11/cambios-en-pension-bienestar-el-regalo-de-amlo-para-los-adultos-mayores-en-2024-403570.html.

Proceso. 1998. "Los nuevos dueños del Caribe." 12 July 1998.

Proceso. 2011. "Los Hank: Estribe de corrupción." 4 June 2011. www.proceso.com.mx/nacional/2011/6/4/los-hank-estirpe-de-corrupcion-87788.html.

Proceso. 2015. "Denuncia candidato del PRI 'Bloqueo' de su rival del PAN en Yucatán." 5 May 2015. www.proceso.com.mx/nacional/2015/5/5/denuncia-candidato-del-pri-bloqueo-de-su-rival-del-pan-en-yucatan-146632.html.

Proceso. 2021. "Zapatistas e indígenas, foco rojo para el Tren Maya." 14 January 2021. www.proceso.com.mx/reportajes/2021/1/14/zapatistas-indigenas-foco-rojo-para-el-tren-maya-256287.html.

Quintanilla, Susana, and Mary Kay Vaughan. 2003. *Escuela y sociedad en el periodo cardenista*. Mexico City: Fondo de Cultura Económica.

Ramírez Carrillo, Luis Alfonso. 2004. *Las redes del poder: Corrupción, maquiladoras y desarrollo regional en México. El caso de Yucatán*. Mexico City: Miguel Ángel Porrúa.

Ramos, Rolando. 2020. "Congreso declara válida la reforma al artículo 4to de la Constitución en materia de bienestar." *El Economista*, 1 May 2020. www.eleconomista.com.mx/politica/Congreso-declara-valida-la-reforma-al-articulo-4-de-la-Constitucion-en-materia-de-bienestar-20200501-0038.html.

Rankin, Monica. 2009. *México, la Patria! Propaganda and Production during World War II*. Lincoln: University of Nebraska Press.

Re Cruz, Alicia. 1996. *The Two Milpas of Chan Kom*. Albany: SUNY Press.

Redclift, Michael. 2004. *Chewing Gum: The Fortunes of Taste*. New York: Routledge.

Redfield, Robert. 1941. *The Folk Culture of Yucatan*. Chicago: University of Chicago Press.

Reed, Nelson. 1977. *The Caste War of Yucatan*. Stanford, CA: Stanford University Press.

Restall, Matthew. 1997. *The Maya World: Yucatec Culture and Society, 1550–1850*. Stanford, CA: Stanford University Press.

Revista Yucatán. 2010. "Víctor Cervera Pacheco: Ruta al poder." 18 August 2010. www .revistaYucatán.com/v1/politica/victor-cervera-pacheco-ruta-al-poder.

Reyes-Foster, Beatriz. 2019. *Psychiatric Encounters: Madness and Modernity in Yucatán, Mexico*. New Brunswick, NJ: Rutgers University Press.

Reyes-Foster, Beatriz, and Rachael Kangas. 2016. "Unraveling Ix Tab: Revisiting the 'Suicide Goddess' in Maya Archaeology." *Ethnohistory* 63 (1): 1–27.

Rios, Viri. 2021. "La élite tropical." In *4T: Claves para descifrar el rompecabezas*, edited by Blanca Heredia and Hernán Gómez Bruera, 77–93. Mexico City: Grijalbo.

Rivera Hernández, Raúl Diego. 2016. Introduction to *Del Internet a las calles*, edited by Raúl Diego Rivera Hernández, 2–22. Raleigh, NC: A Contracorriente.

Rob, Clifford. 2005. *The Marketing of Rebellion*. Cambridge: Cambridge University Press.

Rodríguez Cano, César Augusto. 2015. "Articulación y contrapoder: Los protagonistas del activismo digital en México (2009-2014)." In *Redes sociodigitales en México*, edited by Rosalía Wincour and José Alberto Sánchez, 81–113. Mexico City: Fondo de Cultura Económica.

Rodríguez Gómez, Katya. 2020. "De Progresa-Oportunidades-Prospera a las Becas Benito Juárez: Un análisis preliminar de los cambios en la política social en el sexenio 2018-2024 en México." *Revista Mexicana de Análisis Político y Administración Pública* 9 (1): 81–91.

Rojas Ubaldo, Amado. 1972. "Investigación regional del territorio de Quintana Roo, para el aprovechamiento del turismo ecológico planificado, que sirva de base para el desarrollo de la zona turística de Cancún." Tesis de Escuela de Ingeniería Municipal, Universidad Autónoma de México.

Romano, Ernesto. 1974. "Los límites de Yucatán y Quintana Roo." *Diario de Yucatán*, 25 May 1974.

Romero Mayo, Rafael, and Jazmín Benítez López. 2014. "El proceso histórico de conformación de la antiguo Payo Obispo (hoy Chetumal) como espacio urbano durante la etapa de Quintana Roo como territorio federal." *Península* 9 (1): 125–40.

Rosado Vega, Luis. 1940. *Quintana Roo: Un pueblo y un hombre*. Mérida: Rosado Vega.

Rosenstein, Carole. 2018. *Understanding Cultural Policy*. New York: Routledge.

Rovira, Guiomar. 2009. *Zapatistas sin fronteras: Las redes de solidaridad con Chiapas y el altermundismo*. Mexico City: Era.

Rugeley, Terry. 1996. *Yucatán's Maya Peasantry and the Origins of the Caste War*. Austin: University of Texas Press.

Sabino, Carlos. 2013. *Los tiempos de Jorge Ubico en Guatemala y el mundo*. Mexico City: Fondo de Cultura Económica.

Salinas de Gortari, Carlos. 2017. *Aliados y Adversarios: TLCAN 1988-2017*. Mexico City: DEBATE.

Salmón Perrilliat, Esteban. 2021. "Política económica: Bases para una prosperidad compartida." In *4T: Claves para Descifrar el Rompecabezas*, edited by Jorge Zepeda Patterson, 197–214. Mexico City: Grijalbo.

Santana, Estrella. 2024. "¿Quiénes serían los nuevos alcaldes de Yucatán, según el PREP?" *Diario de Yucatán*, 3 June 2024.

Santos Corral, Maria Josefa. 2008. *Cien Mil Llamadas por el Ojo de una Aguja: Un analisis antropologico de la apertura de las telecomunicaciones en Mexico*. Madrid: Plaza y Valdes.

Saucedo Ramos, Claudia Lucy, and Carlota Guzmán Gómez. 2018. "La investigación sobre la violencia escolar en México: Tendencias, tensiones y desafíos." *Cultura y Representaciones Sociales* 12 (24): 213–45.

Schantz, Eric M. 2010. "Behind the Noir Border: Tourism, the Vice Racket, and Power Relations in Baja California's Border Zone, 1938–65." In *Holiday in Mexico*, edited by Dina Berger and Andrew Grant Wood, 130–61. Durham, NC: Duke University Press.

Schettino, Macario. 2022. *México en el precipicio: El fracaso de la 4T*. Mexico City: Ariel.

Schuler, Friedrich. 1999. *Mexico between Roosevelt and Hitler: Mexican Foreign Relations in the Age of Cardenas, 1934–1940*. Albuquerque: University of New Mexico Press.

Schwartz, Norman B. 1990. *Forest Society: A Social History of Petén, Guatemala*. Philadelphia: University of Pennsylvania Press.

SEP (Secretaría de Educación Pública). n.d. "Reconocimientos de validez oficial de estudios del tipo superior." Accessed 16 March 2025. www.sirvoes.sep.gob.mx/sirvoes /mvc/consultas.

Shifman, Limor. 2013. *Memes in Digital Culture*. Cambridge, MA: MIT Press.

Smith, Benjamin T. 2018. *The Mexican Press and Civil Society, 1940–1976: Stories from the Newsroom, Stories from the Street*. Chapel Hill: University North Carolina Press.

Smith, Daniel Jordan. 2010. *A Culture of Corruption*. Princeton, NJ: Princeton University Press.

Steiner, Christopher B. 1994. *African Art in Transit*. Cambridge: Cambridge University Press.

Stephen, Lynn. 2002. *Zapata Lives!* Berkeley: University of California Press.

Stern, Alexandra Minna. 1999. "Buildings, Boundaries and Blood. Medicalization and Nation-Building on the U.S.-Mexico Border, 1910–1930." *Hispanic American Historical Review* 79 (1): 41–81.

Suárez Zozaya, María Herlinda. 2010. "Desafíos de una relación en crisis: Educación y jóvenes mexicanos." In *Los jóvenes en México*, edited by Rossana Reguillo, 90–123. Mexico City: Fondo de Cultura Económica.

Súbele al Volumen. 2011. "Estudiantes de la Universidad de Oriente (Valladolid) exigen destituir autorizados." Blog, 2 April 2011. http://subelealvolumen.blogspot.com/2011/04 /estudiantes-de-la-universidad-de.html.

Sullivan, Paul. 1991. *Unfinished Conversations: Mayas and Foreigners between Two Wars*. Berkeley: University of California Press.

Sullivan, Paul. 2004. *Xuxub Must Die: The Lost Histories of Murder on the Yucatán*. Pittsburgh: University of Pittsburgh Press.

Taylor, Sarah H. 2018. *On Being Maya and Getting By*. Boulder: University Press of Colorado.

Telmex (Teléfonos de México). 1991. *Historia de la telefonía en México, 1878-1991*. Mexico City: Telmex.

Thompson, J. Eric. 1963. *Maya Archaeologist*. Norman: University of Oklahoma Press.

Tribuna. 2015. "Justifica Evelio Mis los bloqueros en Pisté." 13 March 2015. https:// tribunacampeche.com/Yucatán/2015/03/13/justifica-evelio-mis-los-bloqueos-en-piste.

UADY (Universidad Autónoma de Yucatán). n.d. "Los orígenes de la radio en Yucatán y fundación de Radio Universidad: Radios y ondas del viejo siglo." Accessed 10 August 2021. www.radio.uady.mx/historia.html.

UAM (Universidad Anáhuac Mayab). n.d. "Modelo educativo." Accessed 15 July 2021. https://merida.anahuac.mx/nosotros/modelo-educativo.

Unión Yucatán. 2018. "Más profesionistas de Yucatán se suman a las filas del desempleo." 20 February 2018. www.unionYucatán.mx/articulo/2018/02/20/economia/mas-profesionistas-de-Yucatán-se-suman-las-filas-del-desempleo.

Urry, John, and Mimi Scheller. 2004. "Places to Play / Places in Play." In *Tourism Mobilities,* edited by Mimi Scheller and John Urry, 1–11. New York: Routledge.

UVY (Universidad Valladolid Yucatán). n.d. "Acerca de . . ." Accessed 27 March 2025. www.uvy.edu.mx/acerca-de-universidad-valladolid-yucatan.

Varela Petito, Gonzalo. 2008. *La educación superior en México: Planeación, evaluación y entorno.* Buenos Aires: Mino y Dávila.

Vidal-Bonifaz, Francisco. 2019. "La historia del monopolio de la televisión abierta en México (1950-1993)." In *Expresión, cultura y participación ciudadana.* Monterrey: Universidad Autónoma de Nuevo León.

Villamil, Jenaro. 2012a. *El sexenio de Televisa: Conjuras del poder mediático.* Mexico City: Grijalbo.

Villamil, Jenaro. 2012b. "Ivonne Ortega: La acaparadora de Dzemul." *Proceso,* 10 October 2012. www.proceso.com.mx/reportajes/2012/10/10/ivonne-ortega-la-acaparadora-de-dzemul-109431.html.

Villamil, Jenaro. 2017. *La rebelión de las audiencias.* Mexico City: Grijalbo.

Villamil, Jenaro, and Julio Scherer Ibarra. 2006. *La guerra sucia de 2006.* Mexico City: Grijalbo.

Villanueva, Eric. 1985. *Crisis henequenero y movimientos campesinos en Yucatán, 1966-1983.* Mexico City: INAH.

Villa Rojas, Alfonso. 1934. "The Yaxunah-Coba Causeway." *Contributions to Archaeology,* no. 9. Washington, DC: CIW.

Villa Rojas, Alfonso. (1978) 1992. *Los elegidos de Dios.* Mexico City: Conaculta.

Wark, McKenzie. 2019. *Capital Is Dead.* New York: Verso.

Waters, Wendy. 1998. "Revolutionizing Childhood: Schools, Roads, and the Revolutionary Generation Gap in Tepoztlán, Mexico, 1928 to 1944." *Journal of Family History* 23 (3): 292–311.

Waters, Wendy. 1999. "Re-mapping the Nation: Road Building as State Formation in Post-Revolutionary Mexico, 1925–1940." PhD diss., University of Arizona.

Watson, Irene. 2014. *Aboriginal People, Colonialism and International Law.* New York: Routledge.

Wells, Allen, and Gilbert Joseph. 1996. *Summer of Discontent, Seasons of Upheaval: Elite Politics and Rural Insurgency in Yucatán, 1876–1915.* Stanford, CA: Stanford University Press.

Wilkins, David E., and K. Tsianina Lomawaima. 2001. *Uneven Grounds: American Indian Sovereignty and Federal Law.* Norman: Oklahoma University Press.

Wutich, Amber, and Alexandra Brewis. 2014. "Food, Water and Scarcity: Towards a Broader Anthropology of Resource Precarity." *Current Anthropology* 55 (4): 444–68.

Xiu Cachón, Gaspar Antonio. 1974a. "Al Presidente de Mexico." *Diario de Yucatán,* 8 November 1974.

Xiu Cachón, Gaspar Antonio. 1974b. "El Plan Tabi." *Diario de Yucatán,* 20 July 1974.

Xiu Cachón, Gaspar Antonio. 1974c. "Los límites de Yucatán y Quintana Roo." *Diario de Yucatán*, 21 September 1974.

Xiu Cachón, Gaspar Antonio. 1974d. "Yucatán y Quintana Roo: Carta abierta al Lic. Echeverría." *Diario de Yucatán*, 11 May 1974.

Yucatán, Gobierno del Estado. n.d. "Flora." Accessed 2 September 2021. www.Yucatán.gob.mx/?p=flora.

Zaid, Javier. (1987) 2012. *La economía presidencial.* Mexico City: Debolsillo.

INDEX

Page numbers in italics refer to illustrations.

Confederación Nacional Campesina (CNC), 56, 64, 73, 79, 82, 84. *See also* Partido Revolucionario Institucional (PRI); clientelism

Confederation of Mexican Workers. *See* Confederación de Trabajadores de México (CTM)

Constitution, of Mexico, 33, 73, 78, 105, 134, 158, 189

construction, 9, 21, 28–29, 61, 80–81, 99–100, 128–29, 141–43, 147–51, 177, 182–85; heavy transport, 182; labor, 75, 99, 151, 191

consumerism, 161, 167–68, 173, 178

Convergencia Nacional, 84

Córdova Lira, Francisco, 80. *See also* Xcaret

corruption, 55, 60, 62, 116, 118, 150, 179, 186, 189

COVID-19 pandemic, 1, 23, 138, 157, 185

Cozumel, 9, 27, 32, 35, 45

crime, 66, 130

Cruzo'ob Maya people, 27, 31, 33, 35–36, 38–39, 41; relationship to road construction, 26, 36–39

CULTUR, 140–43, 145, 154–55

cultural infrastructure, 3, 134, 136, 138, 142–43, 145, 157

cybercafé, 163, 165

debt, 128, 139, 183, 201n13

democracy, 14, 53, 69, 100, 189

development banks, 6, 46, 75, 103, 115

Diario de Yucatán, 50–52, 54–55, 57–70, 82–85, 105, 127–28, 147–48, 171–72, 184–86, 191–92

Díaz Mena, Joaquín "Huacho," 187

direct transfer programs, 88, 115–16, 122–25, 188–89

Dirty War, 64, 196n1

Dzitas, 93, 117, 145, 146

Dzonot Abán, 143, 145, 147, 151–52, 157

Echeverría Álvarez, Luis, 54–58, 61, 67, 78, 100, 171, 196n4

economic crises, 7, 14, 54, 72, 74, 99, 109, 111–12

economic development, 2, 4, 11, 19, 26–27, 34, 45, 50, 91, 167, 190

economists, 7, 16–17, 46, 54, 60, 74–77, 87, 90–91, 94, 100, 183

economy, 3, 5, 7, 10–11, 18–19, 23, 53–54, 73, 96, 129–30, 190

education, 22–26, 104, 106, 110–33, 137, 163, 188–89; and bullying, 128–29, 166; and dropouts, 119, 130; preparatory, 116, 119–20, 122, 125; rural teachers, 114, 118, 125, 142; schools, 66–67, 107, 110, 114–20, 129–30, 164–65; secondary, 116, 119, 123, 125; telesecundaria, 118; and youth culture, 124–25, 129

Ejército Zapatista de Liberación Nacional (EZLN), 4, 159, 180; and expectations of Indigenous activism, 19, 124, 166–67, 192; transnational solidarity networks and, 192

ejido committee, 56, 63, 153–55

ejido communities, 56, 59, 63

elections, 2, 6–7, 13–15, 22–24, 81–88, 104, 126, 154–57, 175–80, 202n2; election-year spending, 16, 54, 68; gift-giving in, 79, 88; municipal, 6, 18, 83, 154, 161, 184, 188, 192; rural voting patterns, 175, 188, 202n2; and "sexenio curse," 16; strategies of electioneering, 7, 14, 23, 72–73, 88, 192, 202n2; and violence, 23, 102, 154, 156

email, 160, 163–65

engineers, 30, 50, 107, 181

Escárcega, 9, 11, 28, 40–43, 182

Escárcega-Chetumal road, 41, 43–44, 60. *See also* Mexican federal highways

ethnic entrepreneurship, 5, 101, 103. *See also* vernacular neoliberalism

executive branch, Mexico, 187

Facebook, 23, 156, 159–77, 187; anonymous troll accounts, 176–77; and local meme creation, 160, 173, 175–76, 178, 205n19; "low" social status, 167

fashion, 95, 163, 167

federal highways. *See* Mexican federal highways

feminism, 180

forests, 11, 26, 28, 30, 37–40, 42–43, 184

Foster, George, 102

Fox Quesada, Vicente, 14, 81, 121, 150

fraud, 14

Frente Ciudadano por México, 180, 183

globalization, 74, 76

governors, Mexico, 15–16, 138–39, 153, 156, 159, 187

Green Ecological Party, 187

Grupo Carso, 183

Grupo Hermes, 141–42

Grupo SIPSE, 205n18

Guatemala City, 41

Guatemala-Mexico border, 29, 41

Guevara, Gabriel, 42

haciendas, 33, 34, 55, 57, 62, 168, 203n6

Hacienda Tabi, 62

Hacienda Xuxub, 33

hammock, 59, 79, 174

handicraft trade, 1–2, 20, 77, 94–97, 101, 106, 109–10, 114, 123–25, 130–31, 133, 136, 149–52, 155, 165, 196n5

Hank González, Carlos, 139

henequen industry, 17, 26, 39, 50–51, 54–62, 64, 69, 74, 91, 100, 138; geopolitical zone of, 40, 51, 58, 63, 73, 105; laborers in, 59, 201n13; obsolescence of, 7, 85; vs. synthetic fibers, 58, 60. *See also* agriculture; industry; parastatal industries; subsidies

Henequeneros de Yucatán, 56

higher education, 113–17, 119, 121, 123, 125, 127, 129–31, 133, 189. *See also* education

Holcá, 8, 12, 28

Hotel Mayaland, 110

hotels, 6, 45–46, 68, 60, 93–94, 99–100, 110, 130, 163–64

human rights, 103, 184

"idea of limited good" (Foster), 98

illegal drugs, 53, 124, 202n14; drug war, 53

Indigenous peoples of Mexico: as agriculturalists, 18; and market autonomy, 103; as models of leadership, 202n1. *See also* Maya people

industry, 6–8, 17–19; chicle, 26, 28–29, 32–34, 36–42, 47, 60, 67, 197n3; cordage, 55, 58; fishing, 113; maquila, 73, 77, 80, 92; regulation, 62–63, 186. *See also* henequen industry; tourism

infrastructure, 5–6, 15, 26–27, 46, 73, 75, 90, 126, 134, 142–43, 181–82; cellular, 169, 177–78; communication, 158, 162; municipal buildings, 68, 122, 153, 156; and regional development, 3, 5, 8, 21–22, 24, 44, 46, 49, 107, 181; telephone, 168; transport, 2, 27, 47. *See also* negative infrastructure

Institutional Revolutionary Party. *See* Partido Revolucionario Institucional (PRI)

Instituto Nacional de Antropología e Historia, 140, 186

Instituto Tecnológico Autónomo de Mexico, 76

Inter-American Development Bank, 6, 46, 75

Isla Mujeres, 28–30, 34–35, 45, 81

job creators, 99. *See also* ethnic entrepreneurship; vernacular neoliberalism

judicial branch, Mexico, 14

Kakalná, 100. *See also* agriculture: sugar; Catmis

Kantunil, 8, 12–13, 28

Kantunilkín, 31–34, 32

Krauze, Enrique, 15, 205n1. *See also* Frente Ciudadano por México

legislative branch, Mexico, 14, 180, 187

López Mateos, Adolfo, 45–46, 61, 196n3

López Obrador, Andres Manuel, 179–85; education reform of, 189; pension reform of, 188–89; promotion of Tren Maya by, 190. *See also* Movimiento de Renovación Nacional (MORENA)

Loret de Mola, Carlos, 54–55, 57, 61–69, 78–79, 82–83, 105, 141, 147, 149, 192, 198n2
Luna Kan, Francisco, 69

Madrid, Miguel de la, 69, 72, 75, 78–79, 91. *See also* "moral renovation," in Mexican politics
maize, 10, 31, 34, 39, 59–63, 85, 93, 122
Mancera, Miguel, 74–77, 87, 90–91, 94
Marxism in Mexico, 64, 66, 76
Maxcanú, 9, 63
"Mayab, The" 105–7, 109
"Maya Disneyland," 134–35, 137, 139, 141, 143–45, 144, 147, 149, 151–55, 157–58, 184
Maya lowlands, 11. *See also* forests
Mayan speakers, 31, 46, 50, 77, 99, 112, 113, 138, 163, 169, 171, 178. *See also* Yukatek Maya language
Maya people, 17, 88; changing marriage customs of, 124; cosmology of, 101, 109; as entrepreneurs, 5, 99, 101–3, 112; ethnic identity of, 19, 23, 33, 101, 103, 109; historical settlement patterns of, 16, 37–39; humor traditions of, 111, 171, 173–76; and *nojoch mama*, 122–23, 174; political representation of women by, 82, 122, 184; pre-Hispanic, 30, 34, 105, 107, 128, 184; and *tatich*, 102, 104, 202n2; territorial autonomy of, 14, 33, 38, 105–6, 197n8, 199nn3–4; and Yukatek Maya language, 59, 105, 108, 135–36, 169, 171, 201n10, 204n13. *See also* Indigenous peoples of Mexico; Mayan speakers
May Pech, Francisco, 38
Mediz Bolio, Antonio, 105–7
Melgar, Rafael, 39–40, 42
Mérida-Chetumal road, 10–11, 27, 36, 38–39, 41–44. *See also* Mexican federal highways
Mérida–Puerto Juárez road, 27, 29, 36, 43–44. *See also* Mexican federal highways

Mexican federal highways, 8–12, 27–28, 32, 43–44, 117, 144, 182–83; Federal Highway 180, 8–12, 27–28, 31–35, 40, 43–46, 51, 94, 117, 135–36, 143–45, 147–48, 150, 180, 182–83; Federal Highway 186, 11, 28, 105, 182, 186, 19; and Pan American Highway, 27
Mexican peso, 59, 75, 89–99, 101, 103, 107, 109–11, 125, 141, 148–50, 152, 175, 186, 189; and "December mistake," 77, 95; devaluation of, 75, 77, 90, 92, 96–98; inflation of, 90–94, 98
Mexican Revolution, 26, 38, 134, 158
Mexico, 3–9, 15–17; Constitution of 1917, 33, 73, 78, 105, 134, 158, 189; economy, 14, 16–17, 72, 91; informal political networks, 14, 125, 139; military, 28–31, 35–36, 41, 160; political system in, 4, 13, 15–16, 72, 180, 189; relationship of, with United States, 26–27, 29, 75–76, 98, 115
migration, 94–95, 105
Mis Mex, Natalia, 156
Mis Tun, Evelio, 107, 152–56, 158, 176–77, 184–88, 190; as charismatic leader, 181, 186; and municipal infrastructure, 154–55; political followers, 153, 155, 157, 159
Molotov (rap-metal group), 172
Monsiváis, Carlos, 166
moral panics, 10, 92, 116, 125, 128–30, 165
"moral renovation," in Mexican politics, 72, 79, 84–85, 87, 91
Movement for National Renovation. *See* Movimiento de Renovación Nacional (MORENA)
Movimiento de Renovación Nacional (MORENA), 180–81, 184–92; expansion of, in rural areas, 2, 187; Fourth Transformation, 180–81, 186. *See also* López Obrador, Andres Manuel
Muna, 9, 145
municipalities, Yucatán, 15, 20, 77, 117–19, 126, 145, 147–51, 157. *See also* elections: municipal

National Action Party. *See* Partido Acción Nacional (PAN)

National Chamber of the Transformation Industry, 44

nationalism, 52, 195n1, 206n2

National Peasant Confederation. *See* Confederación Nacional Campesina (CNC)

navy, Mexican, 28, 45

negative infrastructure, 6–13, 21–23, 32–33, 36, 40–43, 61–64, 70–71, 134, 136, 190–91; at the community level, 12, 151, 185; defined, 3, 11; on nontouristic sectors, 22, 113–16, 120–21, 125, 129, 189; as regional phenomenon, 31, 191

neoliberalism, 3–7, 18–19, 21–23, 69, 71–79, 81, 83, 85, 87, 89–90, 157, 191–93; and *prianismo*, 53, 179–80, 189; and privatization, 17, 72, 78, 80, 102, 112, 163, 168–70, 172. *See also* vernacular neoliberalism

newspapers, 20, 50–53, 59, 64, 66, 68, 82–83, 152. See also *Diario de Yucatán*; *Por Esto!*

North American Free Trade Agreement (NAFTA), 22, 75, 77, 115, 117

nutrition, 115, 122

Oportunidades. *See* direct transfer programs

Ortega Pacheco, Ivonne, 139, 150–52, 154, 157, 182–83, 191; conflict with political factions in Pisté, 154; and Gran Museo del Mundo Maya, 141; and Palacio de la Cultura Maya, 143, 151–52

Ortiz Mena, Antonio, 46, 74–77, 91

Panistas, 81–87, 102, 138, 150–51, 153–54, 156, 158, 176, 187, 190, 198n3, 202n2

parastatal industries, 19, 21, 24; agriculture, 71; Cordemex, 56–60, 63; henequen, 54, 58, 70, 100; sugar, 61; Telmex, 162–63, 168, 170, 183, 204n11

Partido Acción Nacional (PAN), 52, 55, 81–85, 87–88, 151–54; as political faction in Pisté, 83–87, 102, 145, 150,

153–54, 156–58, 176, 186–87, 190, 202n2; and right-of-center national base, 50, 52, 69, 82–85, 87–88

Partido de la Revolución Democrática (PRD), 175, 179–80, 187

Partido Revolucionario Institucional (PRI), 13–14, 50–58, 69–74, 83–89, 139, 150–51, 154–57; association with populism of, 22, 54, 75, 77–78, 81, 83, 85, 139; *pax priísta*, 14, 69, 192, 195n1; Priístas, 52, 83–84, 151, 155–56, 176–77, 187; and rural clientelism, 14, 64–65, 102, 161, 166, 178; and rural loyalists, 52, 82–83, 150–51, 155, 176, 187; and single-party rule, 13–14, 53, 69, 180, 195nn1–2

Partido Verde Ecologista, 187

Party of the Democratic Revolution. *See* Partido de la Revolución Democrática (PRD)

pax priísta, 14, 69, 192, 195n1

Peña Nieto, Enrique, 154; and #YoSoy132, 166–67; and "Televisa sexenio," 203n3

personalism, 84. *See also* clientelism; Mexico: informal political networks

peso crisis, 95

petroleum, 60

Pisté, 1–3, 12–14, 20–24, 51–52, 66–68, 82–102, 108–36, 143–53, 159–68, 180–89; downtown, 13, 69, 96, 151; ejido in, 153–54, 184; handicrafts merchants in, 18, 20, 77, 98, 102, 110, 113, 126, 149–50; origins of tourism industry in, 93–94; Pisteños, 89–95, 103, 158, 161–67, 175–76, 178, 185, 192; relation to Chichén Itzá, 1, 18, 134, 145, 151, 153, 155, 161, 185

Pisteños, 89–95, 103, 158, 161–67, 175–76, 178, 185, 192

Playa del Carmen, 33, 163

Po'ot Mena, Eusebio, 147–48

Popolá, 79, 117, 118, 143–44, 147–51, 182

popular music, 57, 163, 171–72, 174; trova, 171

populism, 22, 54, 71, 73, 75, 77–79, 81, 83, 85, 87, 139. *See also* Cervera Pacheco, Victor; Echeverría Álvarez, Luis;

Por Esto!, 52, 83, 128, 172, 185
precarity, 17, 116, 120, 128
presidentialism, 15, 72. *See also* Mexico: political system
prianismo, 53, 179–80, 189
Priístas, 52, 83–84, 151, 155–56, 176–77, 187
Procampo. *See* direct transfer programs
Progresa. *See* direct transfer programs
Progreso, 9, 168
protests, 65–67, 70, 77–78, 85, 127, 180, 184–86
public health, 31, 115–16, 119, 122–23, 128–29
public intellectuals, 52, 115, 159, 166, 172
Puerto Juárez, 30, 32, 34–36, 44–46, 148
Puerto Morelos, 32, 34, 37

Quintana Roo, 20, 35, 38–43, 79–80, 120, 155; border dispute with Yucatán, 105, 108; as federal territory, 30, 33, 36, 38–39; independence from Yucatán, 105

radio, 162, 170–71, 204n14, 205n18; origins of, in Yucatán, 171, 204n11
Reagan-era policies, 18, 130
real estate, 5, 79–80, 134, 138
Redfield, Robert, 40
remittances, 96, 98
restaurants, 46, 100–101, 135, 151, 164
Rio Hondo, 26
Riviera Maya, 80, 182
roadblock, as political tactic, 65, 67, 134, 138, 155, 176, 186, 192. *See also* protests
roads, 7–13; asphalt, 144, 152, 155; construction of, 10, 25, 36, 41–42, 64, 93, 149, 155; labor in construction of, 11, 43, 93, 148; paving of dirt roads, 7, 44, 144, 155; routing of, 8, 10–12, 17, 27–30, 32, 36–38, 41–42, 44–45, 107, 144–45, 181–86
Rosado Vega, Luis, 107
Rotary Club, 45. *See also* civil society
Ruiz Cortines, Adolfo, 44, 45, 198n15

Salinas de Gortari, Carlos, 73, 75–80, 150
San Salvador Atenco, 203n4
scarcity, 94, 98, 161
schools. *See* education
security, 28–29, 196n1
service sector, 3, 22, 80, 120, 201n6
Sheinbaum Pardo, Claudia, 181, 187
Slim Helú, Carlos, 169, 204n12; and Grupo Carso, 183. *See also* Telmex
single-party rule, 13–14, 53, 69, 180, 195nn1–2
social mobility, 22, 114, 116
Spanish language, 50, 93, 107, 128–29, 152, 163, 174–76
sports, 46, 172
Stabilizing Development, 7, 16, 21, 74–75, 87, 91, 109, 111; and exhaustion as national strategy, 54, 91, 196n4; as historical period, 169, 193; and protectionism, 75, 90–91; and state subsidies, 19, 21, 26, 40, 47, 57, 59, 61, 69, 92, 168, 183, 195n1. *See also* Ortiz Mena, Antonio
state police, 154–56, 176. *See also* elections; security
subsidies, 19–21, 26, 40, 47, 59–61, 69, 92, 168. *See also* industry; parastatal industries
suicide, 128–29, 201n13
swidden agriculture, 38

teachers. *See* education
telephones, 163, 168–69, 171, 204n10; origins of, in Mexico, 204n7; Telmex, 162–63, 168, 170, 183, 204n11. *See also* cell phones; infrastructure
Televisa, 166, 171–74, 203n4, 205n18
Telmex, 162–63, 168, 170, 183, 204n11
television, 51, 118, 162, 166, 170–73, 175–76, 205n17; and paid cable service, 172; Televisa, 166, 171–74, 203n4, 205n18; TV Azteca, 172–73. *See also* radio
Thompson, Edward, 10, 114, 168
Thompson, J. Eric, 199n5
Tinum, municipality of, 20, 23, 83–84, 147–48, 150, 154, 156, 160, 188

Tizimín, 9, 27, 57
Tlatelolco Massacre (1968), 54, 65
tour guides, 186
tourism, 16–23; ambulant vendors, 51,
109–10, 130; beaches, 28, 33, 35, 91,
106; branding, 80, 101, 134–37, 157, 166;
development of, 16, 45, 88, 92, 101, 103,
108, 129, 145; food service, 12, 20, 96,
99, 106, 152; handicrafts trade, 20, 94,
96, 106, 123, 125, 130, 133, 136, 149–50,
196n5; hotels, 6, 45–46, 68, 60,
93–94, 99–100, 110, 130, 163–64; and
paid commissions, 110, 151, 184; restaurants, 46, 100–101, 135, 151, 164; teenagers and, 109–10, 130; tour guides,
19–21, 51, 73–77, 80, 91–92, 101, 107–8,
113–14, 129, 135–40, 151–53; and vectorial
capitalism, 137, 157
train stations, 2, 28, 145, 183, 203n6
Tren Maya, 1–3, 6, 11, 14, 23, 157, 179,
181–88
Tulum, 33
Twitter, 160, 165–67, 175. *See also*
#YoSoy132

Ubico, Jorge, 29, 41
unions, 65–66, 200n4
Universidad Anahuac Mayab, 127
Universidad Autónoma de Yucatán,
65, 125
Universidad Autónoma Nacional de
México, 76
Universidad del Oriente, 119, 127,
201n12
universities, 2, 115–16, 119, 121, 125, 127–28,
16; and career outcomes, 116, 120, 128;
dismissed as *escuelas patitos*, 120; and
mental health, 128–29; ranked by
profile, 120. *See also names of specific
universities*
US dollar, 90, 95; "grabbing" exchanges,
96–97; as prestige object, 96; and
remittances, 96, 98; and treasure
tales, 97
Uxmal, 57, 68, 140, 145

Valladolid, 8, 9, 10, 28, 30, 35–36, 44, 86,
93, 116–17, 119, 125–27, 164–65
vernacular neoliberalism, 5–6, 16, 18–19,
21–23, 47, 50, 69, 71, 74, 89, 111, 167,
178, 193; associated with "postpeasant"
lifestyle, 86, 88, 95, 158, 161, 167; and
critique of government waste, 47, 55,
58; as political "awakening," 71, 86–89,
102, 126, 161, 193; and sentimentaliza-
tion of tradition, 174, 177; and "welfare
queen" stereotype, 18, 130. *See also* consumerism, Maya people; neoliberalism
Villamil, Genaro, 139, 166–67, 172. *See also*
#YoSoy132
Villa Rojas, Alfonso, 39, 44, 107
violence, 24, 41, 154, 156, 184
Voz del Mayab, 171. *See also* radio

Xcaret, 23, 80–81, 102, 110, 135–38, 143, 152,
157, 185; and "captive" tourism, 110, 134,
151; company busses, 22; Xcaret Group,
22, 80–81, 102, 135, 137–38, 143, 152, 157
Xel-ha, 81, 135
Xiu Cachón, Gaspar Antonio, 62–63,
105, 108

Yaxcabá, 79, 117, *117,* 119, 143–44, 147–52,
157, 182
Yucatán (Mexican State), 26–27, 33, 61,
67, 104, 107, 138–40, 142–43, 168, 172;
colonial heritage in, 2, 12, 27, 142, 145;
and environmental harm, 17, 113, 184;
henequen zone in, 40, 51, 58, 63, 73,
105; maize zone in, 60; northeast, 33;
regional arts and culture in, 171, 177
Yukatek Maya language, 59, 105, 108, 128,
135–36, 169, 171, 201n10, 204n13; ethno-
botanical terms, 30

Zaid, Javier, 15, 54
Zapata Bello, Rolando, 106, 154
Zapatista Army of National Liberation.
See Ejército Zapatista de Liberación
Nacional (EZLN)
Zedillo, Ernesto, 78–79